# FRENCH
## AT A GLANCE

**PHRASE BOOK & DICTIONARY FOR TRAVELERS**

# FRENCH
## AT A GLANCE

**PHRASE BOOK & DICTIONARY FOR TRAVELERS**

BY GAIL STEIN, M.A.
Teacher of French
Department of Foreign Languages
Martin Van Buren High School
New York

HEYWOOD WALD, Coordinating Editor
Chairman, Department of Foreign Languages
Martin Van Buren High School
New York

BARRON'S EDUCATIONAL SERIES, INC.
New York ■ London ■ Toronto ■ Sydney

**Cover and Book Design**  Milton Glaser, Inc.

**Illustrations**  Juan Suarez

© Copyright 1984 by Barron's Educational Series, Inc.

*All inquiries should be addressed to:*
Barron's Educational Series, Inc.
250 Wireless Boulevard
Hauppauge, New York 11788

*Library of Congress Catalog Card No. 84-2877*

Paper Edition
International Standard Book No. 0-8120-2712-4

**Library of Congress Cataloging in Publication Data**
Stein, Gail.
  French at a glance.

  Includes index.
  1. French language—Conversation and phrase books—
English. 2. French language—Dictionaries—English.
3. English language—Dictionaries—French. I. Wald,
Heywood. II. Title.
PC2121.S67  1984      448.3′421      84-2877
ISBN 0-8120-2712-4 (pbk.)

PRINTED IN THE UNITED STATES OF AMERICA
012      900  18 17

# CONTENTS

# **PREFACE**

So you're taking a trip to one of the many fascinating countries of the world. That's exciting! In more ways than one, this new phrase book will prove an invaluable companion that will make your stay far more interesting and truly unforgettable.

This phrase book is part of a new series being launched by Barron's Educational Series, Inc. In these books we present the phrases and words that a traveler most often needs for a brief visit to a foreign country, where the customs and language are often different. Each of the phrase books highlights the terms particular to that country, in situations that the tourist is most likely to encounter. With a specially developed key to pronunciation, this book will enable you to communicate quickly and confidently in colloquial terms. It is intended not only for beginners with no knowledge of the language, but also for those who have already studied it and have some familiarity with it.

Some of the unique features and highlights of the Barron's series are:

■ Easy-to-follow *pronunciation keys* and complete phonetic transcriptions for all words and phrases in the book.

■ Compact *dictionary* of commonly used words and phrases—built right into this phrase book so there's no need to carry a separate dictionary.

■ Useful phrases for the *tourist*, grouped together by subject matter in a logical way so that the appropriate phrase is easy to locate when you need it.

■ Special phrases for the *business traveler*, including banking terms, trade and contract negotiations, and secretarial services.

■ Thorough section on *food and drink*, with comprehensive food terms you will find on menus; these terms are often difficult or impossible to locate in dictionaries, but our section gives you a description of the preparation as well as a definition of what it is.

■ *Emergency phrases* and terms you hope you won't need: legal complications, medical problems, theft or loss of valuables, replacement or repair of watches, camera, and the like.

■ *Sightseeing itineraries*, shopping tips, practical travel tips, and regional food specialties to help you get off the beaten path and into the countryside, to the small towns and cities, and to the neighboring areas.

■ A *reference section* providing: important signs, conversion tables, holidays, abbreviations, telling time, days of week and months of year.

■ A brief *grammar section*, with the basic elements of the language quickly explained.

Enjoy your vacation and travel with confidence. You have a friend by your side.

## ACKNOWLEDGMENTS

We would like to thank the following individuals and organizations for their assistance on this project:
Nora Brossard, Assistant Director Public Relations, French National Tourist Office, New York, New York; Professor Pierre François, SUC New Paltz, New York; Marie-Charlotte Iszkowski, Foreign Service Institute, Washington, D.C.; Michel Lalou, Phonelab, New York, New York; George Lang, George Lang, Inc., New York, New York; Dr. Gladys Lipton, Coordinator of Foreign Languages and ESOL, Anne Arundel County Public Schools, Annapolis, Maryland; François Mead, Alliance Française, New York, New York; Professor Henry Urbanski, Chairman, Department of Foreign Languages, SUC New Paltz, New York; Herta Erville; and Andrée Katz.

Also, Air France, Association of American Travel Writers, French National Tourist Office, *New York Times, Signature Magazine, Travel-Holiday Magazine, Travel and Leisure Magazine*, U.S. Tour Operators, and U.S. Travel Data Center.

# QUICK PRONUNCIATION GUIDE

Although all the phrases in this book are presented with an easy-to-use key to pronunciation, you will find speaking French quite a bit easier if you learn a few simple rules. Below are some tables which give the sounds represented by each French letter along with the symbols used to indicate them in this book. Although a French sound is quite different from ours, with a little practice and repetition you will be able to make yourself understood by native French speakers.

After studying the phonetic pronunciation system below, begin to practice the vocabulary words and then progress to the longer phrases. Bonne chance! *Bohn shah_nss_*

## STRESS

As an aid to pronunciation, words in this book have been divided into syllables. Since all French syllables have approximately the same amount of stress, pronounce each syllable with equal emphasis and put a slightly stronger emphasis on the last syllable of a word group.

## CONSONANTS

In French, final consonants are usually silent, except for final C, R, F, and L (as in CaReFuL), which are usually pronounced.

| FRENCH LETTER | ENGLISH SOUND | SYMBOL | EXAMPLE |
|---|---|---|---|
| b, d, f, k, l, m, n, | same as English | | |
| p, s, t, v, z | same as English | | |
| c (before e, i, y) | SS (S at beginning of word) | S | cigare *see-gahr* |
| ç (before a, o, u) | SS (S at beginning of word) | S | garçon *gahr-ssoh_n_* |
| c (before a, o, u) | K | K | comme *kohm* |

| FRENCH LETTER | ENGLISH SOUND | SYMBOL | EXAMPLE |
|---|---|---|---|
| g (before e, i, y) | S as in pleasure | ZH | rouge *roozh* |
| ge (before a, o) | S as in pleasure | ZH | mangeons *mahn-zhohn* |
| g (before a, o, u) | G | G | gant *gahn* |
| gn | nyuh as in onion | NY | oignon *oh-nyohn* |
| h | always silent | | hôtel *oh-tehl* |
| j | S as in pleasure | ZH | je *zhuh* |
| qu, final q | K | K | cinq *sank* |
| r | Roll the R at the top back of the mouth as if you were gargling or spitting. | R | rue *rew* |
| ss | S | SS | poisson *pwah-ssohn* |
| s | beginning of word | S | six *sees* |
| | next to consonant | SS | disque *deessk* |
| s | between vowels | Z | poison *pwah-zohn* |
| th | T | T | thé *tay* |
| x | S in these words only | SS | six *seess*, dix *deess*, soixante *swah-ssahnt* |
| x | X | KSS | excellent *ehkss-eh-lahn* |

NOTE: When combined with a word beginning with a vowel or *h*, *x* has a *z* sound. Before a word beginning with a consonant, it is silent.

## VOWELS

| FRENCH LETTER | ENGLISH SOUND | SYMBOL | EXAMPLE |
|---|---|---|---|
| a, à, â | A as in yacht or A in after | AH | la *lah* |
| é, final er, final ez, et | A as in day | AY | musée *mew-zay* |
| e+2 consonants e+final pronounced consonant e, ê, è | E as in ever | EH | sept *seht* |
| e | sometimes like E of early with no R sound | UH | le *luh* |
| i (î), y | EE as in meet | EE | île *eel* |
| i+ vowel or ll | Y as in yes | EE | famille *fah-mee* |
| o+final pronounced consonant | O as in for | OH | homme *ohm* |
| o, o before se, o last sound in word, au, eau | O as in open | OH | au *oh* |
| ou | OO as in tooth | OO | où *oo* |
| oy, oi | WA as in watch | WAH | trois *trwah* |
| U | There is none. Round lips and say E and U at same time. | EW | du *dew* |
| U + vowel | WEE as in wee | WEE | huit *weet* |

## NASAL SOUNDS

Nasal sounds are produced through the mouth and the nose at the same time. Nasal sounds occur when N or M follow a vowel in the same syllable. There is NO nasal sound for VOWEL + NN, VOWEL + MM, VOWEL + N + VOWEL, VOWEL + M + VOWEL. NOTE: n̲ means there is a nasalized pronunciation of the "N" sound. The tip of the tongue does not touch the roof of the mouth.

| FRENCH LETTER | ENGLISH SOUND | SYMBOL | EXAMPLE |
|---|---|---|---|
| AN, AM, EN, EM | similar to on | AHN̲ | France *Frahn̲ss* |
| IN, IM, AIN, AIM | similar to an | AN̲ | pain *pan̲* |
| IEN | similar to yan of Yankee | YAN̲ | bien *byan̲* |
| ON, OM | similar to on of long. | OHN̲ | bon *bohn̲* |
| UN, UM | similar to un of under. | UHN̲ | un *uhn̲* |

## LIAISON and ELISION

Liaison and elision are two linguistic devices that add to the beauty and fluidity of the French language.

Liaison means linking. In French, the final consonant of a word is usually not pronounced. Sometimes, however, when the final consonant of one word is followed by a beginning vowel or "H" of the next word, liaison occurs.

EXAMPLE:

**Nous arrivons.** *noo zah-ree-vohn̲*

With the following words in French, the final vowel is dropped if the next word starts with a vowel or "H". The dropped vowel is replaced by an apostrophe. This is called elision.

EXAMPLE:

**la auto = l'auto** *(loh-toh)*

**le homme = l'homme** *(lohm)*

# THE BASICS FOR GETTING BY

## MOST FREQUENTLY USED EXPRESSIONS

The expressions in this section are the ones you'll use again and again—the fundamental building blocks of conversation, the way to express your wants or needs, and some simple question forms which you can use to construct all sorts of questions. It's a good idea to practice these phrases until you know them by heart.

| | | |
|---|---|---|
| yes | **oui** | *wee* |
| no | **non** | *nohn* |
| maybe | **peut-être** | *puh-teh-truh* |
| please | **s'il vous plaît** | *seel voo pleh* |
| thank you very much | **merci beaucoup** | *mehr-ssee boh-koo* |
| you're welcome | **de rien** | *duh ryan* |
| | **Je vous en prie** | *zhuh voo zahn pree* |
| Excuse me. | **Excusez-moi.** | *ehkss-kew-zay mwah* |
| | **Pardon** | *pahr-dohn* |
| I'm sorry. | **Je suis désolé(e).** | *zhuh swee day-zoh-lay* |
| Just a second. | **Un moment.** | *uhn moh-mahn* |
| That's all right, O.K. | **Ça va.** | *sah-vah* |
| | **D'accord.** | *dah-kohr* |
| | **Bien entendu.** | *byan nahn-tahn-dew* |
| It doesn't matter. | **Ça ne fait rien.** | *sah nuh feh ryan* |
| Good morning (afternoon). | **Bonjour.** | *bohn-zhoor* |
| Good evening (night). | **Bonsoir.** | *bohn-swahr* |
| | **Bonne nuit.\*** | *bohn nwee* |

NOTE: Used on leaving for the night

| Sir | **Monsieur** | *muh-ssyuh* |
| Madame | **Madame** | *mah-dahm* |
| Miss | **Mademoiselle** | *mahd-mwah-zehl* |
| Good-bye. | **Au revoir.** | *oh ruh-vwahr.* |
| See you later (so long). | **À tout à l'heure.** | *ah toot ah luhr.* |
| See you tomorrow. | **À demain.** | *ah duh-man* |
| Do you speak English? | **Parlez-vous anglais?** | *pahr-lay voo ahn-gleh* |
| I speak a little French. | **Je parle un peu le français.** | *zhuh pahrl uhn puh luh frahn-sseh* |
| Do you understand? | **Comprenez-vous? (Vous comprenez?)** | *voo kohn-pruh-nay (voo kohn-pruh-nay)* |
| I understand. | **Je comprends.** | *zhuh kohn-prahn* |
| I don't understand. | **Je ne comprends pas.** | *zhuh nuh kohn-prahn pah* |
| What? | **Quoi?** | *kwah* |
| What did you say? | **Qu'est-ce que vous avez dit?** | *kehss kuh voo zah-vay dee* |
| How do you say ____ in French? | **Comment dit-on ____ en français?** | *koh-mahn dee tohn ____ ahn frahn-sseh* |
| What does this (that) mean? | **Que veut dire ceci (cela)?** | *kuh vuh deer suh-see (suh-lah)* |
| Please repeat. | **Répétez, s'il vous plaît.** | *Ray-pay-tay, seel voo pleh* |
| I'm American. | **Je suis Américain/Américaine (f).** | *zhuh swee zah-may-ree-kan/zah-may-ree-kehn* |

| | | |
|---|---|---|
| My name is ____. | **Je m'appelle ____.** | *zhuh mah-pehl* |
| What's your name? | **Comment vous appelez-vous?** | *koh-mahn voo zah-play voo* |
| How are you? | **Comment allez-vous?** | *koh-mahn tah-lay voo* |
| How's everything? | **Comment ça va?** | *koh-mahn sah vah* |
| Very well, thanks. And you? | **Très bien, merci. Et vous?** | *treh byan mehr-ssee. ay voo* |
| Where is ____? | **Où est ____?** | *oo eh* |
| ■ the bathroom | **la salle de bains** | *lah sahl duh ban* |
| ■ the dining room | **la salle à manger** | *lah sahl ah mahn-zhay* |
| ■ the entrance | **l'entrée** | *lahn-tray* |
| ■ the exit | **la sortie** | *lah sohr-tee* |
| ■ the taxi | **le taxi** | *luh tak-ssee* |
| ■ the telephone | **le téléphone** | *luh tay-lay-fohn* |
| I'm lost. | **Je suis perdu(e).** | *zhuh swee pehr-dew* |
| We're lost. | **Nous sommes perdus(ues).** | *noo sohm pehr-dew* |
| Where are my friends? | **Où sont mes amis?** | *oo sohn may zah-mee* |
| Where is the bus? | **Où est le bus?** | *Oo eh luh bewss* |
| Which way did they go? | **Par où sont-ils allés?** | *Pahr oo sohn teel zah-lay* |
| ■ to the left | **à gauche** | *ah gohsh* |
| ■ to the right | **à droite** | *ah drwaht* |
| ■ straight ahead | **tout droit** | *too drwah* |
| How much is it? | **C'est combien?** | *Seh kohn-byan* |

| I'd like _____. | **Je voudrais** _____. *zhuh voo-dreh* |
| Please bring me _____. | **Apportez-moi, s'il vous plaît** _____. *ah-pohr-tay mwah seel voo pleh* |
| Please show me _____. | **Montrez-moi, s'il vous plaît** _____. *Mohn-tray mwah, seel voo pleh* |
| I'm hungry. | **J'ai faim.** *zhay fan* |
| I'm thirsty. | **J'ai soif.** *zhay swahf* |
| I'm tired. | **Je suis fatigué(e)** *zhuh swee fah-tee-gay* |
| What's that? | **Qu'est-ce que c'est?** *kehss-kuh-seh* |
| What's up? | **Qu'est-ce qui se passe?** *kehss kee suh pahss* |
| | **Quoi de neuf?** *kwah duh nuhf* |
| I (don't) know. | **Je (ne) sais (pas).** *zhuh (nuh) seh (pah)* |

## QUESTIONS

| Where is ____? | Où est ____? | oo eh |
| When? | Quand? | kahn |
| How much? | Combien? | kohn-byan |
| Who? | Qui? | kee |
| Why? | Pourquoi? | poor-kwah |
| How? | Comment? | koh-mahn |
| What? | Quoi? | kwah |

## EXCLAMATIONS, SLANG, COLLOQUIALISMS

| Ouch! | Aïe! | ahy |
| That hurts! | Oh, ça fait mal! | oh sah feh mahl |
| Wow! Man alive! (expressing surprise) | Oh là là! | oh lah lah |
| Darn it! (expressing annoyance) | Zut alors! | zewt ah-lohr |
| How about that! (Well!) | Eh bien, mon vieux! | eh byan mohn vyuh |
| How beautiful! | Magnifique! Quelle merveille! | mah-nyee-feek kehl mehr-vehy |
| Ugh! | Pouah! | pwah |
| Phew! | Ouf! | oof |
| That's awful! | C'est affreux! | seh-tah-fruh |
| Great! Wonderful! | Formidable! | fohr-mee-dah-bluh |
| That's it! | C'est ça! | seh sah |
| My goodness! | Mon Dieu! | mohn dyuh |

| Good Heavens! | **Mon Dieu!** | *mohn dyuh* |
| For heaven's sake! | **Par exemple!** | *Pahr ehg-zahn-pluh* |
| Bottoms up! Cheers! | **Santé.** **A votre santé!** | *sahn-tay* *ah voh-truh sahn-tay* |
| Quiet! | **Silence!** | *see-lahnss* |
| Shut up! | **Tais-toi!** | *teh-twa* |
| That's enough! | **Ça suffit!** | *sah sew-fee* |
| | **C'est assez!** | *seh tah-ssay* |
| Never mind! | **N'importe.** | *nan-pohrt* |
| Of course! | **Bien sûr!** | *byan sewr* |
| With pleasure! | **Avec plaisir!** | *ah-vehk pleh-zeer* |
| Let's go! | **Allons-y!** | *ah-lohn zee!* |
| What a shame (pity)! | **Quel dommage!** | *kehl doh-mahzh* |
| What a nuisance (showing annoyance)! | **Que c'est ennuyeux!** | *keh seh tahn-nwee-yuh* |
| Nonsense! No way! | **C'est ridicule!** **Allons, donc.** | *seh ree-dee-kewl* *ah-lohn dohnk* |
| Don't be stupid! | **Ne sois pas bête!** | *nuh swah pah beht* |
| Are you crazy? | **Êtes-vous fou/ folle?** | *eht voo foo/fohl* |
| What a fool! | **Quel imbécile!** | *kehl an-bay-sseel* |
| Good luck! | **Bonne chance!** | *bohn shahnss* |

### PROBLEMS, PROBLEMS, PROBLEMS
### (EMERGENCIES)

| Hurry up! | **Dépêchez-vous!** | *day-peh-shay voo!* |
| Look! | **Regardez!** | *ruh-gahr-day* |

| | |
|---|---|
| Watch out! Be careful! | **Faites attention!** *feht zah-tah<u>n</u>-ssyoh<u>n</u>* |
| | **Soyez prudent(e)!** *swah-yay prew-dah<u>n</u>(t)* |
| Listen! | **Écoutez!** *ay-koo-tay* |
| Wait! | **Attendez!** *ah-tah<u>n</u>-day* |
| Fire! | **Au feu!** *oh fuh* |
| I have lost ____. | **J'ai perdu ____.** *zheh pehr-dew* |
| What's the matter with you? | **Qu'est-ce que vous avez?** *kehss kuh voo zah-vay* |
| What (the devil) do you want? | **Que (diable) voulez-vous?** *kuh (dee-ah-bluh) voo-lay voo* |
| Stop bothering me! | **Laissez-moi tranquille!** *leh-ssay mwah trah<u>n</u>-keel* |
| Go away! | **Allez-vous-en!** *ah-lay voo zah<u>n</u>* |
| | **Va-t-en (fam.)!** *Vah-tah<u>n</u>* |

| | | |
|---|---|---|
| Scram! Beat it! | **Fiche-moi la paix!** | *feesh mwah lah peh* |
| Leave me alone! | **Laissez-moi tranquille!** | *leh-ssay mwah trahn-keel* |
| Help, police! | **Au secours, police!** | *oh suh-koor, poh-leess* |
| I'm going to call a cop! | **Ja vais appeler la police!** | *zhuh veh zah-play lah poh-leess* |
| Get out! | **Sortez!** | *sohr-tay!* |
| That guy is a thief! | **Ce type est un voleur!** | *suh teep eh tuhn voh-luhr* |
| He has stolen _____. | **Il a volé _____.** | *eel ah voh-lay* |
| ■ my car | **ma voiture** | *mah vwah-tewr* |
| ■ my passport | **mon passeport** | *mohn pahss-pohr* |
| ■ my purse | **mon sac** | *mohn sahk* |
| ■ my suitcase | **ma valise** | *mah vah-leez* |
| ■ my wallet | **mon portefeuille** | *mohn pohr-tuh-fuhy* |
| ■ my watch | **ma montre** | *mah mohn-truh* |
| This young man is annoying me. | **Ce jeune homme m'embête.** | *suh zhuhn ohm mahn-beht* |
| | **m'ennuie.** | *mahn-nwee* |
| He keeps following me. | **Il n'arrête pas de me suivre!** | *eel nah-reht pah duh muh swee-vruh* |
| Stop that boy! | **Arrêtez ce garçon!** | *Ah-reh-tay suh gahr-ssohn* |
| I haven't done anything. | **Je n'ai rien fait.** | *zhuh nay ryan feh* |
| It's a lie! | **C'est un mensonge.** | *seh tuhn mahn-ssohnzh* |
| It's not true! | **Ce n'est pas vrai!** | *suh neh pah vreh* |

| I'm innocent. | **Je suis innocent(e)** *zhuh swee zee-noh-sahn(t)* |
| I want a lawyer. | **Je voudrais parler à un avocat.** *zhuh voo-dreh pahr-lay ah uhn nah-voh-kah* |
| I want to go ____. | **Je voudrais aller ____.** *zhuh voo-dreh zah-lay* |
| ■ to the American consulate | **au consulat américain** *oh kohn-sew-lah ah-may-ree-kan* |
| ■ to the police station | **au commissariat de police** *oh koh-mee-ssah-ryah duh poh-leess* |
| I need help, quick! | **Vite. Aidez-moi.** *veet eh-day mwah* |
| | **Vite, au secours!** *veet oh suh-koor* |
| Can you help me, please? | **Pouvez-vous m'aider, s'il vous plaît?** *poo-vay voo meh-day seel voo pleh* |
| Does anyone here speak English? | **Y a-t-il quelqu'un ici qui parle anglais?** *ee ah teel kehl-kuhn ee-ssee kee pahrl ahn-gleh* |
| I need an interpreter. | **Il me faut un interprète.** *eel muh foh tuhn nan-tehr-preht* |

## NUMBERS

You will use numbers the moment you land in France, whether it be to exchange money at the airport, purchase a bus ticket for a ride into town, or describe the length of your stay to a customs official. We list here first the cardinal numbers, then follow with ordinal numbers, fractions, and other useful numbers.

### CARDINAL NUMBERS

| 0 | **zéro** | *zay-roh* |
| 1 | **un** | *uhn* |

| 2  | **deux**         | *duh*          |
|----|------------------|----------------|
| 3  | **trois**        | *trwah*        |
| 4  | **quatre**       | *kah-truh*     |
| 5  | **cinq**         | *sank*         |
| 6  | **six**          | *seess*        |
| 7  | **sept**         | *seht*         |
| 8  | **huit**         | *weet*         |
| 9  | **neuf**         | *nuhf*         |
| 10 | **dix**          | *deess*        |
| 11 | **onze**         | *ohnz*         |
| 12 | **douze**        | *dooz*         |
| 13 | **treize**       | *trehz*        |
| 14 | **quatorze**     | *kah-tohrz*    |
| 15 | **quinze**       | *kanz*         |
| 16 | **seize**        | *sehz*         |
| 17 | **dix-sept**     | *dee-seht*     |
| 18 | **dix-huit**     | *dee-zweet*    |
| 19 | **dix-neuf**     | *deez-nuhf*    |
| 20 | **vingt**        | *van*          |
| 21 | **vingt et un**  | *van-tay-uhn*  |
| 22 | **vingt-deux**   | *van-duh*      |
| 23 | **vingt-trois**  | *van-trwah*    |
| 24 | **vingt-quatre** | *van-kah-truh* |
| 25 | **vingt-cinq**   | *van-sank*     |
| 26 | **vingt-six**    | *van-seess*    |
| 27 | **vingt-sept**   | *van-seht*     |
| 28 | **vingt-huit**   | *van-tweet*    |

| 29 | vingt-neuf | *van-nuhf* |
| 30 | trente | *trahnt* |
| 31 | trente et un | *trahn-tay-uhn* |
| 32 | trente-deux | *trahnt-duh* |
| 40 | quarante | *kah-rahnt* |
| 41 | quarante et un | *kah-rahn-tay-uhn* |
| 42 | quarante-deux | *kah-rahnt-duh* |
| 50 | cinquante | *san-kahnt* |
| 51 | cinquante et un | *san-kahn-tay-uhn* |
| 52 | cinquante-deux | *san-kahnt-duh* |
| 60 | soixante | *swah-ssahnt* |
| 61 | soixante et un | *swah-ssahn-tay-uhn* |
| 62 | soixante-deux | *swah-ssahnt-duh* |
| 70 | soixante-dix | *swah-ssahnt-deess* |
| 71 | soixante et onze | *swah-ssahn-tay-ohnz* |
| 72 | soixante-douze | *swah-ssahnt-dooz* |
| 73 | soixante-treize | *swah-ssahnt-trehz* |
| 74 | soixante-quatorze | *swah-ssahnt-kah-tohrz* |
| 75 | soixante-quinze | *swah-ssahnt-kanz* |
| 76 | soixante-seize | *swah-ssahnt-sehz* |
| 77 | soixante-dix-sept | *swah-ssahnt-dee-seht* |
| 78 | soixante-dix-huit | *swah-ssahnt-dee-zweet* |
| 79 | soixante-dix-neuf | *swah-ssahnt-deez-nuhf* |

| | | |
|---|---|---|
| 80 | **quatre-vingts** | *kah-truh-van* |
| 81 | **quatre-vingt-un** | *kah-truh-van-uhn* |
| 82 | **quatre-vingt-deux** | *kah-truh-van-duh* |
| 90 | **quatre-vingt-dix** | *kah-truh-van-deess* |
| 91 | **quatre-vingt-onze** | *kah-truh-van-ohnz* |
| 92 | **quatre-vingt-douze** | *kah-truh-van-dooz* |
| 100 | **cent** | *sahn* |
| 101 | **cent un** | *sahn-uhn* |
| 102 | **cent deux** | *sahn-duh* |
| 110 | **cent dix** | *sahn-deess* |
| 120 | **cent vingt** | *sahn-van* |
| 200 | **deux cents** | *duh-sahn* |
| 201 | **deux cent un** | *duh-sahn-uhn* |
| 330 | **trois cent trente** | *trwah-sahn-trahnt* |
| 1000 | **mille** | *meel* |
| 1001 | **mille un** | *meel-uhn* |
| 1100 | **mille cent** / **onze cents** | *meel-sahn* / *ohnz-sahn* |
| 1200 | **mille deux cents** / **douze cents** | *meel-duh-sahn* / *dooz-sahn* |
| 1350 | **mille trois cent cinquante** / **treize cent cinquante** | *meel-trwah-sahn-san-kahnt* / *trehz-sahn-san-kahnt* |
| 2000 | **deux mille** | *duh-meel* |
| 5000 | **cinq mille** | *sank-meel* |
| 10,000 | **dix mille** | *dee-meel* |

| 100,000 | **cent mille** | *sahn-meel* |
| 1,000,000 | **un million** | *uhn-mee-lyohn* |
| 198_ | **mille neuf cent quatre-vingt_** | *meel-nuhf-sahn kah-truh van* |

## ORDINAL NUMBERS

| first | **premier/première (1ᵉʳ)** | *pruh-myay/pruh-myehr* |
| second | **deuxième (2ᵉ)** | *duh-zyehm* |
| third | **troisième** | *trwah-zyehm* |
| fourth | **quatrième** | *kah-tree-yehm* |
| fifth | **cinquième** | *san-kyehm* |
| sixth | **sixième** | *see-zyehm* |
| seventh | **septième** | *seh-tyehm* |
| eighth | **huitième** | *wee-tyehm* |
| ninth | **neuvième** | *nuh-vyehm* |
| tenth | **dixième** | *dee-zyehm* |

## QUANTITIES

| a half | **une moitié** | *ewn mwah-tyay* |
| half a | **un/une demi/e** | *uhn/ewn duh-mee* |
| half of | **la moitié de** | *lah mwah-tyay duh* |
| a quarter | **un quart** | *uhn kahr* |
| three quarters | **trois quarts** | *trwah kahr* |
| a third | **un tiers** | *uhn tyehr* |
| two thirds | **deux tiers** | *duh tyehr* |
| a cup of | **une tasse de** | *ewn tahss duh* |
| a dozen of | **une douzaine de** | *ewn doo-zehn duh* |
| a kilo of | **un kilo de** | *unn kee-loh duh* |

| a liter of | **un litre de** | *uhn lee-truh duh* |
| a little bit of | **un peu de** | *uhn puh duh* |
| a lot of | **beaucoup de** | *boh-koo duh* |
| a pair of | **une paire de** | *ewn pehr duh* |
| enough of | **assez de** | *ah-ssay duh* |
| too much of | **trop de** | *troh duh* |

## TRAVEL TIP

Touring on the cheap? You'll find that keeping travel costs under control is a lot easier if you watch your daily expenses on such items as breakfast. Just how important is it for you to have that scrambled egg every morning? If you have the more native "continental breakfast," you'll have the money left over to enjoy a theater performance or buy that special gift you saw in the shop window. Another way to save money and have more fun is to take public transportation. Sure, taxis are easier, but you'll get to the heart of the country a lot faster when you take the bus or metro. You'll observe how everyday people get around town, and you're likely to have some interesting adventures too. Exercise caution, however, and do not travel crowded trains or buses with valuables easily within view. Pick-pockets are everywhere and, as a tourist, you are usually paying more attention to the sights than to riders nearby. Women should keep a firm grasp on their purses.

# WHEN YOU ARRIVE

## PASSPORT AND CUSTOMS

In France at last! Your vacation can't begin until you've shown your passport to the proper authorities and passed through customs.

The following chart shows what duty-free items visitors may bring into France.

| DUTY-FREE ITEMS | OUTSIDE EUROPE | COMMON MARKET (EEC) | NON-COMMON MARKET |
|---|---|---|---|
| cigarettes | 400 | 300 OR | 200 |
| cigars | 100 | 75 OR | 50 |
| pipe tobacco | 500 g | 400 g | 250 g |
| wine | 2L | 3L. AND | 2L |
| over 38 proof sp. | 1L | 1½L | 1L |
| perfume | 50 g | 75 g | 50 g |
| toilet water | 25 cl | 25 cl | 25 cl |

Generally all items for personal use enter the country duty-free and most tourists have little trouble passing through customs. Baggage in hand, you must follow the sign that applies to you: *Articles à déclarer* or *Rien à déclarer* (Nothing to declare). Good luck! You're on your way!

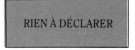

| | |
|---|---|
| My name is _____ | **Je m'appelle** _____ *zhuh mah-pehl* |
| I'm American Canadian, British, Australian. | **Je suis américain(e) canadien(ne), anglais(e), australien(ne).** *zhuh swee zah-may-ree-kahn (kehn) kah-nah-dyan (dyehn), ahn-gleh (glehz), ohs-trah-lyan (yehn)* |

| | |
|---|---|
| My address is _____ | **Mon adresse est** _____ *mohn nah-drehss eh* |
| I'm staying at _____ | **Je loge à** _____ *zhuh lohzh ah* |
| Here is (are) _____. | **Voici** _____. *vwah-ssee* |
| ■ my documents | **mes papiers** *may pah-pyay* |
| ■ my passport | **mon passeport** *mohn pahss-pohr* |
| ■ my identification card | **ma carte d'identité** *mah kahrt dee-dahn-tee-tay* |
| I'm _____. | **Je suis** _____. *zhuh swee* |
| ■ on a business trip | **en voyage d'affaires** *zahn vwah-yahzh dah-fehr* |
| ■ on vacation | **en vacances** *zahn vah-kahnss* |
| ■ on a visit | **en visite** *zahn vee-zeet* |
| I'll be staying here _____. | **Je resterai ici** _____. *zhuh rehss-tray ee-ssee* |
| ■ a few days | **quelques jours** *kehl-kuh zhoor* |
| ■ a few weeks | **quelques semaines** *kehl-kuh suh-mehn* |
| ■ a week | **huit jours** *wee zhoor* |
| ■ two weeks | **quinze jours** *kanz zhoor* |
| ■ a month | **un mois** *uhn mwah* |
| I'm travelling _____. | **Je voyage** _____. *zhuh vwah-yahzh* |
| ■ alone | **seul** *suhl* |
| ■ with my husband | **avec mon mari** *ah-vehk mohn mah-ree* |
| ■ with my wife | **avec ma femme** *ah-vehk mah fahm* |
| ■ with my family | **avec ma famille** *ah-vehk mah fah-mee* |
| These are my bags. | **Voici mes bagages.** *vwah-ssee may bah-gahzh* |

| I have nothing to declare. | **Je n'ai rien à déclarer.** *zhuh nay ryan ah day-klah-ray* |
| I only have a carton of cigarettes. | **J'ai seulement une cartouche de cigarettes.** *zhay suhl-mahn ewn kahr-toosh duh see-gah-reht* |
| ■ a bottle of whisky | **une bouteille de whisky** *ewn boo-tehy duh wheess-kee* |
| They're gifts. | **Ce sont des cadeaux.** *suh sohn day kah-doh* |
| They're for my personal use. | **Ils sont pour usage personnel.** *eel sohn poor ew-zazh pehr-soh-nehl* |
| Do I have to pay duty? | **Dois-je payer des droits de douane?** *dwahzh peh-yay day drwah duh dwahn* |
| May I close my bag now? | **Puis-je fermer ma valise maintenant?** *pweezh fehr-may mah vah-leez mant-nahn* |

## IDENTITY CARD

Upon entering the country you will be required to fill out an identity card, usually with the following information.

**Nom de famille** _____ Last name _____

**Prénom** _____ First name _____

**Nationalité** _____ Nationality _____

**Date de naissance** _____ Birthdate _____

**Profession** _____ Profession _____

**Adresse** _____ Address _____

**Passeport (de)** _____ Passport (from) _____

## BAGGAGE AND PORTERS

If you can find a porter to help you with your luggage, it is customary to give him/her a tip of about five to seven francs per bag. It will probably be simpler and less expensive, however, to avail yourself of the hand carts now in use at most airports and railway stations. You can usually wheel them right through customs and into the street.

| | |
|---|---|
| Where can I find a baggage cart? | **Où puis-je trouver un chariot à bagages?** *oo pweezh troo-vay uhn shah-ryoh ah bah-gahzh* |
| (I need a) porter. | **(Il me faut un) porteur.** *(eel muh foh tuhn) pohr-tuhr* |
| These are our (my) bags. | **Voici nos (mes) valises.** *vwah-ssee noh (may) vah-leez* |
| ■that big one | **cette grande** *seht grahnd* |
| ■these two little ones | **ces deux petites** *say duh puh-teet* |
| Put them here (there). | **Mettez-les ici (là).** *meh-tay lay zee-ssee (lah)* |
| Be careful with that one! | **Faites attention avec celle-là!** *feht zah-tahn-ssyohn ah-vehk sehl lah* |
| I'll carry this one myself. | **Je porterai celle-ci moi-même.** *zhuh pohr-tray sehl see mwah mehm* |

| I'm missing a suitcase. | **Il me manque une valise.** *eel muh mahnk ewn vah-leez* |
| How much do I owe you? | **Combien est-ce que je vous dois?** *kohn-byan ehss kuh zhuh voo dwah* |
| Thank you (very much). | **Merci (beaucoup).** *mehr-ssee (boh-koo)* |
| This is for you. | **C'est pour vous.** *seh poor voo* |

## AIRPORT TRANSPORTATION

| Where can I get a taxi? | **Où puis-je trouver un taxi?** *oo pweezh troo-vay uhn tahk-ssee* |
| What buses go into town? | **Quels bus vont en ville?** *kehl bews vohn tahn veel* |
| Where is the bus stop? | **Où est l'arrêt de bus?** *oo eh lah-reh duh bews* |
| How much is the fare? | **Quel est le tarif?** *kehl eh luh tah-reef* |
| Can I rent a car? | **Puis-je louer une voiture?** *pweezh loo-ay ewn vwah-tewr* |

---

### TRAVEL TIP

Tired of waiting for your suitcase to come off the plane? You can avoid this delay by packing all your belongings into a small carry-on bag. Especially for those who travel light, the carry-on bag is sufficient to hold a week or two's clothing and personal goods. Avoid bags that are too large to fit under your seat on the plane, however, since not all airlines use planes with overhead bins capable of holding such bags. Some airlines have limits on the dimensions of carry-on bags, and if your bag exceeds those limits, you must check the item.

# BANKING AND MONEY MATTERS

## BANKS

Most banks are open from 9:30 AM to 4:30 PM. Some close for lunch, especially during the summer months. All banks close at noon the day preceding a holiday. Banks will change foreign currency into francs at the most favorable rate of exchange. There are also *bureaux de change* at airports or railway stations, which keep longer hours but give a less favorable exchange rate. Many hotels will exchange money and travelers' checks for you, but the rate they offer will be the least favorable.

### BANKING TERMS

| | | |
|---|---|---|
| amount | **le montant** | *luh mohn-tahn* |
| bad | **mauvais** | *moh-veh* |
| bad check | **le chèque sans provision** | *luh shehk sahn proh-vee-zyohn* |
| banker | **le banquier** | *luh bahn-kyay* |
| bill | **le billet** | *luh bee-yeh* |
| borrow (to) | **emprunter** | *ahn-pruhn-tay* |
| cashier | **le caissier** | *luh kehss-yay* |
| capital | **le capital** | *luh kah-pee-tahl* |
| cashier's office | **la caisse** | *lah kehss* |
| checkbook | **le carnet de chèques** | *luh kahr-neh duh shehk* |
| endorse (to) | **endosser** | *ahn-doh-ssay* |
| income | **le revenu** | *luh ruh-vuh-new* |
| interest rate | **le taux d'intérêt** | *luh toh dan-tay-reh* |

| investment | **le placement** | *luh plahss-mah<u>n</u>* |
| lend (to) | **preter** | *preh-tay* |
| loss | **la perte** | *la pehrt* |
| make change (to) | **faire de la mon-naie** | *fehr duh la moh-neh* |
| mortgage | **l'hypothèque** (*f.*) | *lee-poh-tehk* |
| open an account (to) | **ouvrir un compte** | *oo-vreer uh<u>n</u> koh<u>n</u>t* |
| poster | **l'affiche** (*f.*) | *lah-feesh* |
| premium | **la prime** | *lah preem* |
| profit | **le bénéfice** | *luh bay-nay-feess* |
| secretary | **le (la) secrétaire** | *luh (lah) seh-kray-tehr* |
| safe | **le coffre-fort** | *luh koh-fruh fohr* |
| signature | **la signature** | *lah see-nyah-tewr* |
| window | **le guichet** | *luh gee-sheh* |

## MONEY

The franc is the basic unit of French currency. The franc consists of 100 centimes. French money is issued in the following denominations:

- Five (*un sou*), ten and twenty copper-colored centime coins.
- Fifty centime (one-half franc), one franc, two franc, and five franc silver-colored coins.
- Ten franc, dark, copper-colored coin that is replacing the ten franc note which is still in circulation.
- There are 50, 100, and 500 franc bills.

## EXCHANGING MONEY

| | |
|---|---|
| Where can I (change) _____? | **Où puis-je (changer) _____?** *oo pweezh (shahn-zhay)* |
| ■ money | **de l'argent** *duh lahr-zhahn* |
| ■ dollars | **des dollars** *day doh-lahr* |
| ■ travelers' checks | **des chèques de voyage** *day shehk duh vwah-yahzh* |
| ■ cash a personal check | **toucher un chèque personnel** *too-shay uhn shehk pehr-soh-nehl* |
| Where is there a bank? | **Où se trouve une banque?** *Oo suh troov ewn bahnk* |
| ■ money exchange | **un bureau de change** *uhn bew-roh duh shahnzh* |
| At what time do they open (close)? | **À quelle heure ouvre (ferme)-t-on?** *ah kehl uhr oo-vruh (fehrm) tohn* |
| Where is the cashier's window? | **Où est la caisse** *oo eh la kehss* |

The current exchange rates are available in the banks which exchange money, and are also published daily in the newspapers. Since the rates fluctuate from day to day, you may find it helpful to convert the following amounts in francs into their equivalent in your own currency.

| FRENCH FRANCS | YOUR CURRENCY |
|---|---|
| 1 | |
| 5 | |
| 10 | |
| 50 | |
| 100 | |
| 500 | |

| BELGIAN FRANCS | YOUR CURRENCY |
|---|---|
| 10 | |
| 20 | |
| 50 | |
| 100 | |
| 500 | |
| 1000 | |

| SWISS FRANCS | YOUR CURRENCY |
|---|---|
| 1 | |
| 2 | |
| 5 | |
| 10 | |
| 20 | |
| 50 | |
| 1000 | |

| | |
|---|---|
| What's the current exchange rate? | **Quel est le cours (du change) le plus récent?** *kehl eh luh koor (dew shahnzh) luh plew ray-sahn* |
| I'd like to cash this check. | **Je voudrais toucher ce chèque.** *zhuh voo-dreh too-shay suh shehk* |

| Where do I sign? | **Où dois-je signer?** *oo dwahzh see-nyay* |
| Where do I endorse it? | **Où est-ce que je l'endosse?** *oo ehss kuh zhuh lahn-dohss* |
| I'd like the money in (large) bills. | **Je voudrais l'argent en grosses coupures.** *zhuh voo-dreh lahr-zhahn ahn grohss koo-pewr* |
| ■ in small change | **en petite monnaie** *ahn puh-teet moh-nay* |
| Give me two twenty-franc bills. | **Donnez-moi deux billets de vingt francs.** *doh-nay mwah duh bee-yeh duh van frahn* |
| ■ fifty | **cinquante** *san-kahnt* |
| ■ one hundred | **cent** *sahn* |
| Do you accept credit cards? | **Acceptez-vous les cartes de crédit?** *ahk-ssehp-tay voo lay kahrt duh kray-dee* |

## TIPPING

In many instances, service charges are included in the price of the service rendered. These usually come to about 10 to 15% and should be indicated on the bill.

Usually a customer will leave some small change in addition to any charge that has been included if the service has been satisfactory. At times, a set amount should be given.

The following table is merely a suggested guide. Tips will vary from time to time due to inflation and other factors. It is therefore advisable to ask some knowledgeable person (hotel manager, tour director, etc.) once you get to the country, for proper tipping information, or you should check the rate of exchange.

| SERVICE | TIP |
| --- | --- |
| Waiter | 12–15% |
| Bellboy, porter | 5–6 francs/bag |
| Chambermaid | 8–10 francs/day |
| Usher | 3–4 francs |
| Taxi driver | 10–15% of the fare |
| Guide | 10% |
| Barber, hairdresser | 10–15% |
| Shoeshine | small change |
| Bathroom attendant | 1–2 francs |

## TIPPING AT HOTELS

Check to see whether the service charge (usually 10–15%) is included in the room price. The words "service compris" or "toutes taxes comprises" indicate that your tipping obligations have been fulfilled except for the bellboy carrying your luggage and the concierge who may perform special services for you. Should any other employee go out of his way to help you, then a small additional tip would be in order.

---

### TRAVEL TIP

It is possible, through diet and habit, to ease the transition to a new time zone, commonly referred to as "jet lag." Up to four days prior to your departure, begin accustoming your body to its future schedule by gradually changing the times you eat until they more closely match that of your destination. Eat lightly and avoid carbohydrates. If you are taking a night flight, eat very little the day of your departure and avoid alcohol and even dinner on the plane if it is offered. Instead, ask to have your breakfast earlier, then rest until it is served. When you arrive, you will have had your breakfast about the same time as people in that country, and be ready for your next meal at the appropriate time. When you do have your next meal, try to eat a lot of protein, followed in the next meal by a high-carbohydrate diet. Avoid taking a nap during your first day, and instead go to bed a little earlier than usual.

# AT THE HOTEL

## LODGING

Accommodations are varied, plentiful and are available in different price ranges. If you have not made a reservation and are looking for a place to stay, it is best to go to a tourist information center called le Syndicat d'Initiative (SI) or Office du Tourisme (OT). Someone there will gladly help you find a room to suit your needs and your budget. You will find yourself staying at one of the following:

## HOTEL

Although there are hotel rooms in every price range, it is best to make an advance reservation. Festivals, exhibitions, shows and trade fairs attract many visitors and rooms are quickly filled. The French government rates hotels by using a star system ranging from * inexpensive to **** expensive (*luxe*). A hotel receives its rating based on room price and the conveniences it provides: size of room, telephone availability, bathroom facilities. A continental breakfast, consisting of rolls, butter and jam and coffee or tea is often included in the price of the room. English is spoken in the larger, more exclusive hotels, and American style breakfasts are usually available there.

## MOTEL

Motels have recently spread to France. They are located near main roads outside towns and cities and at the airport.

## PENSION

Pensions resemble rooming houses where the visitor pays for a room and all or part of his meals.

## AUBERGE (LOGIS)

This is usually a small, modest and inexpensive country inn found off the main roads in rural areas.

## CHAMBRES D'HÔTE

In towns or villages rooms are made available in the homes of local families who will supply bed and breakfast for a fee.

## GÎTES RURAUX

If you visit the countryside, you may rent a gîte, a private residence—house or apartment.

You should be aware that in France, especially outside of Paris, it is customary and expected that a guest eat dinner at his hotel. Many smaller hotels will charge you for dinner whether you eat it or not, or refuse to rent the room unless you eat in the hotel. You may inquire about this at the desk.

## GETTING TO YOUR HOTEL

| | |
|---|---|
| I'd like to go to the ____ Hotel. | **Je voudrais aller à l'hôtel ____.** *zhuh voo-dreh zah-lay ah loh-tel* |
| Is it near (far)? | **C'est près (loin) d'ici?** *seh preh (lwan) dee-ssee* |
| Where can I get a taxi? | **Où puis-je trouver un taxi?** *oo pweezh troo-vay uhn tahk-see* |
| How much is the fare? | **Quel est le tarif?** *kehl eh luh tah-reef* |
| Where is the bus stop? | **Où est l'arrêt de bus?** *oo eh lah-reh duh bews* |

## CHECKING IN

When you register, it will be necessary to fill out a form (une fiche) with your name, address and passport number at the registration desk of any establishment.

| | |
|---|---|
| I'd like a single (double) room for tonight ____. | **Je voudrais une chambre à un lit (à deux lits) pour ce soir ____.** *zhuh voo-dreh zewn shahn-bruh ah uhn lee (ah duh lee) poor suh swahr* |

| | | |
|---|---|---|
| ■with a shower | **avec douche** *ah-vehk doosh* | |
| ■with a bath | **avec salle de bains** *ah-vehk sahl duh ban* | |
| ■with a balcony | **avec balcon** *ah-vehk bahl-kohn* | |
| ■facing the ocean | **qui donne sur l'océan** *kee dohn sewr loh-ssay-ahn* | |
| ■facing the street | **qui donne sur la rue** *kee dohn sewr lah rew* | |
| ■facing the court-yard | **qui donne sur la cour** *kee dohn sewr lah koor* | |
| Does it have ____? | **Y a-t-il ____?** *ee ah teel* | |
| ■air conditioning | **la climatisation** *lah klee-mah-tee-zah-ssyohn* | |
| ■hot water | **l'eau chaude** *loh shohd* | |
| ■television | **une télévision** *ewn tay-lay-vee-zyohn* | |
| ■a private bathroom | **une salle de bain privée** *ewn sahl duh ban pree-vay* | |
| ■shower | **une douche** *ewn doosh* | |
| I (don't) have a reservation. | **J'ai (Je n'ai pas) retenu une (de) chambre.** *zhay (zhuh nay pah) ruh-tuh-new ewn (duh) shahn-bruh* | |
| Could you call another hotel to see if they have something? | **Pourriez-vous appeler un autre hôtel pour voir s'ils ont une chambre de libre?** *poo-ree-yay voo zah-play uhn noh-truh oh-tehl poor vwahr seel zohn tewn shahn-bruh duh lee-bruh* | |
| May I see the room? | **Puis-je voir la chambre?** *pweezh vwahr lah shahn-bruh* | |
| I (don't) like it. | **Elle me plaît.** *ehl muh pleh* | |
| | **Elle ne me plaît pas.** *ehl nuh muh pleh pah* | |

| | |
|---|---|
| Do you have something ____? | **Avez-vous quelque chose ____?** *ah-vay voo kehl-kuh shohz* |
| ■ better | **de meilleur** *duh meh-yuhr* |
| ■ larger | **de plus grand** *duh plew grahn* |
| ■ smaller | **de plus petit** *duh plew puh-tee* |
| ■ cheaper | **de meilleur marché** *duh meh-yuhr mahr-shay* |
| On what floor is it? | **C'est à quel étage?** *seht ah kehl ay-tahzh* |
| Is there an elevator? | **Y a-t-il un ascenseur?** *ee ah teel uhn nah-sahn-suhr* |
| How much do you charge for ____? | **Quel est le tarif ____?** *kehl eh luh tah-reef* |
| ■ the American plan | **pension complète** *pahn-ssyohn kohn-pleht* |
| ■ bed and breakfast | **petit déjeuner compris** *puh-tee day-zhuh-nay kohn-pree* |

| | |
|---|---|
| ■breakfast and dinner | **en demi-pension** *ahn duh-mee pahn-ssyohn* |
| ■the room without meals | **pour la chambre sans repas** *poor lah shahn-bruh sahn ruh-pah* |
| Is it necessary to eat here? | **Faut-il manger ici?** *foh-teel man-zhay ee-see* |
| Is everything included? | **Est-ce que tout est compris?** *ehss kuh too teh kohn-pree* |
| The room is very nice. I'll take it. | **Cette chambre me plaît. Je la prends.** *seht shahn-bruh muh pleh. Zhuh lah prahn* |
| I prefer a room in the back. | **Je préfère une chambre sur la cour.** *zhuh pray-fehr ewn shahn-bruh sewr lah koor* |
| Is there a reduction for children? | **Accordez-vous des réductions aux enfants?** *ah-kohr-day voo day ray-dewk-ssyohn oh zahn-fahn* |
| Could you put another bed in the room? | **Pourriez-vous mettre un autre lit dans la chambre?** *poo-ree-yay voo meh-truh uhn noh-truh lee dahn lah shahn-bruh* |
| Is there a charge? How much? | **Faut-il payer pour cela? Combien?** *foh teel peh-yay poor suh-lah? kohn-byan* |

## OTHER ACCOMMODATIONS

| | |
|---|---|
| I'm looking for ____. | **Je cherche** ____. *zhuh shehrsh* |
| ■a boarding house | **une pension** *ewn pahn-ssyohn* |
| ■a private house | **une maison particulière** *ewn meh-zohn pahr-tee-kew-lyehr* |
| I want to rent an apartment. | **Je voudrais louer un appartement.** *zhuh voo-dreh loo-ay uhn nah-pahr-tuh-mahn* |

| | |
|---|---|
| I need a living room, bedroom and kitchen. | **Il me faut un salon, une chambre à coucher et une cuisine.** *eel muh foh uhn sah-lohn, ewn shahn-bruh ah koo-shay ay ewn kwee-zeen* |
| Do you have a furnished room? | **Avez-vous une chambre meublée? (garnie?)** *ah-vay voo zewn shahn-bruh muh-blay (gahr-nee)* |
| How much is the rent? | **C'est combien le loyer?** *seh kohn-byan luh lwah-yay* |
| I'll be staying here for _____. | **Je resterai ici _____.** *zhuh rehss-tray ee-ssee* |
| ■ two weeks | **quinze jours** *kahnz zhoor* |
| ■ one month | **un mois** *uhn mwah* |
| ■ the whole summer | **tout l'été** *too lay-tay* |
| I want a place that's centrally located near public transportation. | **Je voudrais (avoir) une résidence située au centre de la ville près des transports publics.** *zhuh voo-dreh zah-vwahr ewn ray-zee-dahnss see-tew-ay oh sahn-truh duh lah veel preh deh trahnss-pohr pew-bleek* |
| Is there a youth hostel around here? | **Y a-t-il une auberge de jeunesse par ici?** *ee ah teel ewn oh-behrzh duh zhuh-nehss preh dee-ssee* |

## ORDERING BREAKFAST

The French or Continental breakfast is usually simple—coffee or chocolate, a croissant or brioche with jam or marmalade. At the larger hotels you will be able to order an English-style breakfast (juice, eggs, bacon, toast). You may enjoy having breakfast in your room.

| | |
|---|---|
| We'll have breakfast in the room. | **Nous prendrons le petit déjeuner à la chambre.** *noo prahn-drohn luh puh-tee day-zhuh-nay ah lah shahn-bruh* |

| Please send up ____ | **Faites monter ____ s'il vous plaît** *feht mohn-tay seel voo pleh* |
|---|---|
| ■ One (two) coffee(s) | **Un (deux) café(s)** *uhn (duh) kah-fay* |
| ■ Tea | **Un thé** *uhn tay* |
| ■ Chocolate | **Un chocolat** *uhn shoh-koh-lah* |
| ■ A (some) croissant(s) | **Un (des) croissant(s)** *uhn (day) krwah-ssahn* |
| ■ Fruit | **Des fruits** *day frwee* |
| ■ Fruit juice | **Du jus de fruit** *dew zhew duh frwee* |
| I'll (we'll) eat breakfast in the dining room. | **Je (nous) prendrai (prendrons) le petit déjeuner à la salle à manger.** *zhuh (noo) prahn-dray (prahn-drohn) luh puh-tee day-zhuh-nay ah lah sahl ah mahn-zhay* |
| We'd like ____ | **Nous voudrions ____** *noo voo-dree-yohn* |
| ■ Scrambled (fried) (boiled) eggs | **Des oeufs brouillés (au plat) (à la coque)** *day zuh broo-yay (oh plah) (ah lah kohk)* |
| ■ Toast | **Du pain grillé** *dew pan gree-yay* |
| ■ Jam | **De la confiture** *duh lah kohn-fee-tewr* |

NOTE: See Food section (pp. 77–107) for more phrases for ordering meals

## HOTEL SERVICE

| Where is ____? | **Où est ____?** *oo eh* |
|---|---|
| ■ the dining room | **la salle à manger** *lah sahl ah mahn-zhay* |
| ■ the bathroom | **la salle de bains** *lah sahl duh ban* |

| | | |
|---|---|---|
| ■ the elevator | **l'ascenseur** *lah-ssahn-ssuhr* | |
| ■ the phone | **le téléphone** *luh tay-lay-fohn* | |
| What is my room number? | **Quel est le numéro de ma chambre?** *kehl eh luh new-may-roh duh mah shahn-bruh* | |
| May I please have my key? | **Pourrais-je avoir la clef?** *poo-rehzh ah-vwahr lah klay* | |
| I need ____. | **Il me faut ____.** *eel muh foh* | |
| ■ a bellboy | **un chasseur** *tuhn shah-ssuhr* | |
| ■ a chambermaid | **une femme de chambre** *tewn fahm duh shahn-bruh* | |
| Please send ____ to my room | **Veuillez envoyer ____ à ma chambre** *vuh-yay ahn-vwah-yay ah mah shahn-bruh* | |
| ■ breakfast | **le petit déjeuner** *luh puh-tee day-zhuh-nay* | |
| ■ a towel | **une serviette** *ewn sehr-vyeht* | |
| ■ a bar of soap | **une savonnette** *ewn sah-voh-neht* | |
| ■ some hangers | **des cintres** *day san-truh* | |
| ■ a pillow | **un oreiller** *uhn noh-reh-yay* | |
| ■ a blanket | **une couverture** *ewn koo-vehr-tewr* | |
| ■ some ice | **de la glace** *duh lah glahss* | |
| ■ ice cubes | **des glaçons** *day glah-ssohn* | |
| ■ some ice water | **de l'eau glacée** *duh loh glah-ssay* | |
| ■ an ashtray | **un cendrier** *uhn sahn-dree-yay* | |
| ■ toilet paper | **un rouleau de papier hygiénique** *uhn roo-loh duh pah-pyay ee-zhyay-neek* | |
| ■ a bottle of mineral water | **une bouteille d'eau minérale** *ewn boo-tehy doh mee-nay-rahl* | |

| | |
|---|---|
| ■ a reading lamp | **une lumière pour lire** *ewn lew-myehr poor leer* |
| ■ an electric adaptor | **un transformateur** *uhn trahnss-fohr-mah-tuhr* |

NOTE: Electrical current is usually 220 volts. A European-style adaptor plug or an adaptable appliance is necessary for electric hair dryers or clocks. Large international hotels may have an adaptor plug at the reception desk, but smaller hotels or pensions are unlikely to be able to provide one.

| | |
|---|---|
| Just a minute. | **Un moment.** *uhn moh-mahn* |
| Come in. | **Entrez.** *ahn-tray* |
| Put it on the table. | **Mettez-ça sur la table.** *meh-tay sah sewr lah tah-bluh* |
| Will you wake me? | **Voulez-vous bien me réveiller?** *voo-lay voo byan muh ray-veh-yay* |
| Please wake me to-morrow at ___ | **Réveillez-moi demain matin à ___, s'il vous plaît.** *ray-veh-yay mwah duh-man mah-tan ah seel voo pleh* |
| There is no ___. | **Il n'y a pas ___.** *eel nyah pah* |
| ■ running water | **d'eau courante** *doh koo-rahnt* |
| ■ hot water | **d'eau chaude** *doh shohd* |
| ■ electricity | **d'électricité** *day-lehk-tree-ssee-tay* |
| The ___ doesn't work. | **___ ne fonctionne pas.** *nuh fohnk-ssyohn pah* |
| ■ air conditioning | **le climatiseur** *luh klee-mah-tee-zuhr* |
| ■ fan | **le ventilateur** *luh vahn-tee-lah-tuhr* |
| ■ faucet | **le robinet** *luh roh-bee-neh* |
| ■ lamp | **la lampe** *lah lahnp* |
| ■ light | **la lumière** *lah lew-myehr* |

| | |
|---|---|
| ■radio | **la radio** *lah rah-dyoh* |
| ■socket | **la prise de courant** *lah preez duh koo-rahn* |
| ■switch | **le commutateur** *luh koh-mew-tah-tuhr* |
| ■television | **la télévision** *lah tay-lay-vee-zyohn* |
| Can you fix it? | **Pouvez-vous la réparer** *poo-vay voo lah ray-pah-ray* |
| ■now | **maintenent** *mant-nahn* |
| ■as soon as possible | **aussitôt que possible** *oh-ssee-toh kuh poh-ssee-bluh* |
| The room is dirty. | **La chambre est sale.** *lah shahn-bruh eh sahl* |
| Are there any _____ for me? | **Y a-t-il _____ pour moi.** *ee ah teel poor mwah* |
| ■letters | **des lettres** *day leh-truh* |
| ■messages | **des messages** *day meh-ssahzh* |
| ■packages | **des colis** *day koh-lee* |
| ■post cards | **des cartes postales** *day kahrt pohss-tahl* |
| Did anyone call for me? | **Est-ce que quelqu'un m'a téléphoné?** *ehss kuh kehl kuhn mah tay-lay-foh-nay* |
| Who is it? | **Qui est-ce?** *kee ehss* |
| Can you make a phone call for me? | **Pouvez-vous faire un appel téléphonique pour moi?** *poo-vay voo fehr uhn nah-pehl tay-lay-foh-neek poor mwah* |
| I'd like to put this in the hotel safe. | **Je voudrais mettre ceci dans le coffre-fort de l'hôtel.** *zhuh voo-dreh meh-truh ssuh-ssee dahn luh koh-fruh-fohr duh loh-tehl* |

## CHECKING OUT

| | |
|---|---|
| I'd like the bill, please. | **Je voudrais l'addition, si'il vous plaît.** *zhuh voo-dreh lah-dee-ssyohn̲ seel voo pleh* |
| I'm leaving today (tomorrow). | **Je pars aujourd'hui (demain).** *zhuh pahr oh-zhoor-dwee (duh-man̲)* |
| Please send someone up for the baggage. | **Faites monter quelqu'un pour les valises, s'il vous plaît.** *feht mohn̲-tay kehl-kuhn̲ poor lay vah-leez seel voo pleh* |

---

### TRAVEL TIP

Now that many airlines allow you to reserve your seat in advance, you can ensure that you have the place you want without arriving at the airport well in advance. But what a good seat is depends on the type of aircraft and your personal preferences. Familiarize yourself with the layouts of the major types of planes, especially the wide-bodies, so you know what to ask for. If you prefer nonsmoking, you may wish to avoid the seats in that section which are immediately in front of or behind the smoking section. Also, some overseas airlines divide the plane lengthwise, so nonsmokers are only across the aisle from smokers. If you want to see the movie, avoid the bulkhead seats; if you want to walk around and stretch your legs frequently, choose an aisle seat. If you wish to sleep, avoid a seat near the galley.

# GETTING AROUND TOWN

In villages or out in the country you may want to stroll around to do your sightseeing. Although walking in the city is also rewarding, you'll want to be familiar with the types of public transportation available.

For information on plane, train or boat travel, see pp. 53–58.

## THE SUBWAY

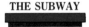

The subway (LE MÉTRO), is the clean, inexpensive, and efficient underground train system in Paris. Above ground, a big "M" indicates a metro stop. Trains run very frequently—about every five minutes. Large, clear subway maps help you locate the correct line to take to reach your destination. At the ticket window (**guichet**) you can purchase a first or second class ticket. (First class cars are in the middle of the train.) For convenience and economy, a book of 10 tickets (**un carnet**) is available for regular riders. Frequent riders may wish to purchase an orange card (**carte orange**) which permits unlimited rides for a month. The Métro closes at 1 A.M.

| | |
|---|---|
| Is there a subway in this city? | **Y a-t-il un métro dans cette ville?** *ee ah teel uhn may-troh dahn seht veel* |
| Where is there a subway station? | **Où se trouve une station de métro?** *oo suh troov ewn stah-ssyohn duh may-troh* |
| How much is the fare? | **Quel est le prix du trajet?** *kehl eh luh pree dew trah-zheh* |
| Where can I buy a ticket? | **Où puis-je acheter un billet?** *oo pweezh ahsh-tay uhn bee-yeh* |
| Which line goes to _____? | **Quelle ligne va à _____?** *kehl lee-nyuh vah ah* |
| Does this train go to _____? | **Est-ce que ce train va à _____?** *ehss kuh suh tran vah ah* |

| | |
|---|---|
| How many more stops? | **Il nous reste combien d'arrêts?** *eel noo rehsst kohn-byan dah-reh* |
| What's the next station? | **Quelle est la prochaine station?** *kehl eh lah proh-shehn stah-ssyohn* |
| Where should I get off to go to ___? | **Où dois-je descendre pour aller à ___?** *oo dwahzh day-sahn-druh poor ah-lay ah* |
| Do I have to change? | **Faut-il prendre une correspondance?** *foh teel prahn-druh ewn koh-rehss-pohn-dahnss* |
| Please tell me when we get there. | **S'il vous plaît, dites-moi quand nous y arriverons.** *seel voo pleh, deet mwah kahn noo zee ah-ree-vrohn* |

| | |
|---|---|
| Défense de cracher | No spitting |

In the trains, buses, and metro, certain seats with numbers are reserved. You may sit in one of those seats if there are enough seats vacant. A war veteran may come up to you and show you his ID card, and in that case, you have to give him your seat. You may see the following notices posted:

| LES PLACES NUMÉROTÉES SONT RÉSERVÉES: | NUMBERED SEATS ARE RESERVED FOR: |
|---|---|
| 1. Aux invalides de guerre | Disabled veterans |
| 2. Aux invalides civils | Handicapped persons |
| 3. Aux femmes enceintes | Pregnant women |
| 4. Aux personnes accompagnées d'enfants de moins de 4 ans | Persons with children under 4 years of age. |

## THE BUS (STREETCAR, TRAM)

European Express and Europabus serve major European cities. They are less expensive, but slower, than trains. If you plan to travel around the city by bus, you may purchase a discount book of tickets *(un carnet)*. Be sure to have some small change on entering the bus.

| | |
|---|---|
| Défense de parler au conducteur | Do not speak to the driver |

| Where is the bus stop? (bus terminal)? | **Où est l'arrêt de bus?/le terminus?** *oo eh lah-reh dew bewss/luh tehr-mee-newss* |
|---|---|
| Which bus do I take to get to _____? | **Quel bus faut-il prendre pour aller à _____?** *kehl bewss foh teel prahn-druh poor ah-lay ah* |
| In which direction do I have to go? | **Dans quel sens dois-je aller?** *dahn kehl sahnss dwahzh ah-lay* |
| How often do the buses run? | **Quelle est la fréquence des bus?** *kehl eh lah fray-kahnss day bewss* |
| Do you go to _____? | **Est-ce que vous allez à _____?** *ehss kuh voo zah-lay ah* |
| I want to go to _____. | **Je voudrais aller à _____.** *zhuh voo-dreh zah-lay ah* |
| Is it far from here? | **C'est loin d'ici?** *seh lwan dee-ssee* |
| How many stops are there? | **Il y a combien d'arrêts?** *eel yah kohn-byan dah-reh* |
| Do I have to change? | **Faut-il changer de bus?** *foh teel shahn-zhay duh bewss* |
| How much is the fare? | **Quel est le prix du trajet?** *kehl eh luh pree dew trah-zheh* |

| Could you tell me where to get off? | **Pourriez-vous me dire quand je dois descendre?** *poo-ree-yay voo muh deer kahn zhuh dwah day-sahn-druh* |
| Where do I get off? | **Où dois-je descendre?** *oo dwahzh day-sahn-druh* |

## TAXIS

Taxis, except for certain ones making trips to and from the airport, which give a flat rate, are metered. Look for the sign **Stationnement de Taxis** indicating a taxi stand. You cannot hail a taxi on the street within 100 meters of a stand. There is a supplement (indicated on the meter) after 11 p.m.

| Is there a taxi stand around here? | **Y a-t-il une station de taxis près d'ici?** *ee ah teel ewn stah-ssyohn duh tahk-ssee preh dee-ssee* |
| Where can I get a taxi? | **Où puis-je trouver un taxi?** *oo pweezh troo-vay uhn tahk-ssee* |
| Taxi! Are you available? | **Taxi! Êtes-vous libre?** *tahk-ssee eht voo lee-bruh* |
| Take me (I want to go) _____. | **Conduisez-moi (Je voudrais aller)** _____. *kohn-dwee-zay mwah (zhuh voo-dreh zah-lay)* |
| ■ to the airport | **à l'aéroport** *ah lahy-roh-pohr* |
| ■ to this address | **à cette adresse** *ah seht ah-drehss* |
| ■ to the hotel | **à l'hôtel** *ah loh-tehl* |
| ■ to the station | **à la gare** *ah lah gahr* |
| ■ to _____ Street | **à la rue** _____ *ah lah rew* |
| Do you know where it is? | **Savez-vous où ça se trouve?** *sah-vay voo oo sah suh troov* |
| How much is it to _____? | **C'est combien pour aller à _____?** *seh kohn-byan poor ah-lay ah* |

| Faster! I'm in a hurry. | **Allez plus vite! Je suis pressé(e)!** *ah-lay plew veet zhuh swee preh-ssay* |
| Please drive slower. | **Conduisez plus lentement, s'il vous plaît.** *kohn-dwee-zay plew lahnt-mahn seel voo pleh* |
| Don't go so fast. | **Ne conduisez pas si vite, s'il vous plaît.** *Nuh kohn-dwee-zay pah see veet seel voo pleh* |
| Stop here at the corner. | **Arrêtez-vous ici, au coin.** *ah-reh-tay voo zee-ssee, oh kwan* |
| Stop at the next block. | **Arrêtez-vous à la prochaine rue.** *ah-reh-tay voo ah lah proh-shehn rew* |
| Wait for me. I'll be right back. | **Attendez-mois, s'il vous plaît. Je reviens tout de suite.** *ah-tahn-day mwah seel voo pleh zhuh ruh-vyan toot sweet* |
| How much do I owe you? | **Combien est-ce que je vous dois?** *kohn-byan ehss kuh zhuh voo dwah* |
| This is for you. | **Voilà pour vous.** *vwah-lah poor voo* |

| | |
|---|---|
| Where is the Tourist Office? | **Où est le Syndicat d'Initiative?** *oo eh luh sa<u>n</u>-dee-kah dee-nee-ssyah-teev* |
| I need an (English speaking) guide. | **J'ai besoin d'un guide (qui parle anglais).** *zhay buh-zwa<u>n</u> duh<u>n</u> geed (kee pahrl ah<u>n</u>-gleh)* |
| How much does he charge ____? | **Quel est le prix ____?** *kehl eh luh pree* <br> **C'est combien ____?** *seh koh<u>n</u>-bya<u>n</u>* |
| ■ per hour | **à l'heure** *ah luhr* |
| ■ per day | **à la journée** *ah lah zhoor-nay* |
| There are two (four, six) of us. | **Nous sommes deux (quatre, six).** *noo sohm duh (kah-truh, seess)* |
| Where can I buy a guide book? (a map) | **Où puis-je acheter un guide touristique? (une carte)** *oo pweezh ahsh-tay uh<u>n</u> geed too-reess-teek (ewn kahrt)* |
| What are the main attractions? | **Qu'est-ce qu'il y a de plus intéressant?** *kehss keel yah duh plew za<u>n</u>-tay-reh-ssah<u>n</u>* |
| What are things of interest here? | **Qu'est-ce qu'il y a d'intéressant à voir par ici?** *kehss keel yah da<u>n</u>-tay-reh-ssah<u>n</u> ah vwahr pahr ee-ssee* |
| Are there trips through the city? | **Y a-t-il des visites guidées à travers la ville?** *ee ah teel day vee-zeet gee-day ah trah-vehr lah veel* |
| Where do they leave from? | **D'où partent-elles?** *doo pahr tehl* |
| We want to see ____. | **Nous voudrions voir ____.** *noo vood-ree-yoh<u>n</u> vwahr* |
| ■ the botanical garden | **le jardin botanique** *luh zhahr-da<u>n</u> boh-tah-neek* |
| ■ the business center | **le quartier des affaires** *luh kahr-tyay day zah-fehr* |
| ■ the castle | **le château** *luh shah-toh* |

| | | |
|---|---|---|
| ■ the cathedral | **la cathédrale** | *lah kah-tay-drahl* |
| ■ the church | **l'église** | *lay-gleez* |
| ■ the concert hall | **la salle de concert** | *lah sahl duh kohn-ssehr* |
| ■ the downtown area | **le centre de la ville** | *luh sahn-truh duh la veel* |
| ■ the fountains | **les fontaines** | *lay fohn-tehn* |
| ■ the library | **la bibliothèque** | *lah bee-blee-oh-tehk* |
| ■ the main park | **le parc principal** | *luh pahrk pran-ssee-pahl* |
| ■ the main square | **la place principale** | *lah plahss pran-ssee-pahl* |
| ■ the market | **le marché** | *luh mahr-shay* |
| ■ the mosque | **la mosquée** | *lah mohss-kay* |
| ■ the museum (of fine arts) | **le musée des beaux arts** | *luh mew-zay day boh **zahr*** |
| ■ a nightclub | **une boîte de nuit** | *ewn bwaht duh nwee* |
| ■ the old part of town | **la vieille ville** | *lah vyehy veel* |
| ■ the opera | **l'opéra** | *loh-pay-rah* |
| ■ the palace | **le palais** | *luh pah-leh* |
| ■ the stadium | **le stade** | *luh stahd* |
| ■ the synagogue | **la synagogue** | *lah see-nah-gohg* |
| ■ the university | **l'université** | *lew-nee-vehr-**ssee**-tay* |
| ■ the zoo | **le zoo** | *luh zoh* |
| Is it all right to go in now? | **Peut-on entrer maintenant?** | *puh tohn ahn-tray mant-nahn* |
| Is it open? | **C'est ouvert?** | *seh too-vehr* |
| Is it closed? | **C'est fermé?** | *seh fehr-may* |

| At what time does it open? | **À quelle heure ouvre -t-il / elle?** *ah kehl uhr oo-vruh teel/ tehl* |
| At what time does it close? | **À quelle heure ferme-t-il/elle?** *ah kehl uhr fehrm teel/tehl* |
| What are the visiting hours? | **Quelles sont les heures de visite?** *kehl sohn lay zuhr duh vee-zeet* |
| What's the admission price? | **Combien coûte un billet d'entrée?** *kohn-byan koot uhn bee-yeh dahn-tray* |
| How much do children pay? | **C'est combien pour les enfants?** *seh kohn-byan poor lay zahn-fahn* |
| Can they go in free? Until what age? | **Est-ce gratuit pour les enfants? Jusqu'à quel âge?** *ehss grah-twee poor lay zahn-fahn. zhewss-kah kehl ahzh* |
| Is it all right to take pictures? | **Peut-on prendre des photos?** *puh tohn prahn-druh day foh-toh* |

## A SIGHTSEEING ITINERARY

France is a country overwhelmingly rich in places and things to be seen. Its cities and countryside overflow with sites and institutions redolent of historic, intellectual and artistic tradition. Few indeed are the areas not commemorated by a general's triumph, a king's passage, an artist's inspiration or a philosopher's wit. To attempt an exhaustive tour in the usual short vacation span would be foolhardy. We try here simply to suggest, in broad outline, some of the highlights, the best-known and most popular attractions to which visitors are drawn. Modern France has an extensive and sophisticated system of public transportation, enabling the traveler to get quickly to whatever area most interests him.

### PARIS

Paris is the cultural, economic, political and social center of France. Among its museums are: The *Louvre,* which contains the Venus de Milo, the Winged Victory of Samothrace and the Mona Lisa. Also on display are antiquities, sculpture, art objects, furniture and paintings from every European school; the *Army Museum* adjacent to the *Invalides,* in which stands the tomb of Napoleon; the *Jeu de Paume Museum* with its vast collection of Impressionist paintings; the *Panthéon,* which has paintings and the mausoleums of many illustrious French; the *Cluny Museum,* renowned for medieval art.

Those with an interest in church sculpture and architecture will be particularly interested in the Cathedral of *Notre-Dame.* Its spires, portals, stained glass windows and flying buttresses make it a milestone in Gothic architecture. Vividly colored stained glass windows dating back to the 13th century and portraying over 1,000 biblical scenes make the *Sainte-Chapelle* church unique. *Sacré-Coeur,* the domed white church dominating Montmartre, resembles a mosque and is decorated on the interior with mosaics. The 18th-19th century church of the *Madeleine* with its colonnade is also of some interest.

Noted public squares frequented by tourists include: the *Place de la Concorde,* where many historical figures, including Louis XVI and Marie Antoinette, were guillotined during the French Revolution. The obelisk in the middle of the square comes from the ruins of the temple at Luxor in Egypt and is covered with hieroglyphics. The *Place Vendôme* is the site of the Vendôme column, which has scenes depicting Napoleon's military campaigns at its center. On top of the column is a statue of the emperor. The *Place de l'Opéra,* dominated by the Opéra, is the home of the national opera and ballet companies and renowned for its architecture and decor. The *Place de la Bastille* is the site of the once famous prison, since destroyed, where the first shots of the Revolution are commemorated every July 14. The *Place Charles de Gaulle,* upon which stands the *Arc de Triomphe,* is one of France's best known landmarks. Under the arch is the tomb of the Unknown Soldier. Twelve avenues fan out from the arch, creating the pattern of a star. Leading to the arch, the Champs Elysées is lined with trees, cafés and luxurious shops.

The *Centre National d'Art et de Culture Georges Pompidou,* on the site of the old Les Halles market, is a national museum with frequent expositions and a voluminous research library. From the observation deck on the roof you can see all of Paris.

The *Eiffel Tower* stands over 1,000 feet tall and acts as a radio and television transmitter. From any of its three different levels one gets a panoramic view of Paris. At its base there is a popular restaurant. Walking along the *quais* of the *Seine* you will find the parapets lined with quaint bookshops. *Montmartre,* or the "Butte," as it is commonly known, is a center of artistic life where bohemianism may be said to have its roots. The *Latin Quarter* is the home of the Sorbonne University and an intellectual hub.

At the *Palais de Justice,* the seat of the courts and all the judicial system, you will see the *Conciergerie* which served as a prison during the Revolution. Also not to be missed are *La Bourse* or Stock Exchange, and *Le Marché aux puces,* the Paris flea market.

When your feet hurt and you want to take a break, relax in the *Tuileries* gardens, beside the Seine. Statues, figures and decorative vases line these formal French gardens. The *Bois de Boulogne* is a vast park containing ornamental lakes, flower gardens, cafés, restaurants, two racetracks and a children's amusement park. Best, however, not to frequent it at night. The *Bois de Vincennes* contains museums and a zoo. The *Luxembourg* gardens, on the left bank, are much used by students.

Just outside of Paris is *Versailles,* the luxurious palace known for its architecture, style, and gardens. A bus tour from Paris to Versailles might also include side trips to *Fontainebleau* and *Chantilly* castles. The *Basilica of Saint Denis,* and the small city of *Sèvres,* known for its multicolored porcelain, are also not far from the capital.

## FARTHER AFIELD

A bus tour of the *Loire* valley enables one to visit many splendid castles, among them *Chambord* and *Chenonceaux.* This tour might include a trip to the *Chartres* cathedral, which contains sculptures representing biblical personages. The stained glass windows of the cathedral are unique, drawing visitors who travel to France just to see them.

The beaches of *Normandy,* where the Allies landed in 1944, will be of special interest to history buffs.

*Mont-Saint-Michel,* a monastery surrounded by a medieval

fortress, is situated on a small island in the English Channel, between Normandy and Brittany.

A visit to the *wine country*, the regions of Bordeaux, Champagne and Languedoc, will be interesting and informative.

*Strasbourg*, an industrial city, has a cathedral famous for its astronomical clock. It also contains the offices of the EEC, the European Economic Community known as the Common Market.

The cities of *Chamonix* and *Grenoble*, and the *French Alps*, are extremely popular and offer a wide variety of winter activities.

*Nice*, capital of the *Riviera*, vacation spot of the jet-set and refuge from the ravages of winter, has pebble beaches and a casino. If you prefer a sand beach, *Cannes*, also on the *Côte d'Azur*, is a pleasant alternative.

On a side trip to *Monaco*, a visit to Prince Rainier's palace provides a view of the harbor and the yachts moored there. The casino at *Monte Carlo* is its principal attraction.

In *Avignon* there is the *Palace of the Popes* and the *Bridge of St. Bénézet*. *Nîmes* and *Arles*, quaint cities noted for their Roman ruins, have amphitheaters still in their original form. *Lourdes* has a shrine that attracts religious pilgrims and those seeking relief from illness or injury.

## OUTSIDE FRANCE

For a glimpse of France closer to the United States, visit *Québec* with its magnificent beaches, parks, mountains, forests and lakes. Participate in your favorite summer or winter sport. See the old and the new cities and visit the charming castles.

If you prefer a tranquil vacation, visit a tropical island. Rest in the shade of the palm and coconut trees of *Martinique* or *Guadeloupe* in the Lesser Antilles. Enjoy the beaches, the languorous life style and the fruit-flavored daiquiris. In Martinique, tour the capital, *Fort-de-France*, see the ruins of *Saint-Pierre* and *Mt. Pelée*, and the luxuriant rain forest. In Guadeloupe, the town of *Gosier* is the heart of vacation life. At *Le Moule*, the horseshoe beach is one of the island's most popular attractions. Or visit *Haiti*, on the island of Hispaniola, in the Greater Antilles. Horseback ride to the famed *Citadelle*, tour *Port-au-Prince*, the capital, relax by the *waterfalls of Cayes* and lie on the beautiful beaches of *Port Salut.*

## RELIGIOUS SERVICES

France has many cathedrals and churches that you may wish to visit. There are churches and synagogues in major cities that do conduct some services in English. For more information, speak to the concierge at your hotel.

| | |
|---|---|
| Is there a ____ near here? | **Y a-t-il ____ près d'ici?** *ee ah teel ____ preh dee-ssee* |
| ■ Catholic church | **une église catholique** *ewn ay-gleez kah-toh-leek* |
| ■ Protestant church | **un temple** *uhn tahn-pluh* |
| ■ synagogue | **une synagogue** *ewn see-nah-gohg* |
| ■ mosque | **une mosquée** *ewn mohss-kay* |
| At what time is the service (mass)? | **À quelle heure commence le service/la messe?** *ah kehl uhr koh-mahnss luh sehr-veess/lah mehss* |
| I would like to speak to a ____. | **Je voudrais parler à un ____.** *zhuh voo-dreh pahr-lay ah uhn* |
| ■ priest | **prêtre** *preh-truh* |
| ■ minister | **pasteur** *pahss-tuhr* |
| ■ rabbi | **rabbin** *rah-ban* |

---

### TRAVEL TIP

When you are packing to leave home, leave a little space in your suitcase to hold the small purchases you will make while you are away. If you can't manage this, then pack a collapsible tote bag in your suitcase, to be filled up and carried separately on your return trip.

---

# PLANNING A TRIP

During your stay, you may want to plan some longer excursions. In France you can get around by moped **(mobilette)**, bicycle or even hiking. For more extensive trips, boats, planes, and trains are all readily available, as are rental cars (see Driving a Car). You may even rent a barge to travel through France on an elaborate canal system.

## AIR SERVICE

| | |
|---|---|
| When is there a flight to _____? | **Quand y a-t-il un vol pour _____?** *kahn tee ah teel uhn vohl poor* |
| I would like a round trip (one way) ticket in tourist class (first class). | **Je voudrais un aller et retour (un aller) en seconde classe (première classe).** *zhuh voo-dreh zuhn ah-lay ay ruh-toor (uhn nah-lay) ahn suh-gohnd klahss (pruh-myehr klahss)* |
| A seat _____. | **Une place _____.** *ewn plahss* |
| ■ in the smoking section | **dans la section fumeurs.** *dahn lah sehk-ssyohn few-muhr* |
| ■ in the non-smoking section | **dans la section non-fumeurs** *dahn lah sehk-ssyohn nohn few-muhr* |
| ■ next to the window | **à côté de la fenêtre** *ah koh-tay duh lah fuh-neh-truh* |
| ■ on the aisle | **côté couloir** *koh-tay koo-lwahr* |
| What is the fare? | **Quel est le tarif?** *kehl eh luh tah-reef* |
| Are meals served? | **Sert-on des repas?** *sehr tohn day ruh-pah* |
| At what time does the plane leave? | **À quelle heure part l'avion?** *ah kehl uhr pahr lah vyohn* |
| At what time do we arrive? | **À quelle heure arrivons-nous?** *ah kehl uhr ah-reev-ohn noo* |

| When do we land in ___? | **Quand est-ce que l'avion atterrit en ___?** *kahn tehss kuh lah-vyohn ah-teh-ree ahn* |
|---|---|
| What is my flight number? | **Quel est le numéro de mon vol?** *kehl eh luh new-may-roh duh mohn vohl* |
| What gate do we leave from? | **De quelle porte partons-nous?** *duh' kehl pohrt pahr-tohn noo* |
| I want to confirm (cancel) my reservation for flight ___. | **Je voudrais confirmer (annuler) ma réservation pour le vol numéro ___.** *zhuh voo-dreh kohn-feer-may (ah-new-lay) mah ray-zehr-vah-ssyohn poor luh vohl new-may-roh* |
| I'd like to check my bags. | **Je voudrais enregistrer mes bagages.** *zhuh voo-dreh zahn-ruh-zheess-tray may bah-gahzh* |
| I have only carry-on baggage. | **J'ai seulement des bagages à main.** *zhay suhl-mahn day bah-gazh ah man* |
| Please pass my film (camera) through by hand.* | **Passez mon film (appareil) à la main, s'il vous plaît.** *pah-ssay mohn film (ah-pah-rehy) ah lah man seel voo pleh* |

NOTE: Some high-speed film can be damaged by airport security X-rays. It is best to pack film in your suitcase, protected in a lead insulated bag. If you have film in your camera or carry-on baggage, avoid problems and ask the guard to pass it through by hand instead. If the guard refuses, bow to his wishes.

## SHIPBOARD TRAVEL

| Where is the dock? | **Où est le dock?** *oo eh luh dohk* |
|---|---|
| When does the next boat leave for ___? | **Quand part le prochain bateau pour ___?** *kahn pahr luh proh-shan bah-toh poor* |

| | |
|---|---|
| How long does the crossing take? | **La traversée dure combien de temps?** *lah trah-vehr-ssay dewr kohn-byan duh tahn* |
| Do we stop at any ports? | **Dans quels ports est-ce qu'on fait escale?** *dahn kehl pohr ehss kohn feh ehss-kahl* |
| How long will we remain in the port? | **L'escale dure combien de temps?** *lehss-kahl dewr kohn-byan duh tahn* |
| When do we land? | **Quand est-ce qu'on y arrive?** *kahn tehss kohn nee ah-reev* |
| At what time do we have to be back on board? | **À quelle heure faut-il retourner au bateau?** *ah kehl uhr foh teel ruh-toor-nay oh bah-toh* |
| I'd like a _____ ticket. | **Je voudrais un billet _____.** *zhuh voo-dreh zuhn bee-yeh* |
| ■ first class | **de première classe** *duh pruh-myehr klahss* |
| ■ tourist class | **de deuxième classe** *duh duh-zyehm klahss* |
| ■ cabin | **de cabine** *duh kah-been* |

| | |
|---|---|
| I don't feel well. | **Je ne me sens pas bien.** *zhuh nuh muh sah_n_ pah bya_n_* |
| Can you give me something for sea sickness? | **Pouvez-vous me donner quelque chose contre le mal de mer?** *poo-vay voo muh doh-nay kehl-kuh shohz koh_n_-truh luh mahl duh mehr* |

## TRAIN SERVICE

The French railway system is extensive, serving small as well as large cities. Trains have first and second class. The new TGV makes the regions of Rhône-Alps, Savoy, Rhône Valley, Provence, Languedoc and even western Switzerland only a few hours' journey from Paris. There are also special tourist trains (CEVENOL) running from Paris to Marseilles.

### TYPES OF TRAINS

| | |
|---|---|
| **TEE (Trans-Europ-Express)** | Has only first-class seating, plus supplementary charge. |
| **TGV (Très grande vitesse)** | High speed train with first and second class seating. |
| **Rapide** | Express that stops only at major stations. Luxury accommodations are available. |
| **Express** | Long-distance train. |
| **Omnibus** | Local train. |

If you have to sleep on a train you will find the following expressions useful:

| | |
|---|---|
| **Wagon-lit** | A first-class private sleeping compartment for one or two (with sink and mirror). |
| **Couchette** | A second-class sleeping compartment with 6 bunks. If you are not a party of six, you may have to share it with |

| | |
|---|---|
| | strangers. You sleep in your clothes. |
| **Coach** | You sleep, if possible, fully dressed, sitting in your first or second class seat. |

## EATING ON A TRAIN

You can get anything from a full meal to a light snack and drinks on the train. Use the **wagon-restaurant** (dining car). Also, when the train pulls into a large station, call out the window to the vendors of sandwiches, cheeses and drinks. You may, if you prefer, carry on your own meals and refreshments, as the dining car can be very expensive.

## STATION

| | |
|---|---|
| Where is the train station? (the ticket office) | **Où est la gare? (le guichet)** *oo eh lah gahr (luh gee-sheh)* |
| I'd like to see the schedule. | **Je voudrais voir l'horaire.** *zhuh voo-dreh vwahr loh-rehr* |
| A first class (second class) ticket to ____, please. | **Un billet de première classe (seconde classe) pour ____, s'il vous plaît.** *uhn bee-yeh duh pruh-myehr klahss (suh-gohnd klahss) poor ____ seel voo pleh* |
| ■ half-price ticket | **un billet de demi-tarif** *uhn bee-yeh duh duh-mee tah-reef* |
| ■ one-way (round-trip) ticket | **un aller simple (aller et retour)** *uhn nah-lay san-pluh (nah-lay ay ruh-toor)* |
| I would like a (no) smoking compartment. | **Je voudrais un compartiment (non-) fumeurs.** *zhuh voo-dreh zuhn kohn-pahr-tee-mahn (nohn) few-muhr* |
| When does the train arrive (leave)? | **À quelle heure est-ce que le train arrive (part)?** *ah kehl uhr ehss kuh luh tran ah-reev (pahr)* |

| From what platform does it leave (arrive)? | **Dè (À) quel quai (De quelle voie) part (arrive) -t-il?** *duh (ah) kehl kay (duh kehl vwah) pahr (ah-reev) teel* |
|---|---|
| Does this train stop at ____? | **Est-ce que ce train s'arrête à ____?** *ehss kuh suh tran sah-reht ah* |
| Is the train late? | **Est-ce que le train a du retard?** *ehss kuh luh tran ah dew ruh-tahr* |
| How long does it stop? | **Il s'arrête pendant combien de temps?** *eel sah-reht pan-dan kohn-byan duh tahn* |
| Is there time to get a bite? | **A-t-on le temps de prendre quelque chose?** *ah tohn luh tahn duh prahn-druh kehl-kuh shohz* |
| Do we have to stand in line? | **Faut-il faire la queue?** *foh teel fehr lah kuh* |
| All aboard! | **En voiture, s'il vous plaît!** *ahn vwah-tewr seel voo pleh* |
| Is there a dining car (sleeping car)? | **Y a-t-il un wagon restaurant (un wagon-lit)?** *ee ah teel uhn vah-gohn rehss-toh-rahn (uhn vah-gohn lee)* |
| Is it a ____? | **Est-ce ____?** *ehss* |
| ■ a through train | **un rapide** *uhn rah-peed* |
| ■ a local | **un omnibus** *uhn nohm-nee-bewss* |
| ■ an express | **un express** *uhn nehkss-prehss* |
| Do I have to change trains? | **Dois-je changer de train?** *dwahzh shahn-zhay duh tran* |
| Is this seat taken? | **Est-ce que cette place est occupée?** *ehss kuh seht plahss eh toh-kew-pay* |
| Where are we now? | **Où sommes-nous maintenant?** *oo sohm noo mant-nahn* |
| Will we arrive on time? (late)? | **Arriverons-nous à l'heure? (en retard?)** *ah-reev-rohn noo ah luhr? (ahn ruh-tahr)* |

# ENTERTAINMENT AND DIVERSION

## MOVIES

Movies are generally shown from 2 p.m. to 10 p.m. with late night schedules on Saturday. "Pariscope" and "L'Officiel des Spectacles" are two guides to the movies in Paris, indicating the time and place of the film showing. The abbreviation V. O. (**version originale**) means that the original version of the movie in the language in which it was made is being shown. V. F. (**version française**) means that the movie is dubbed in French. In the movies or theater it is customary to tip the usher or usherette. Movies generally change on Wednesday. The bigger, more expensive, more comfortable movie houses are on the Champs-Elysées in Paris.

| | | |
|---|---|---|
| Let's go to the ____. | **Allons au ____.** | *ah-lohn zoh* |
| ■movies | **cinéma** | *see-nay-mah* |
| ■museum | **musée** | *mew-zay* |
| ■theater | **théâtre** | *tay-ah-truh* |
| What are they showing today? | **Qu'est-ce qu'on joue aujourd'hui?** | *kehss kohn zhoo oh-zhoor-dwee* |
| It's a ____. | **C'est ____.** | *seh* |
| ■mystery | **un mystère** | *tuhn mee-sstehr* |
| ■comedy | **une comédie** | *tewn koh-may-dee* |
| ■drama | **un drame** | *tuhn drahm* |
| ■musical | **une comédie musicale** | *tewn koh-may-dee mew-zee-kahl* |
| ■romance | **une histoire d'amour** | *tewn eess-twahr dah-moor* |
| ■Western | **un western** | *tuhn wehss-tehrn* |

| | |
|---|---|
| ■ war film | **un film de guerre** *tuhn feelm duh gehr* |
| ■ science fiction film | **une histoire de science fiction** *tewn eess-twahr duh see-yahnss feek-ssyohn* |
| Is it in English? | **Est-ce en anglais?** *ehss ahn nahn-gleh* |
| Are there English subtitles? | **Y-t-il des sous-titres en anglais?** *ee ah teel day soo-tee-truh ahn nahn-gleh* |
| Where is the box office (time schedule)? | **Où est le bureau de location (l'horaire)?** *oo eh luh bew-roh duh loh-kah-ssyohn (loh-rehr)* |
| What time does the (first) show begin? | **À quelle heure commence le (premier) spectacle?** *ah kehl uhr koh-mahnss luh (pruh-myay) spehk-tah-kluh* |
| What time does the (last) show end? | **À quelle heure se termine le (dernier) spectacle?** *ah kehl uhr suh tehr-meen luh (dehr-nyay) spehk-tah-kluh* |
| I'd like to speak to an usher. | **Je voudrais parler à une ouvreuse.** *zhuh voo-dreh pahr-lay ah ewn oo-vruhz* |

## THEATER

France has several national theaters like the **Comédie Française** or the **Théatre National de l'Odéon.** There are also about fifty private playhouses. Theaters are closed one day a week. The day is listed in the newspapers. Booking offices are generally open from 11 a.m. to 6 p.m. Most of the theaters are closed one month in the summer, usually August.

For entertainment information in Paris 24 hours a day, call 720-88-98.

| | |
|---|---|
| I need tickets for tonight. | **Il me faut des billets pour ce soir.** *eel muh foh day bee-yeh poor suh swahr* |
| Two _____ seats | **Deux places _____** *duh plahss* |

| | |
|---|---|
| ■ orchestra | **à l'orchestre** *ah lohr-kehss-truh* |
| ■ balcony | **au balcon** *oh bahl-koh<u>n</u>* |
| ■ first balcony | **au premier balcon** *oh pruh-myay bahl-koh<u>n</u>* |
| ■ mezzanine | **au parterre** *oh pahr-tehr* |

## OPERA-BALLET-CONCERT

| | |
|---|---|
| We would like to attend ____. | **Nous voudrions assister à ____.** *noo voo-dree-yoh<u>n</u> ah-sseess-tay ah* |
| ■ a ballet | **un ballet** *uh<u>n</u> bah-leh* |
| ■ a concert | **un concert** *uh<u>n</u> koh<u>n</u>-ssehr* |
| ■ an opera | **un opéra** *uh<u>n</u> noh-pay-rah* |
| Is there a ____ nearby? | **Y a-t-il par ici ____?** *ee ah teel pahr ee-ssee* |
| ■ concert hall | **une salle de concert** *ewn sahl duh koh<u>n</u>-ssehr* |
| ■ opera house | **un opéra** *uh<u>n</u> noh-pay-rah* |
| ■ ballet | **un ballet** *uh<u>n</u> bah-leh* |
| What are they playing? | **Que joue-t-on?** *kuh zhoo toh<u>n</u>* |
| Who is the conductor? | **Qui est le chef d'orchestre?** *kee eh luh shehf dohr-kehss-truh* |
| I prefer ____. | **Je préfère ____.** *zhuh pray-fehr* |
| ■ classical music | **la musique classique** *lah mew-zeek klah-sseek* |
| ■ modern music | **la musique moderne** *lah mew-zeek moh-dehrn* |
| ■ folk dances | **les danses folkloriques** *lay dahnss fohl-kloh-reek* |

| Are there any seats for tonight's performance? | **Y a-t-il des places pour ce soir?** *ee ah teel day plahss poor suh swahr* |
| When does the season end? | **Quand se termine la saison théâtrale?** *kahn suh tehr-meen lah seh-zohn tay-ah-trahl* |
| Should I get the tickets in advance? | **Faut-il acheter les billets d'avance?** *foh teel ahsh-tay lay bee-yeh dah-vahnss* |
| Do I have to dress formally? | **La tenue de soirée est-elle de rigueur?** *lah tuh-new duh swah-ray eh tehl duh ree-guhr* |
| How much are the front row seats? | **Combien coûtent les places au premier rang?** *kohn-byan koot lay plahss oh pruh-myay rahn* |
| What are the least expensive seats? | **Quelles sont les places les moins chères?** *kehl sohn lay plahss lay mwan shehr* |
| May I have a program? | **Un programme, s'il vous plaît.** *uhn proh-grahm seel voo pleh* |

| What opera are they putting on? | **Quel opéra jouent-ils?** *kehl oh-pay-rah zhoo teel* |
| Who's singing? | **Qui chante?** *kee shahnt* |
| Who's playing the lead? | **Qui joue le rôle principal?** *kee zhoo luh rohl pran-ssee-pahl* |
| Who are the members of the cast? | **Qui sont les membres de la troupe?** *kee sohn lay mahn-bruh duh lah troop* |
| Who is _____? | **Qui est _____?** *kee eh* |
| ■ the tenor | **le ténor** *luh tay-nohr* |
| ■ the baritone | **le baryton** *luh bah-ree-tohn* |
| ■ the soprano | **le soprano** *luh soh-prah-noh* |
| ■ the bass | **la basse** *lah bahss* |

## NIGHT CLUBS

If it's entertainment you want, try the bars, nightclubs and discos in the major cities. Paris, of course, offers the widest selection of things to do. Nightclubs, providing dinner and a show, are very expensive. A late night drink at a jazz spot or bar might interest you. Discos abound with the latest song hits and special lighting effects.

| Let's go to a nightclub! | **Allons dans une boîte de nuit!** *ah-lohn dahn zewn bwaht duh nwee* |
| Is a reservation necessary? | **Faut-il réserver?** *foh teel ray-zehr-vay* |
| I feel like dancing. | **J'ai envie de danser.** *zhay ahn-vee duh dahn-ssay* |
| Is there a discotheque here? | **Y a-t-il une discothèque par ici?** *ee ah teel ewn deess-koh-tehk pahr ee-ssee* |
| Is there a dance at the hotel? | **Y a-t-il un bal à l'hôtel?** *ee ah teel uhn bahl ah loh-tehl* |

| I'd like a table near the dance floor. | **Je voudrais avoir une table près de la piste (de danse).** *zhuh voo-dreh zah-vwahr ewn tah-bluh preh duh lah peesst (duh dahnss)* |
| Is there a minimum (cover charge)? | **Y a-t-il un prix d'entrée?** *ee ah teel uhn pree dahn-tray* |
| Where is the check-room? | **Où est le vestiaire?** *oo eh luh vehss-tyehr* |
| At what time does the floor show go on? | **À quelle heure commence le spectacle?** *ah kehl uhr koh-mahnss luh spehk-tah-kluh* |

## DANCING

| May I have this dance? | **M'accordez-vous cette danse?** *mah-kohr-day voo seht dahnss* |
| Yes, all right. With pleasure. | **Oui, d'accord. Avec plaisir.** *wee dah-kohr. ah-vehk pleh-zeer* |
| Would you like a cigarette (a drink)? | **Voudriez-vous une cigarette (une boisson)?** *voo-dree-yay voo zewn see-gah-reht (ewn bwah-ssohn)* |
| Do you have a light? | **Avez-vous du feu?** *ah-vay voo dew fuh* |
| Do you mind if I smoke? | **Ça vous dérange si je fume?** *sah voo day-rahnzh see zhuh fewm* |
| May I take you home? | **Puis-je vous raccompagner chez vous?** *pweezh voo rah-kohn-pah-nyay shay voo* |

## CASINOS

While on the Côte d'Azur you must visit the world-famous Casino of Monte-Carlo in Monaco. Unlike most other casinos, admission is free. There are other casinos throughout France. All are licensed, regulated and monitored by the French government. A passport is needed to enter. Admission is restricted to adults (over 21 years of age).

# QUIET RELAXATION

Do you want to play cards? — **Voulez-vous jouer aux cartes?** *voo-lay voo zhoo-ay oh kahrt*

- bridge — **au bridge** *oh breedzh*

- black jack — **au black-jack** *oh blahk zhahk*

- poker — **au poker** *oh poh-kehr*

I have the highest card. — **J'ai la meilleure carte.** *zhay lah meh-yuhr kahrt*

- an ace — **un as** *uhn nahss*

- a king — **un roi** *uhn rwah*

- a queen — **une dame** *ewn dahm*

- a jack — **un valet** *uhn vah-leh*

Do you want to cut? — **Voulez-vous couper les cartes?** *voo-lay voo koo-pay lay kahrt*

Where can I get a deck of cards? — **Où puis-je obtenir des cartes à jouer?** *oo pweezh ohp-tuh-neer day kahrt ah zhoo-ay*

Do you want to shuffle? — **Voulez-vous battre les cartes?** *voo-lay voo bah-truh lay kahrt*

I pass. — **Parole.** *pah-rohl*

Do you have clubs, hearts, spades, diamonds? — **Avez-vous du trèfle, du coeur, du pique ou du carreau?** *ah-vay voo dew treh-fluh, dew kuhr, dew peek oo dew kah-roh*

It's your turn to deal. — **À vous de donner.** *ah voo duh doh-nay*

Who opens? — **Qui commence?** *kee koh-mahnss*

What's your score? — **Combien de points avez-vous?** *kohn-byan duh pwan ah-vay voo*

| I win (lose). | **Je gagne (Je perds).** *zhuh gah-nyuh (zhuh pehr)* |
|---|---|
| You win (lose). | **Vous gagnez (Vous perdez).** *voo gah-nyay (voo pehr-day)* |
| Do you want to play _____? | **Voulez-vous jouer _____?** *voo-lay voo zhoo-ay* |
| ■ checkers | **aux dames** *oh dahm* |
| ■ chess | **aux échecs** *oh zay-shehk* |
| ■ dominoes | **aux dominos** *oh doh-mee-noh* |
| We need a board (dice). | **Il nous faut un échiquier (des dés).** *eel noo foh tuhn nay-shee-kyay (day day)* |
| We need the pieces. | **Il nous faut les pièces.** *eel noo foh lay pee-yehss* |
| ■ the king | **le roi** *luh rwah* |
| ■ the queen | **la reine** *lah rehn* |
| ■ the rook | **la tour** *lah toor* |
| ■ the bishop | **le fou** *luh foo* |
| ■ the knight | **le cavalier** *luh kah-vah-lyay* |
| ■ the pawn | **le pion** *luh pee-yohn* |
| Checkmate. | **Échec et mat.** *ay-shehk ay maht* |
| Check. | **Échec.** *ay-shehk* |

## SPORTS

Golf, tennis, swimming, cycling, skiing, basketball, ice-skating, fishing, hiking and sailing are recreational activities in which you can participate throughout the country.

Boxing and wrestling matches, soccer, rugby and pelote (jai alai) matches draw large crowds of spectators.

Two special events that attract natives and tourists alike are Le Tour de France, a three week bicycle race across France (held each June) and Le Mans, a 24 hour Formula One auto race (also in June).

## SPECTATOR SPORTS

### SOCCER

| | |
|---|---|
| I'd like to see a soccer match. | **Je voudrais voir un match de football.** *zhuh voo-dreh vwahr uhn mahtch duh foot-bohl* |
| Where's the stadium? | **Où est le stade?** *oo eh luh stahd* |
| When does the first half begin? | **Quand commence la première mi-temps?** *kahn koh-mahnss lah pruh-myehr mee-tahn* |
| When are they going to kick off? | **Quand vont-ils donner le coup d'envoi?** *kahn vohn teel doh-nay luh koo dahn-vwah* |
| What teams are going to play? | **Quelles équipes vont jouer?** *kehl zay-keep vohn zhoo-ay* |
| Who is playing ____? | **Qui joue ____?** *kee zhoo* |
| ■center | **au centre** *oh sahn-truh* |
| ■fullback | **à l'arrière** *ah lah-ryehr* |
| ■halfback | **en demi** *ahn duh-mee* |
| ■wing | **à l'aile** *ah lehl* |
| What was the score? | **Quel a été le score?** *kehl ah ay-tay luh skohr* |

### JAI ALAI

| | |
|---|---|
| Are you a jai alai fan? | **Êtes-vous un fana de la pelote (basque)?** *eht voo zuhn fah-nah duh lah puh-loht (bahssk)* |

| | |
|---|---|
| I'd like to see a jai alai match. | **Je voudrais voir un match de pelote.** *zhuh voo-dreh vwahr uhn mahtch duh puh-loht* |
| Where can I get tickets? | **Où puis-je me procurer des billets?** *oo pweezh muh proh-kew-ray day bee-yeh* |
| Where is the jai alai court? | **Où est le fronton?** *oo eh luh frohn-tohn* |
| Who are the players? | **Qui sont les joueurs?** *kee sohn lay zhoo-uhr* |
| Each team has a forward end (a back end). | **Chaque équipe a un avant (un arrière).** *shahk ay-keep ah uhn nah-vahn (uhn nah-ryehr)* |
| I bet that the blue team will win. | **Je parie que l'équipe bleue va gagner.** *zhuh pah-ree kuh lay-keep bluh vah gah-nyay* |
| Where do I place my bet? | **Où fait-on les paris?** *oo feh-tohn lay pah-ree* |
| At that window. | **À ce guichet.** *ah suh gee-sheh* |

## HORSE RACING

| | |
|---|---|
| Is there a racetrack here? | **Y a-t-il un champ de courses par ici?** *ee ah teel uhn shahn duh koorss pahr ee-ssee* |
| I want to see the horse races. | **Je voudrais voir les courses de chevaux.** *zhuh voo-dreh vwahr lay koorss duh shuh-voh* |

## ACTIVE SPORTS

### TENNIS

| | |
|---|---|
| Do you play tennis? | **Jouez-vous au tennis?** *zhoo-ay voo oh teh-neess* |

| | | |
|---|---|---|
| I like the game. | **J'aime bien ce sport.** *zhehm byan suh spohr* | |
| I (don't) play very well. | **Je (ne) joue (pas) bien.** *zhuh (nuh) zhoo (pah) byan* | |
| I need practice. | **Je dois m'entraîner.** *zhuh dwah mahn-treh-nay* | |
| Do you know where there is a (good) court? | **Savez-vous où se trouve un bon court de tennis?** *sah-vay voo oo suh troov uhn bohn koohr duh teh-neess* | |
| Can I rent rackets and balls? | **Puis-je louer des raquettes et des balles?** *pweezh loo-ay day rah-keht ay day bahl* | |
| How much do they charge per hour (per day)? | **Quel est le tarif à l'heure/à la journée?** *kehl eh luh tah-reef ah luhr/ ah lah zhoor-nay* | |
| I serve (You serve) first. | **C'est à moi (à vous) le premier service.** *seh tah mwah (tah voo) luh pruh-myay sehr-veess* | |
| You play very well. | **Vous jouez très bien.** *voo zhoo-ay treh byan* | |
| You've won. | **Vous avez gagné.** *voo zah-vay gah-nyay* | |
| I've won. | **J'ai gagné.** *zhay gah-nyay* | |
| It's a tie. | **Match nul.** *mahtch newl* | |

## BEACH OR POOL

| | |
|---|---|
| Oh! It's hot. | **Oh là là! Quelle chaleur!** *oh lah lah kehl shah-luhr* |
| Let's go to the beach (to the pool). | **Allons à la plage (à la piscine).** *ah-lohn zah lah plahzh (ah lah pee-sseen)* |

| | |
|---|---|
| Is it a sand beach? | **Est-ce une plage de sable?** *ehss ewn plahzh duh sah-bluh* |
| How do you get there? | **Comment y va-t-on?** *koh-mahn tee vah tohn* |
| Which bus will take us to the beach? | **Quel bus faut-il prendre pour aller à la plage?** *kehl bewss foh teel prahn-druh poor ah-lay ah lah plahzh* |
| Is there a pool in the hotel? | **Y a-t-il une piscine à l'hôtel?** *ee ah teel ewn pee-sseen ah loh-tehl* |
| Is it an indoor (outdoor) pool? | **Est-ce une piscine couverte (en plein air)?** *ehss ewn pee-sseen koo-vehrt (ahn pleh nehr)* |
| I (don't) know how to swim well. | **Je (ne) sais (pas) bien nager.** *zhuh (nuh) seh (pah) byan nah-zhay* |
| I just want to stretch out in the sand. | **Je voudrais tout simplement m'allonger sur le sable.** *zhuh voo-dreh too san-pluh-mahn mah-lohn-zhay sewr luh sah-bluh* |
| Is it safe to swim here? | **Peut-on nager ici sans danger?** *puh-tohn nah-zhay ee-ssee sahn dahn-zhay* |
| Are the waves big? | **Y a-t-il de grandes vagues?** *ee ah teel duh grahnd vahg* |
| Are there sharks? | **Y a-t-il des requins?** *ee ah teel day ruh-kan* |
| Is there any danger for children? | **Y a-t-il du danger pour les enfants?** *ee ah teel dew dahn-zhay poor lay zahn-fahn* |
| Is there a lifeguard? | **Y a-t-il un maître-nageur?** *ee ah teel uhn meh-truh nah-zhuhr* |
| I'm going in the water now. | **Je vais entrer dans l'eau maintenant.** *zhuh veh zahn-tray dahn loh mant-nahn* |

| | |
|---|---|
| Where can I get _____? | **Où puis-je obtenir _____?** *oo pweezh ohp-tuh-neer* |
| ■ an air mattress | **un matelas pneumatique** *uhn maht-lah pnuh-mah-teek* |
| ■ a bathing suit | **un maillot de bain** *uhn mah-yoh duh ban* |
| ■ a beach ball | **un ballon de plage** *uhn bah-lohn duh plahzh* |
| ■ a beach chair | **une chaise longue pour la plage** *ewn shehz lohng poor lah plahzh* |
| ■ a beach towel | **une serviette de plage** *ewn sehr-vyeht duh plahzh* |
| ■ a chaise longue | **une chaise longue** *ewn shehz lohng* |
| ■ sunglasses | **des lunettes de soleil** *day lew-neht duh soh-leh* |
| ■ suntan lotion | **la lotion pour bronzer** *lah loh-ssyohn poor brohn- zay* |
| ■ a surfboard | **une planche de surf** *ewn plahnsh duh sewrf* |
| ■ water skis | **des skis nautiques** *day skee noh-teek* |

## ON THE SLOPES

| | |
|---|---|
| Which ski area do you recommend? | **Quelle station de ski recommandez-vous?** *kehl stah-ssyohn duh skee ruh-koh-mahn-day voo* |
| I am a novice (intermediate, expert) skier. | **Je suis un(e) débutant(e) (un skieur moyen; un expert).** *zhuh swee zuhn (zewn) day-bew-tahn(t) (uhn skee-uhr mwah-yan/uhn ehks-pehr)* |

| What kind of lifts are there? | **Quel type de téléski y a-t-il?** *kehl teep duh tay-lay-sskee ee-yah-teel* |
| How much does the lift cost? | **Combien coûte le trajet?** *kohn-byan koot luh trah-zheh* |
| Do they give lessons? | **Donne-t-on des leçons?** *dohn-tohn day luh-ssohn* |
| Where can I stay at the summit? | **Où puis-je loger au sommet?** *oo pweezh loh-zhay oh soh-meh* |
| Is there any cross country skiing? | **Est-ce qu'on fait du ski de promenade?** *ehss-kohn feh dew skee duh proh-muh-nahd* |
| Is there enough snow this time of year? | **Y a-t-il assez de neige en ce moment?** *ee ah teel ah-ssay duh nehzh ahn suh moh-mahn* |
| How would I get to that place? | **Comment aller à cet endroit-là?** *koh-mahn tah-lay ah seht ahn-drwah lah* |

| Can I rent _____ there? | **Peut-on y louer _____?** *puh-tohn nee loo-ay* |
| ■ equipment | **un équipement de ski** *uhn nay-keep-mahn duh skee* |
| ■ poles | **des bâtons** *day bah-tohn* |
| ■ skis | **des skis** *day skee* |
| ■ ski boots | **des chaussures de ski** *day shoh-ssewr duh skee* |

## ON THE LINKS

| Is there a golf course here? | **Y a-t-il un terrain de golf par ici?** *ee ah teel uhn teh-ran duh gohlf pahr ee-ssee* |
| Can one rent clubs? | **Peut-on louer des clubs?** *puh tohn loo-ay day kluhb* |

## CAMPING

Campgrounds are located all over France. They are often crowded, especially in the month of August when most Frenchmen are on vacation. Arrive early to insure a spot. Campsites are rated by stars; the fewer the stars, the less desirable the site. Most sites have adequate facilities. Students are sometimes offered discounts. A camping permit is sometimes required. You may camp unofficially in a suitable place as long as you have permission from the land owner. Be sure to leave the property in the same condition as you found it.

| Is there a camping site near here? | **Y a-t-il un terrain de camping par ici?** *ee ah teel uhn teh-ran duh kahn-peeng pahr ee-ssee* |
| Can you show me how to get there? | **Pouvez-vous m'indiquer comment y aller?** *poo-vay voo man-dee-kay koh-mahn tee ah-lay* |

| | |
|---|---|
| Where is it on the map? | **Où se trouve-t-il sur la carte?** *oo suh troov teel sewr lah kahrt* |
| Where can we park our trailer? | **Où pouvons-nous installer notre caravane?** *oo poo-vohn noo an-stah-lay noh-truh kah-rah-vahn* |
| Can we camp for the night? | **Pouvons-nous camper cette nuit?** *poo-vohn noo kahn-pay seht nwee* |
| Where can we spend the night? | **Où pouvons-nous passer la nuit?** *oo poo-vohn noo pah-ssay lah nwee* |
| Is there ____? | **Y a-t-il ____?** *ee ah teel* |
| ■ drinking water | **de l'eau potable** *duh loh poh-tah-bluh* |
| ■ running water | **de l'eau courante** *duh loh koo-rahnt* |
| ■ gas | **du gaz** *dew gahz* |
| ■ electricity | **de l'électricité** *duh lay-lehk-tree-ssee-tay* |
| ■ a children's playground | **un terrain de jeu pour enfants** *uhn teh-ran duh zhuh poor ahn-fahn* |
| ■ a grocery store | **une épicerie** *ewn ay-peess-ree* |
| Are there ____? | **Y a-t-il ____?** *ee ah teel* |
| ■ toilets | **des toilettes** *day twah-leht* |
| ■ showers | **des douches** *day doosh* |
| ■ washrooms | **des lavabos** *day lah-vah-boh* |
| ■ tents | **des tentes** *day tahnt* |
| ■ cooking facilities | **des installations pour faire la cuisine** *day zan-stah-lah-ssyohn poor fehr lah kwee-zeen* |
| How much do they charge per person? (per car)? | **Quel est le tarif par personne/pour une caravane?** *kehl eh luh tah-reef pahr pehr-ssohn/poor ewn kah-rah-vahn* |

| We intend staying ____ days/weeks. | **Nous pensons rester ____ jours/semaines.** *noo pahn-ssohn rehss-tay ____ zhoor/suh-mehn* |

## IN THE COUNTRYSIDE

| I'd like to drive through the countryside. | **Je voudrais conduire dans la campagne.** *zhuh voo-dreh kohn-dweer dahn lah kahn-pah-nyuh* |
| Where can I rent a car for the day? | **Où puis-je louer une voiture à la journée?** *oo pweezh loo-ay ewn vwah-tewr ah lah zhoor-nay* |
| Are there tours to the country? | **Y a-t-il des excursions à la campagne?** *ee ah teel day zehkss-kewr-zyohn ah lah kahn-pah-nyuh* |
| When do they leave? | **Quand sont les départs?** *kahn ssohn lay day-pahr* |
| From where do they leave? | **D'où partent-elles?** *doo pahrt-ehl* |
| Is there anyone who can take me? | **Y a-t-il quelqu'un qui puisse me conduire?** *ee ah teel kehl kuhn kee pweess muh kohn-dweer* |
| What a beautiful landscape! | **Quel beau paysage!** *kehl boh pay-zahzh* |
| Look at ____. | **Regardez ____.** *ruh-gahr-day* |
| ▪the barn | **la grange** *lah grahnzh* |
| ▪the bridge | **le pont** *luh pohn* |
| ▪the farm | **la ferme** *lah fehrm* |
| ▪the fields | **les champs** *lay shahn* |
| ▪the flowers | **les fleurs** *lay fluhr* |
| ▪the forest | **la forêt** *lah foh-reh* |
| ▪the hill | **la colline** *lah koh-leen* |

| | | |
|---|---|---|
| ■ the lake | **le lac** *luh lahk* | |
| ■ the mountains | **les montagnes** *lay mohn-tah-nyuh* | |
| ■ the ocean | **l'océan (m.)** *loh-ssay-ahn* | |
| ■ the plants | **les plantes** *lay plahnt* | |
| ■ the pond | **l'étang (m.)** *lay-tahn* | |
| ■ the river | **la rivière** *lah ree-vyehr* | |
| ■ the stream | **le ruisseau** *luh rwee-ssoh* | |
| ■ the trees | **les arbres** *lay zahr-bruh* | |
| ■ the valley | **la vallée** *lah vah-lay* | |
| ■ the village | **le village** *luh vee-lahzh* | |
| ■ the waterfall | **la cascade** *lah kahss-kahd* | |
| Where does this ____ lead to? | **Où mène ____?** *oo mehn* | |
| ■ road | **ce chemin** *suh shuh-man* | |
| ■ path | **ce sentier** *suh sahn-tyay* | |
| ■ highway | **cette grande route** *seht grahnd root* | |
| How far away is ____? | **À quelle distance est ____?** *ah kehl deess-tahnss eh* | |
| ■ the city | **la ville** *lah veel* | |
| ■ the crossroads | **le carrefour** *luh kahr-foor* | |
| ■ the inn | **l'auberge (f.)** *loh-behrzh* | |
| How long does it take to get to ____? | **Combien de temps faut-il pour aller à ____?** *kohn-byan duh tahn foh teel poor ah-lay ah* | |
| I'm lost. | **J'ai perdu mon chemin.** *zhay pehr-dew mohn shuh-man* | |
| Can you show me the way to ____? | **Pouvez-vous m'indiquer le chemin pour ____?** *poo-vay voo man-dee-kay luh shuh-man poor* | |

# FOOD AND DRINK

The world has only a few truly great cuisines, and French is one of them. Respected for its extensive selection of dishes, its inventive uses of ingredients, and its exactness in preparation, French food is always reliably appetizing. French people are inherently great cooks, for they have been developing the elements of good taste since childhood. Wherever you eat in France, whether it be in Paris or Lyons, in the country or in the city, the food you will be offered will be carefully and lovingly prepared.

The past masters—especially Carême and Escoffier—defined and codified French food, so that you will not find the variations in ingredients or preparations that you notice in most other foods; a hollandaise sauce, for example, will always be made with egg yolks, into which are whisked butter and a dash of vinegar or lemon juice; it will be the same sauce, whether you are enjoying it in a Paris bistro or a country inn. What will vary will be particularly the regional dishes—dishes from the provinces of France that are made chiefly by the cooks in small restaurants and inns.

France's restaurants are famous, and they alone are worth a trip to that country. The most famous ones are those graded with one, two, or three (best) stars in the red Michelin guide. There are other ratings, too, especially from Gault & Millau, which tend to favor restaurants whose chefs prepare the nouvelle cuisine dishes. Three-star restaurants are also among the most expensive and the most formal, for these are the towers of **haute cuisine,** and all other restaurants strive to be in that category some day.

Eating in France is a somewhat structured affair. To make your stay enjoyable and to gather a bit of the French flavor, we suggest you follow the French manner of eating. First, here are the types of restaurants you are likely to encounter.

| | |
|---|---|
| **Auberge, Relais, Hostellerie** | a country inn. |
| **Bistro** | a small neighborhood restaurant in town, similar to a pub or tavern and usually very informal. |

| | |
|---|---|
| **Brasserie** | a large café which serves quick meals throughout the day or evening; most meals involve only the entrée, such as a steak or chop. |
| **Cabaret** | a nightclub where you may also eat a meal. |
| **Café** | a neighborhood spot to socialize, either indoors or out, where you can linger over a coffee or glass of wine or beer and perhaps have a little snack. Cafés also serve breakfast (usually a **croissant** and **café au lait**) and later in the day serve soft drinks and ice cream. |
| **Casse-croûte** | a restaurant specializing in sandwiches. |
| **Crêperie** | a small stand specializing in the preparation of crêpes—thin pancakes dusted with sugar or covered with jam and rolled up. |
| **Fast-food place** | a small place to eat an American-style snack, mostly hamburgers and French fries; most are in Paris along the Champs-Elysée and many are American chains such as McDonald's and Burger King. |
| **Restaurant** | can range from a small, family-owned inn, where mom seats you, dad cooks the meal, and the children serve you, to a formal, three-star palace where you receive the most elegant service and most beautifully garnished foods. |
| **Self** | a cafeteria, popular with students and mostly located near a university. |
| **Troquet** | a wine shop where you can also have a snack. |

By law, all establishments serving food must post a menu showing the prices. Most often, you will see posted two menus—one which is a listing of the *à la carte* offerings, and the other as one, two, or three different *prix fixe* meals. You can, of course, order the dishes you wish following the *à la carte* menu, but the resulting cost will be higher than if you choose one of the menus. The menus are a good choice since they always feature a freshly prepared entrée and usually reflect the specialty of the chef. When there is more than one menu from which to choose, they will differ depending upon the number of courses or the relative value of the entrée; lower-priced menus usually include a grilled steak or chicken dish as entrée, while the higher-priced might feature an additional cheese course or perhaps both fish and meat courses. In some regions, especially those that receive a number of tourists, you'll often see a special "tourist" menu, which will feature a specialty of the region—cassoulet in Languedoc or truffles in Perigord, for example. Wherever you eat, look for the **plat du jour** (day's specialty) or the **spécialités de la maison** (chef's specialties).

Most menus include a line at the bottom stating that the service charge is included in the price of the meal; it is usually about 12%. It is also customary to leave some small change on the table for the waiter, usually what would round off your bill. If you order a wine other than the house wine, you should also tip the steward, although the service for wine is sometimes also included in the bill. Oftentimes, especially in very casual restaurants, the wine is included in the menu **(boisson comprise).** If you want a simple, inexpensive wine, select the house wine, which will usually be a regional wine; if you want advice in a casual restaurant, ask the waiter—as a Frenchman, he will have been brought up to know wines and will recommend one that you will enjoy with what you are eating (see also pages on wine, 104–107).

## MEALS OF THE DAY

Most tourists will have their breakfast in the hotel, so much of the information that follows applies to lunch and dinner. Breakfast, **le petit déjeuner,** is usually small, consisting of a croissant or part of a loaf of day-old French bread, with butter and jam. It is usually served with **café au lait**—a large cup or bowl of hot coffee mixed half-and-half with steamed milk; this breakfast is called **café complet** and it is what you will most often be served, especially if breakfast is included in the cost of your room. You may also order hot tea or hot chocolate for breakfast.

Lunch and dinner in France are about the same in character and courses. Lunch, referred to as **le déjeuner,** is usually served between 12:30 and 3 p.m. Especially in smaller towns or on the road, be sure to stop early (by 12:15 to secure a table for lunch; many local spots have reserved tables for residents—you'll even see their napkins saved from the previous day).

In warm weather, do what many French people do for lunch—picnic. Especially if you are sightseeing and don't want to take the time for a lengthy lunch, buy some French bread in a **boulangerie,** then go next door to the *charcuterie* for 100 grams of *pâté de campagne;* stop in an *épicerie* for some salads or sliced tomatoes and some cheese, and also pick up a bottle of wine or mineral water. Take your goods to a park or stop along the road in a field and enjoy your lunch. In France, you'll find the roads are vacated by 12:30, and everyone has pulled over, set up tables, and begun to eat. In town, they will go to the **Jardin des Plantes** or **Bois de Boulogne.**

Dinner **(dîner)** is a bit more formal than lunch and usually served more graciously. In Paris, people eat late—8 p.m. is the earliest—while in the country, you can properly begin by 7:30. It is a time for the enjoyment of food and wine, and therefore a meal can carry on for at least two hours. Most French people do not begin their meal with a cocktail, but sometimes will have an apéritif. The meal consists of the following courses, in this order: cold or hot hors d'oeuvres; soup; fish; meat or poultry with accompanying vegetables; cheese; dessert. In recent years, lighter eating patterns have cut down on the number of courses, and you can of course decline to have a particular course.

In the specialty restaurants—those particularly noted for their food—you will often see a **menu dégustation** or a **menu gastronomique.** The former is a dinner whereby you receive a sampling of a large number of items on the menu, so as to try many of the chef's dishes—this is most popular in **nouvelle cuisine** restaurants. The latter is a special menu for food-lovers, which features rare items or very difficult dishes to prepare.

## TYPES OF FRENCH COOKING

The basics of French food were established centuries ago, but there have been developments in recent years that have released this food from its straitjacket. The following is a breakdown of the types of food you are likely to encounter.

**Haute Cuisine**  This is classic French cooking, offered in the top (Michelin starred) restaurants. The food is refined and exquisitely presented.

**Cuisine Bourgeoise**  This is the country food of France, made for centuries in everyday kitchens, and it is from this that **haute cuisine** was developed. This is the food you'll have in most bistros and small restaurants.

**Nouvelle Cuisine**  Developed in the seventies and now less respected, this food represented a break from traditional flour-based sauces and rigid rules. In this style, fruits were combined with meats and fish, sauces were reduced until thickened, and salads with elaborate arrangements were developed. This cuisine was promoted by such leaders as Paul Bocuse, Roger Vergé, and the Troisgros brothers; its influences are still apparent in most restaurants.

**Cuisine Minceur**  A special diet-conscious cuisine developed by Michel Guérard.

Nowadays, you'll find that menus will include a mixture of dishes—some considered *nouvelle cuisine* and others more along the line of traditional provincial food.

## EATING OUT

| | |
|---|---|
| Do you know a good restaurant? | **Connaissez-vous un bon restaurant?** *koh-neh-ssay voo uhn bohn rehss-toh-rahn?* |
| It is very expensive? | **C'est très cher?** *seh treh shehr* |
| Do you know a restaurant that serves regional dishes? | **Connaissez-vous un restaurant de cuisine régionale?** *koh-neh-ssay voo uhn rehss-toh-rahn duh kwee-zeen ray-zhyoh-nahl* |
| I'd like to make a reservation _____. | **Je voudrais retenir une table _____.** *zhuh voo-dreh ruh-tuh-neer ewn tah-bluh* |
| ■for tonight | **pour ce soir** *poor suh swahr* |
| ■for tomorrow evening | **pour demain soir** *poor duh-man swahr* |
| ■for two (four) persons | **pour deux (quatre) personnes** *poor duh (kah-truh) pehr-ssohn* |
| ■at 8 (8:30 P.M.) | **à vingt heures (vingt heures trente)** *ah van-tuhr (van-tuhr trahnt)* |
| Waiter! | **Garçon!** *gahr-ssohn!* |
| Miss! | **Mademoiselle** *mahd-mwah-zehl* |
| A table for two in the corner (near the window). | **Une table pour deux dans un petit coin (près de la fenêtre).** *ewn tah-bluh poor duh dahn zuhn puh-tee kwan (preh duh lah fuh-neh-truh)* |
| We'd like to have lunch (dinner) now. | **Nous voudrions déjeuner (dîner) maintenant.** *noo voo-dree-yohn day-zhuh-nay (dee-nay) mant-nahn* |
| The menu, please. | **La carte (Le menu), s'il vous plaît.** *lah kahrt (luh muh-new) seel voo pleh* |

| | |
|---|---|
| I'd like the fifty-franc menu. | **Je voudrais le menu à cinquante francs.** *zhuh voo-dreh luh muh-new ah san-kahnt frahn* |
| What's today's special? | **Quel est le plat du jour?** *kehl eh luh plah dew zhoor* |
| What do you recommend? | **Qu'est-ce que vous me recommandez?** *kehss kuh voo muh ruh-koh-mahn-day* |
| What's the house specialty? | **Quelle est la spécialité de la maison?** *kehl eh lah spay-ssyah-lee-tay duh lah meh-zohn* |
| Do you serve children's portions? | **Servez-vous des demi-portions pour les enfants?** *sehr-vay voo day duh-mee pohr-ssyohn poor lay zahn-fahn* |
| I'm (not) very hungry. | **J'ai (Je n'ai pas) très faim.** *zhay (zhuh nay pah) treh fan* |
| To begin with, bring us ____. | **Pour commencer, apportez-nous ____.** *poor koh-mahn-ssay, ah-pohr-tay noo* |
| ■ an apéritif | **un apéritif** *uhn nah-pay-ree-teef* |
| ■ a cocktail | **un cocktail** *uhn kohk-tehl* |
| ■ some white (red, rosé) wine | **du vin blanc (rouge, rosé)** *dew van blahn (roozh, roh-zay)* |
| ■ some water | **de l'eau** *duh loh* |
| ■ a bottle of mineral water, with (without) gas | **une bouteille d'eau minérale gazeuse (plate)** *ewn boo-tehy doh mee-nay-rahl gah-zuhz (plaht)* |
| ■ a beer | **une bière** *ewn byehr* |
| I'd like to order now. | **Je voudrais commander maintenant.** *zhuh voo-dreh koh-mahn-day mant-nahn* |
| I'd like ____. | **Je voudrais ____.** *zhuh voo-dreh* |

(see the listings that follow for individual dishes, and also the regional specialties noted on pages 102–103)

| | | |
|---|---|---|
| Do you have a house wine? | **Avez-vous du vin ordinaire?** *ah-vay-voo dew van ohr-dee-nehr* | |
| Is it dry (mellow, sweet)? | **Est-ce sec (moelleux, doux)?** *ehss sehk (mwah-luh, doo)* | |
| Please also bring us ____. | **Apportez-nous aussi, s'il vous plaît** ____. *ah-pohr-tay noo oh-ssee seel voo pleh* | |

- ■ a roll — **un petit pain** *uhn puh-tee pan*
- ■ bread — **du pain** *dew pan*
- ■ butter — **du beurre** *dew buhr*

| | |
|---|---|
| Waiter, we need ____. | **Garçon, apportez-nous** ____, **s'il vous plaît.** *gahr-ssohn ah-pohr-tay noo seel voo pleh* |

- ■ a knife — **un couteau** *uhn koo-toh*
- ■ a fork — **une fourchette** *ewn foor-sheht*
- ■ a spoon — **une cuiller** *ewn kwee-yehr*
- ■ a teaspoon — **une cuiller à café** *ewn kwee-yehr ah kah-fay*
- ■ a glass — **un verre** *uhn vehr*
- ■ a goblet — **un gobelet** *uhn gohb-leh*
- ■ a cup — **une tasse** *ewn tahss*
- ■ a saucer — **une soucoupe** *ewn soo-koop*
- ■ a plate — **une assiette** *ewn ah-ssyeht*
- ■ a napkin — **une serviette** *ewn sehr-vyeht*
- ■ a toothpick — **un cure-dent** *uhn kewr-dahn*

## APPETIZERS (STARTERS)

Appetizers can be either hot or cold; if you order both, have the cold one first. The following are among the most common items you'll see on a menu.

**1.** ARTICHAUTS À LA VINAIGRETTE   artichokes in a vinaigrette dressing.

**2.** CRUDITÉS VARIÉES   assorted vegetables—sliced tomatoes, shredded carrots, sliced cooked beets—in a vinaigrette dressing.

**3.** ESCARGOTS À LA BOURGUIGNONNE   snails cooked and served in the shell, seasoned with a garlic, shallot, and parsley butter.

**4.** FOIE GRAS   fresh, often uncooked liver of a force-fed goose; sliced and served with toasted French bread slices.

**5.** PÂTÉ   any of a number of meat loaves, made from puréed liver and usually also with meat—pork, veal, or chicken. **Pâté de foie gras** is made with goose liver; **pâté de campagne** is "of the country" and is a coarser mixed meat paté; **pâté en croute** is a liver pâté encased in pastry.

**6.** QUICHE LORRAINE   an egg custard tart, sometimes with bacon strips or bits; some versions now also made with Gruyère cheese.

**7.** QUENELLES   light dumplings, usually made from **brochet** (pike) but also from shellfish; served in a white sauce.

**8.** RILLETTES   a pork mixture that has been potted, then served as a spread, usually with French bread.

**9.** TERRINE   A type of pâté, usually served from a deep pot rather than sliced as pâté would be. Terrines can be made from pork, poultry, game, or fish.

## SOUPS

Some of those that appear on menus are the following:

**1.** BISQUE D'ÉCREVISSES   a creamy soup made with crawfish; other bisques are made with lobster, shrimp, or oysters.

**2.** BOUILLABAISSE   a seafood stew, made with a variety of fish and shellfish depending on the region, seasoned with saffron and fennel or pernod.

**3.** CONSOMMÉ   a clear broth, made usually from chicken or beef and flavored with herbs; **en gelée** is consommé that has been jelled and sliced; **madrilène** is with tomatoes; **printanier** has a variety of vegetables.

**4.** CRÈME   A creamy soup, made from any of a number of vegetables and usually enriched with egg yolks. **D'Argenteuil** is cream of asparagus soup; **de volaille** is a creamy chicken soup.

**5.** PETITE MARMITE   a rich consommé served with the meat and vegetables.

**6.** POTAGE   a coarser soup, usually made with a purée of vegetables; some varieties of potage are **parmentier** (leeks and potatoes), **au cresson** (watercress), **julienne** (shredded vegetables).

**7.** SOUPE À L'OIGNON   famous French onion soup, served over French bread and covered with cheese.

**8.** VELOUTÉ   a creamy soup, most common of which is **de volaille** (cream of chicken) and **de tomate** (tomato).

## EGG DISHES

As is true for most of the continent, eggs are not eaten for breakfast but rather are served as a beginning course in a variety of preparations.

**1.** OEUFS BERCY   eggs baked with sausages in a tomato sauce.

**2.** OEUFS EN COCOTTE   eggs gently baked in individual cups until softly cooked, sometimes with cream, then eaten with a spoon.

**3. OEUFS EN GELÉE**   poached eggs that are set into jelled consommé and served chilled as a salad.
**4. OMELETTE**   a French omelette is puffy and contains a variety of fillings—**aux fines herbes** is with a mixture of parsley, chives, and tarragon.
**5. PIPERADE**   scrambled eggs mixed with tomatoes, onions, and sweet peppers.
**6. SOUFFLÉ**   soufflés can be made with almost any ingredients—vegetables, chicken livers, cheese, ham, and so on; they are always light and puffy.

## FISH COURSE

The French often eat a fish course preceding meat or poultry. You can also order the fish course as your main selection. Here are some of the names for fish and shellfish you'll find on menus; for the names of preparations, see pages 92–93. When there is no price on the menu, the abbreviation s.g. *(selon grosseur)* refers to a dish that is sold by weight.

| | | |
|---|---|---|
| **les anchois** | *lay zah<u>n</u>-shwah* | anchovies |
| **les anguilles** | *lay zah<u>n</u>-gee* | eel |
| **le bar** | *luh bahr* | bass (hake) |
| **la barbue** | *lah bahr-bew* | brill |
| **la baudroie** | *lah boh-drwah* | anglerfish, monkfish |
| **le brochet** | *luh broh-sheh* | pike |
| **le cabillaud** | *luh kah-bee-yoh* | cod |
| **le calmar** | *luh kahl-mahr* | squid |
| **la carpe** | *lah kahrp* | carp |
| **le carrelet** | *luh kahr-leh* | flounder |
| **le congre** | *luh koh<u>n</u>-gruh* | conger eel |
| **les crevettes** | *lay kruh-veht* | shrimp |
| **la daurade** | *lah doh-rahd* | porgy |
| **les écrevisses** | *lay zay-kruh-veess* | crawfish |

| | | |
|---|---|---|
| les escargots | *lay zehss-kahr-goh* | snails |
| les harengs (fumés) | *lay ah-rah<u>n</u> (few-may)* | herring (smoked) |
| le homard | *luh oh-mahr* | lobster |
| les huîtres | *lay zwee-truh* | oysters |
| la lamproie | *lah lah<u>n</u>-prwah* | lamprey |
| la langouste | *lah lah<u>n</u>-goosst* | spiny lobster |
| les langoustines | *lay lah<u>n</u>-goo-ssteen* | large shrimp |
| la lotte | *lah loht* | monkfish |
| le loup de mer | *luh loo duh mehr* | sea bass |
| le maquereau | *luh mah-kroh* | mackerel |
| le merlan | *luh mehr-lah<u>n</u>* | whiting |
| la morue | *lah moh-rew* | cod |
| les moules | *lay mool* | mussels |
| les palourdes | *lay pah-loord* | clams |
| la perche | *lah pehrsh* | perch |
| les poulpes | *lay poolp* | octopus |
| la rascasse | *lah rahss-kahss* | scorpionfish |
| les sardines | *lay sahr-deen* | sardines |
| le saumon | *luh soh-moh<u>n</u>* | salmon |
| les scampi | *lay skah<u>n</u>-pee* | large shrimp |
| le thon | *luh toh<u>n</u>* | tuna |
| la truite | *lah trweet* | trout |
| le turbot | *luh tewr-boh* | European turbot |

## POULTRY AND GAME

The French have several names for chicken, depending on its size or age. They also have varying names for duck and some game. Below are some of the more common terms you'll see on menus:

| la caille | *lah kahy* | quail |
| le cerf | *luh sehr* | venison |
| la canard, cane-ton | *luh kah-nahr, kahn-tohn* | duckling |
| le chapon | *luh shah-pohn* | capon |
| le chevreuil | *luh shuh-vruhy* | venison |
| le cochon de lait | *luh koh-shohn duh leh* | suckling pig |
| la dinde | *lah dand* | turkey |
| le faisan | *luh feh-zahn* | pheasant |
| le lapin | *luh lah-pan* | rabbit |
| le lièvre | *luh lyeh-vruh* | hare |
| l'oie *(f.)* | *lwah* | goose |
| le perdreau, la perdrix | *luh pehr-droh, lah pehr-dree* | partridge |
| le pigeon, le pi-geonneau | *luh pee-zhohn, luh pee-zhoh-noh* | squab |
| la pintade, le pintadeau | *lah pan-tahd, luh pan-tah-doh* | guinea fowl |
| la poule | *lah pool* | stewing fowl |
| le poulet, poussin, la volaille | *luh poo-leh, poo-ssan, lah voh-lahy* | chicken |

**Suprême de volaille** is the fillet from a young chicken breast, usually served with a sauce or garnish.

## MEATS

Here are some basic terms for different kinds of meat, followed by a listing of some common cuts of meat and other terms you'll find on a menu:

| l'agneau *(m.)* | *lah-nyoh* | lamb |
| le bœuf | *luh buhf* | beef |

| | | |
|---|---|---|
| **la chèvre** | *lah sheh-vruh* | goat |
| **le jambon** | *luh zhah<u>n</u>-boh<u>n</u>* | ham |
| **le mouton** | *luh moo-toh<u>n</u>* | mutton |
| **le porc** | *luh pohr* | pork |
| **le veau** | *luh voh* | veal |
| | | |
| **les andouilles** | *lay zah<u>n</u>-dooy* | pork sausages |
| **le bifteck** | *luh beef-tehk* | steak |
| **le boudin** | *luh boo-da<u>n</u>* | blood sausage |
| **le carré d'ag-neau** | *luh kah-ray dah-nyoh* | rack of lamb |
| **le cervelas** | *luh sehr-vuh-lah* | garlicky pork sausage |
| **la cervelle** | *lah sehr-vehl* | brains |
| **la charcuterie** | *lah shahr-kew-tree* | assorted sausages, pâtés, and terrines |
| **le chateaubriand** | *luh shah-toh-bree-ah<u>n</u>* | porterhouse steak |
| **la côte de boeuf** | *lah koht duh buhf* | ribs of beef |
| **les côtelettes** | *lay koht-leht* | cutlets |
| **les côtes de porc, de veau** | *lay koht duh pohr, duh voh* | chops, pork or veal |
| **les crépinettes** | *lay kray-pee-neht* | small sausages |
| **l'entrecôte** *(f.)* | *lah<u>n</u>-truh-koht* | sirloin steak |
| **l'escalope** *(f.)* | *lehss-kah-lohp* | cutlet |
| **le filet de bœuf** | *luh fee-leh duh buhf* | fillet of beef |
| **le foie** | *luh fwah* | liver |
| **le gigot d'agneau** | *luh zhee-goh dah-nyoh* | leg of lamb |

| | | |
|---|---|---|
| **la langue** | *lah lahng* | tongue |
| **le lard** | *luh lahr* | bacon |
| **les médaillons de veau** | *lay may-dah-yohn duh voh* | small rounds of veal |
| **les noisettes** | *lay nwah-zeht* | small fillets |
| **les pieds de porc** | *lay pyay duh pohr* | pig's feet |
| **le ris de veau** | *luh ree duh voh* | veal sweetbreads |
| **les rognons d'ag-neau** | *lay roh-nyohn dah-nyoh* | lamb kidneys |
| **le rosbif** | *luh rohss-beef* | roast beef |
| **les saucisses** | *lay soh-sseess* | sausages |
| **la selle d'agneau** | *lah sehl dah-nyoh* | saddle of lamb |
| **le steak** | *luh stehk* | steak |
| **le tournedos** | *luh toor-nuh-doh* | small fillets of beef |
| **les tripes** | *lay treep* | tripe |
| Is it ____? | **C'est ____?** | *seh* |
| ■baked | **au four** | *oh foor* |
| ■boiled | **bouilli(e)** | *boo-yee* |
| ■braised (stewed) | **braisé(e)** | *breh-zay* |
| ■broiled (grilled) | **grillé(e)** | *gree-yay* |
| ■roasted | **rôti(e)** | *roh-tee* |
| ■poached | **poché(e)** | *poh-shay* |
| I like the steak ____. | **Je préfère le steak ____.** | *zhuh pray-fehr luh stehk* |
| ■well-done | **bien cuit(e)** | *byan kwee* |
| ■medium | **à point** | *ah pwan* |
| ■rare | **saignant(e)** | *seh-nyahn* |
| ■tender | **tendre** | *tahn-druh* |

## PREPARATIONS AND SAUCES

Of necessity, these descriptions are very brief and generalized, but they should give you an impression of what to expect.

1. aioli   mayonnaise heavily flavored with garlic
2. allemande   a light (blond) sauce
3. à la bonne femme   white wine sauce with vegetables
4. alsacienne   with sauerkraut
5. béarnaise   a butter-egg sauce flavored with shallots, wine, and tarragon
6. bercy   basic meat or fish sauce
7. beurre blanc   butter sauce flavored with shallots and wine
8. beurre noir   browned butter sauce
9. blanquette   an egg-enriched cream sauce, usually part of a stewed dish
10. bordelaise   a dish prepared with Bordeaux wine
11. bourguignonne   a dish prepared with Burgundy red wine
12. bretonne   a dish that includes beans
13. caen   a dish made with Calvados (apple brandy)
14. chantilly   a sauce of whipped cream and hollandaise; or as a dessert, sweetened whipped cream
15. chasseur   a sauce made with mushrooms, white wine, shallots, and parsley
16. choron   a béarnaise sauce with tomatoes
17. coquilles   a preparation served in a scallop shell
18. coulibiac   a preparation served in a pastry shell
19. crécy   a dish made with carrots
20. daube   a stew, usually beef, made with red wine, onions, and garlic
21. demi-deuil   when slices of truffles are inserted beneath the skin of a chicken
22. diable   a spicy sauce, usually with chili or cayenne pepper
23. duxelles   a mushroom mixture, usually as a stuffing or sauce base
24. estragon   a dish made with tarragon
25. farcie   a stuffing, or forcemeat filling
26. fenouil   a sauce made with fennel
27. financière   madeira sauce with truffles
28. fines herbes   a dish made with a variety of chopped fresh herbs
29. florentine   a dish that includes spinach

**30.** forestière   a dish made with wild mushrooms
**31.** fricassée   a stewed or potted dish, usually chicken
**32.** gratin   a crusty baked dish, named for the dish in which it is cooked
**33.** hollandaise   an egg yolk and butter sauce, with vinegar or lemon juice
**34.** jardinière   a dish with fresh vegetables
**35.** lyonnaise   a preparation made with onions
**36.** madère   a dish made with madeira wine
**37.** maître d'hôtel   a butter sauce with parsley and lemon juice
**38.** marchand de vin   a sauce with a meat stock and red wine
**39.** meunière   a simple dish lightly dusted with flour and sauteed, served in a lemon-butter sauce
**40.** mornay   a simple white sauce with grated cheese, usually gruyère
**41.** mousseline   a hollandaise sauce with whipped cream
**42.** moutarde   with mustard
**43.** nantua   a basic white sauce with cream and shellfish
**44.** normande   either a fish sauce with oysters or shrimp; or a sauce with apples
**45.** parmentier   a dish with potatoes
**46.** périgourdine   with truffles
**47.** poivrade   a dark sauce, seasoned with pepper
**48.** provençale   a vegetable garnish, usually with tomatoes, olives, anchovies, and garlic
**49.** quenelles   light-as-air dumplings made from fish or shellfish
**50.** ragoût   a thick stew
**51.** rémoulade   a mayonnaise flavored with mustard and sometimes capers
**52.** véronique   a dish with grapes
**53.** verte   a green mayonnaise, flavored with parsley and other herbs
**54.** vinaigrette   an oil and vinegar dressing for salads
**55.** vol-au-vent   a puff-pastry shell in which is usually served a creamed meat dish

## VEGETABLES

| l'artichaut *(m.)* | *lahr-tee-shoh* | artichoke |
| **les asperges** | *lay zahss-pehrzh* | asparagus |

| | | |
|---|---|---|
| l'aubergine *(f.)* | *loh-behr-zheen* | eggplant |
| la betterave | *lah beh-trahv* | beet |
| les carottes | *lay kah-roht* | carrots |
| le céleri | *luh sayl-ree* | celery |
| le céleri rave | *luh sayl-ree-rahv* | knob celery |
| les champignons | *lay shahn-pee-nyohn* | mushrooms |
| le chou | *luh shoo* | cabbage (green) |
| le chou-fleur | *luh shoo-fluhr* | cauliflower |
| la courgette | *lah koor-zheht* | zucchini |
| le cresson | *luh kreh-ssohn* | watercress |
| les épinards | *lay zay-pee-nahr* | spinach |
| les flageolets | *lay flah-zhoh-leh* | green shell beans |
| les haricots verts | *lay ah-ree-koh vehr* | green beans |
| les oignons | *lay zoh-nyohn* | onions |
| l'oseille *(f.)* | *loh-zehy* | sorrel |
| le piment | *luh pee-mahn* | green pepper |
| les pois | *lay pwah* | peas |
| le poireau | *luh pwah-roh* | leek |
| les pommes de terre | *lay pohm duh tehr* | potatoes |
| la tomate | *lah toh-maht* | tomato |

## SEASONINGS

Although French food is most often perfectly seasoned, personal preferences sometimes intercede. Here's how to ask for what you want.

| I'd like ___. | **Je voudrais** ___. | *zhuh voo-dreh* |
|---|---|---|
| ■ butter | **du beurre** | *dew buhr* |
| ■ horseradish | **du raifort** | *dew reh-fohr* |
| ■ ketchup | **du ketchup** | *dew keht-chuhp* |
| ■ margarine | **de la marga-rine** | *duh lah mahr-gah-reen* |
| ■ mayonnaise | **de la mayon-naise** | *duh lah mah-yoh-nehz* |
| ■ mustard | **de la moutarde** | *duh lah moo-tahrd* |
| ■ olive oil | **de l'huile d'ol-ive** | *duh lweel doh-leev* |
| ■ pepper (black) | **du poivre (noir)** | *dew pwah-vruh (nwahr)* |
| ■ pepper (red) | **du poivre (rouge)** | *dew pwah-vruh (roozh)* |
| ■ saccharine | **de la saccha-rine** | *duh lah sah-kah-reen* |
| ■ salt | **du sel** | *dew sehl* |
| ■ sugar | **du sucre** | *dew sew-kruh* |
| ■ vinegar | **du vinaigre** | *dew vee-neh-gruh* |
| ■ worcestershire sauce | **de la sauce an-glaise** | *du lah sohss ahn-glehz* |

## CHEESE COURSE

The cheese course is offered after the meat course and before the dessert. Most often, the restaurant will offer a tray of cheeses, from which you select two or three that balance one another. The cheese course is an opportunity to sample some cheeses that never get exported.

| What is that cheese? | **Quel est ce fromage?** | *kehl eh suh froh-mahzh* |
|---|---|---|
| Is it ___? | **Est-il ___?** | *eh-teel* |
| ■ mild | **maigre** | *meh-gruh* |
| ■ sharp | **piquant** | *pee-kahn* |
| ■ hard | **fermenté** | *fehr-mahn-tay* |
| ■ soft | **à pâte molle** | *ah paht mohl* |

Among the more popular cheeses are the following.

**1.** BANON   Made from sheep's or goat's milk, a soft cheese with a natural rind; a mild cheese with a mild nutty flavor.

**2.** BLEU D'AUVERGNE   Made from cow's milk, this soft cheese has an internal mold and when cut, the veins are visible. With a very sharp flavor.

**3.** BOURSIN   A soft cow's milk cheese, with a mild flavor, sometimes enhanced with herbs.

**4.** BRIE   A variety of cheeses made from cow's milk and with a bloomy rind. Varieties range in flavor from mild to very pronounced, some with a fruity flavor.

**5.** CAMEMBERT   Less delicate than brie, but also a cow's milk cheese with a bloomy rind. Should be eaten firm.

**6.** CANTAL   A cow's milk cheese that varies with length of aging. Some varieties are softer and milder, while more aged ones are hard and with a more pronounced flavor.

**7.** CHÈVRE   Any of an almost infinite variety of goat's milk cheeses, which vary from very soft to quite firm, and from mild and creamy to tart and crumbly. There will always be a few chèvres on the cheese tray.

**8.** COLOMBIÈRE   This cow's milk cheese is soft and supple, with a mild flavor.

**9.** MUNSTER   A cow's milk cheese that is soft and spicy, with a tangy flavor. In Alsace, where the cheese comes from, it is eaten young.

**10.** PONT-L'ÉVÊQUE   A cow's milk cheese that is very smooth and supple, with a pronounced flavor.

**11.** PORT-SALUT   The brand name for the Saint-Paulin from the monastery of Port-du-Salut.

**12.** REBLOCHON   A soft cow's milk cheese with a mild and creamy flavor.

**13.** ROQUEFORT   A sheep's milk cheese that is soft and pungent. The cheese is cured in caves, an ancient process with rigid standards for production. Texture is very buttery.

**14.** SAINT-PAULIN   Made from cow's milk, this is a velvety smooth cheese with a mild flavor.

**15.** TOMME DE SAVOIE   A mild cow's milk cheese with a nutty flavor.

**Petit Suisse** is a fresh, unsalted cheese made from cow's milk and enriched with cream, then molded into heart shapes and sprinkled with sugar; it is a common dessert.

**Fromage à la crème** is *fromage blanc,* a rich, creamy white cheese made from unskimmed cow's milk. It is eaten topped with cream and sugar for breakfast.

**Fondue** is a specialty of Switzerland and parts of France that border on Switzerland. It is a large pot of bubbling melted cheese (usually gruyère or emmenthal), into which is dipped cubes of French bread. Fondue is served as a warming lunch or dinner course.

**Raclette** is a specialty of French-speaking Switzerland. It involves the slow melting of a hard cheese, usually alongside a roaring fire, during which the diners scrape off the cheese as it melts onto slices of French bread.

## FRUITS AND NUTS

Here are the names of some common fruits, followed by nuts.

| | | |
|---|---|---|
| **l'abricot** | *lah-bree-koh* | apricot |
| **l'ananas** | *lah-nah-nah* | pineapple |
| **la banane** | *lah bah-nahn* | banana |
| **les cassis** | *lay kah-sseess* | black currants |
| **la cerise** | *lah suh-reez* | cherry |
| **le citron** | *luh see-trohn* | lemon |
| **la datte** | *lah daht* | date |

| la figue | *lah feeg* | fig |
| les fraises | *lay frehz* | strawberries |
| les fraises des bois | *lay frehz duh bwah* | wild strawberries |
| les framboises | *lay frahn-bwahz* | raspberries |
| les groseilles | *lay groh-sehy* | red currants |
| la limette | *lah lee-meht* | lime |
| la mandarine | *lah mahn-dah-reen* | tangerine |
| le melon | *luh muh-lohn* | melon |
| les mûres | *lay mewr* | mulberries |
| les myrtilles | *lay meer-tee* | blueberries |
| l'orange | *loh-rahnzh* | orange |
| la noix de coco | *lah nwah duh koh-koh* | coconut |
| le pample-mousse | *luh pahn-pluh-mooss* | grapefruit |
| la pêche | *lah pehsh* | peach |
| la poire | *lah pwahr* | pear |
| la pomme | *lah pohm* | apple |
| la prune | *lah prewn* | plum |
| le pruneau | *luh prew-noh* | prune |
| le raisin | *luh reh-zan* | grape |
| l'amande *(f.)* | *lah-mahnd* | almond |
| le marron | *luh mah-rohn* | chestnut |
| la noisette | *lah nwah-zeht* | hazelnut |
| les noix | *lay nwah* | nuts |

## DESSERTS—SWEETS

Often, a restaurant will display its desserts on a table in the dining room or the waiter will roll the cart to your table so you can make a selection. On the cart will be a variety of tarts, fruits in light syrup, and pastries. Here are some common items you might consider for dessert.

**1.** BAVAROISE   A bavarian cream; mont-blanc is a bavarian cream made with chestnuts.
**2.** BEIGNETS   Fritters, often made from fruit such as apple.
**3.** BOMBE   An ice cream construction, often with different flavors and sometimes also with sherbet.
**4.** CHARLOTTE   An assemblage of sponge fingers and pudding; usually the sponge cake is used to line the dish and pudding is in the center.
**5.** CRÈME CARAMEL   An egg custard served with a caramel sauce.
**6.** CRÊPES   Dessert crêpes, the most famous of which are **Crêpes Suzette,** made with orange flavoring and served flaming with Grand Marnier.
**7.** GÂTEAU   An elaborate layer cake, made with thin layers of sponge cake and pastry cream, and decorated.
**8.** MOUSSE AU CHOCOLAT   An airy pudding made with chocolate, cream, eggs, and brandy, garnished with whipped cream.
**9.** MACÉDOINE DE FRUITS   A fresh fruit salad.
**10.** OEUFS À LA NEIGE   Soft meringue ovals served floating on a custard sauce.
**11.** OMELETTE NORVÉGIENNE   Baked Alaska.
**12.** PÂTISSERIE   Pastry selection of any variety, including éclairs, millefeuilles, savarin, Saint-Honoré (cream puff cake).
**13.** POIRES HÉLÈNE   A poached pear, served with vanilla ice cream and chocolate sauce.
**14.** PROFITEROLES   Cream puffs, served with chocolate sauce.
**15.** SOUFFLÉ   An endless variety of sweet soufflés, the famous one being the Grand Marnier soufflé.
**16.** TARTE   Open-faced fruit pies, often made with apples or plums.

In addition, ice cream is a French favorite, as is sherbet and granité (fruit ice). Here's how to ask for these:

| ice cream | **une glace** | *ewn glahss* |
| chocolate | **au chocolat** | *oh shoh-koh-lah* |
| vanilla | **à la vanille** | *ah lah vah-nee* |
| strawberry | **aux fraises** | *oh frehz* |
| sundae | **une coupe** | *ewn koop* |
| sherbet | **un sorbet** | *uhn sohr-beh* |
| fruit ice | **un granité** | *uhn grah-nee-tay* |

## SPECIAL CIRCUMSTANCES

Many travelers have special dietary requirements, so here are a few phrases that might help you get what you need or avoid what does you wrong.

| I don't want anything fried (salted). | **Je ne veux rien de frit (salé).** *zhuh nuh vuh ryan duh free (sah-lay)* |
| I cannot eat anything made with ___. | **Je ne peux rien manger de cuisiné au (à la) ___.** *zhuh nuh puh ryan mahn-zhay duh kwee-zee-nay oh (ah lah)* |
| Do you have any dishes without meats? | **Avez-vous des plats sans viande?** *ah-vay voo day plah sahn vyahnd* |

## BEVERAGES

See pages 103–107 for information on French apéritifs, wines, and brandies. As for other beverages, we give you the following phrases to help you ask for exactly what you wish.

| Waiter, please bring me ___. | **Garçon, apportez-moi ___.** *gahr-ssohn ah-pohr-tay mwah* |
| coffee | **du café** *dew kah-fay* |
| with milk (morning only) | **du café au lait** *dew kah-fay oh leh* |
| espresso | **du café-express** *dew kah-fay ehkss-prehss* |
| with cream | **du café-crème** *dew kah-fay krehm* |

| | | |
|---|---|---|
| ■ black coffee | **du café noir** | *dew kah-fay nwahr* |
| ■ iced coffee | **du café glacé** | *dew kah-fay glah-ssay* |
| cider (alcoholic) | **du cidre** | *dew see-druh* |
| juice | **du jus** | *dew zhew* |
| lemonade | **de la citronnade** | *duh lah see-troh-nahd* |
| milk | **du lait** | *dew leh* |
| ■ cold | **froid** | *frwah* |
| ■ hot | **chaud** | *shoh* |
| ■ milk shake | **un frappé** | *uhn frah-pay* |
| orangeade | **une orangeade** | *ewn oh-rahn-zhahd* |
| punch | **un punch** | *uhn puhnsh* |
| soda | **un soda** | *uhn soh-dah* |
| tea | **un thé** | *uhn tay* |
| ■ with milk | **au lait** | *oh leh* |
| ■ with lemon | **au citron** | *oh see-trohn* |
| ■ with sugar | **sucré** | *sew-kray* |
| ■ iced | **glacé** | *glah-ssay* |
| water | **de l'eau** *(f.)* | *duh loh* |
| ■ cold | **de l'eau fraîche** | *duh loh frehsh* |
| ■ ice | **de l'eau glacée** | *duh loh glah-ssay* |
| ■ mineral | **de l'eau minérale** | *duh loh mee-nay-rahl* |
| ■ with gas | **gazeuse** | *gah-zuhz* |
| ■ without gas | **plate** | *plaht* |

### SETTLING UP

The bill normally includes a surcharge for service. In addition, most people leave the small change from the bill as a token of appreciation.

| The check, please. | **L'addition, s'il vous plaît.**  *lah-dee-ssyohn seel voo pleh* |
| Separate checks. | **Des notes séparées.**  *day noht say-pah-ray* |
| Is the service (tip) included? | **Le service est compris?**  *luh sehr-veess eh kohn-pree* |
| I haven't ordered this. | **Je n'ai pas commandé ceci.**  *zhuh nay pah koh-mahn-day suh-ssee* |
| I don't think the bill is right. | **Je crois qu'il y a une erreur dans l'addition.**  *zhuh krwah keel yah ewn ehr-ruhr dahn lah-dee-ssyohn* |
| We're in a hurry. | **Nous sommes pressés.**  *noo sohm preh-ssay* |
| Is it ready? | **Est-elle prête?**  *eh-tehl preht* |
| Will it take long? | **Il faudra longtemps?**  *eel foh-drah lohn-tahn* |
| This is for you. | **Ceci est pour vous.**  *suh-ssee eh poor voo* |

## REGIONAL FRENCH SPECIALTIES

French food is noted for its ingredients: wild mushrooms such as **chanterelles, cèpes,** and morels; truffles; fresh **foie gras;** chickens from Bresse; butter and cream from Normandy; cheese from all parts of France. Below we give you some of the notable dishes from some of the provinces of France, most of which are famous for their regional ingredients.

**1. ALSACE-LORRAINE**  This region has a strong German influence in its food and the most famous dish is **choucroute garnie,** a sauerkraut, pork and sausage mixture; also **pâté de foie gras, quiche lorraine,** and **chicken in riesling wine.** The food is hearty, with much emphasis on fish, fruit, and pork.

**2. BORDEAUX**  Food from here is prepared simply, with use of Bordeaux wine, **cèpes,** and **confit d'oie,** a potted goose, preserved in its own fat. This is a noted wine-producing area.

**3.** BRITTANY  **Crêpes** are the best-known food from here, with a variety of sweet and savory fillings. There is also much seafood and sausages. Cider is the popular beverage.

**4.** BURGUNDY  With Lyons in the gastronomic center, this region has some of the best food in France. The chickens from Bresse are world famous, as is the beef; from Burgundy we also get the savory mustards, spiced gingerbread, and black-currant liqueur—cassis. This is also a major wine-producing region.

**5.** NORMANDY  Foods from here are marked by a use of apples or apple **eau de vie.** The omelettes from Mère Poulard are famous; the fish dishes in this region are also noteworthy.

**6.** PROVENCE  This is a southern region that uses much olive oil and garlic in its dishes. Fish and seafood predominate, with a generous use of vegetables and fruits. The most famous dish is **bouillabaisse,** a fish stew; **salade niçoise,** with lettuce, tuna, hard-cooked eggs, olives, and anchovies, and **pissaladière,** a pizza made with anchovies are also popular.

**7.** PARIS  Food from all parts of France influences the dishes that are served in Paris. Those especially Parisian are **boeuf à la mode** (boiled beef with vegetables) and brie cheese.

## APÉRITIFS, WINES, AND AFTER-DINNER DRINKS

### APÉRITIFS

Most French people prefer to drink an apéritif before a meal rather than a cocktail. An apéritif is an appetite stimulant, and can be a variety of drinks, ranging from a simple vermouth or vermouth mixed with a liqueur (such as cassis), to a distilled drink such as Cynar, made from artichoke hearts. Among the most popular are:

| | |
|---|---|
| **Byrrh** **Dubonnet** **Saint-Raphaël** | wine-and-brandy–based, flavored with herbs and bitters |
| **Pernod** **Ricard** | anise-based, licorice-flavored |
| **Vermouth** | fortified wine made from red or white grapes |

**Cynar**  bitter tasting, distilled from artichoke hearts

## WINE

The high quality of the soil and the moderate climate have given French vineyards their historically unique position among wine-producing countries. Wine served with meals follows a progression from the light white wines to richer, heartier reds. (One wouldn't drink a Mâcon after a Pommard, or a Bordeaux after a Burgundy.)

White wines and rosés are served very cold (52°F). Beaujolais, although red, should be lightly chilled. Bordeaux is served at room temperature (62°), Burgundy just above room temperature. Sweet wines should be chilled, and Champagne iced. The chart below will help you select a wine to suit your tastes and your food.

| wine | **le vin** | *luh van* |
|---|---|---|
| ■ red wine | **le vin rouge** | *luh van roozh* |
| ■ rosé | **le vin rosé** | *luh van roh-zay* |
| ■ sparkling wine | **le vin mousseux** | *luh van moo-ssuh* |
| ■ sherry | **un sherry** | *uhn sheh-ree* |
| ■ white wine | **le vin blanc** | *luh van blahn* |

## AFTER-DINNER DRINKS

Brandy is often enjoyed after a lengthy, especially fine meal. **Cognac,** the finest of brandies, is distilled from grapes grown in the Charente district, the principal city of which is Cognac. It is usually aged for 20 years in barrels made from Limousin oak trees. Four different types that differ in character and taste are Remy-Martin, Martel, Courvoisier, and Hennessy. Ordering these cognacs in France is considerably less expensive than elsewhere.

**Armagnac** comes from the Basque region. It is often bottled straight, rather than blended as cognac is.

**Eaux-de-vie** are distilled fruit brandies. Unlike cognac and other brandies, they are aged in crockery, not wood, so their taste is harsher. Some eaux-de-vie are **kirsch** (black cherry), **framboise** (wild raspberries), **poire william** (Swiss William pears), **mirabelle** (yellow plum), **calvados** (apple), and **marc** (from stems, pits, and skins of certain grapes).

Some liqueurs to choose from are:

| | |
|---|---|
| **absinthe** | light drink with a pronounced anise aroma. |
| **anisette** | clear, sweet aromatic liqueur made from aniseeds and herbs. |
| **Bénédictine** | a blend of 150 different herbs and plants. |
| **B & B** | a combination of Bénédictine and brandy. |
| **Chambord** | raspberry-flavored, combined with honey. |
| **Chartreuse** | a combination of 130 herbs, in green and yellow. |
| **Cointreau** | made from sweet and bitter tropical orange peels blended with cognac. |
| **Crème de Cassis** | made from black currants. |
| **Grand Marnier** | an orange-flavored liqueur made from the peel of bitter Curaçao oranges and blended with cognac. |

---

### TRAVEL TIP

Every traveler has a few small items that he or she never fails to carry along on a trip. Some of these are a small flashlight, a tiny tube of spot remover, a Swiss army knife, some twine, Scotch tape, a small screwdriver, corkscrew, sewing kit, rubber bands and paper clips, extra plastic bags, and a washcloth.

| WINE | REGION | DESCRIPTION | ORDER WITH |
|---|---|---|---|
| Anjou | Loire | semisweet rosé | fish, meat, game, poultry, esp. ham |
| Beaujolais | Burgundy | light, young, fruity red wine | meat, poultry, fowl, cheese |
| Chablis | Burgundy | dry white, flinty bouquet, nutty taste | fish, seafood, esp. lobster |
| Champagne | Champagne | delicate, sparkling white wine | |
| | | Extra Dry (fruity)—medium dry | aperitif |
| | | Brut—driest | aperitif |
| | | Sec—least dry | dessert |
| Châteauneuf-du-Pape | Rhône | full-bodied red wine | game, poultry, meat |
| Côte de Beaune | Burgundy | very delicate light red wine | meat, esp. prime ribs, fowl, poultry |
| Côte de Bourg | Bordeaux | medium, full-bodied red wine | meat, poultry, fowl, cheese |
| Côtes du Rhône | Rhone | light, fruity, red wine | meat, poultry, fowl |
| | | full-bodied white wine | fish, fowl, veal |
| Gewürztraminer | Alsace | light, crisp white wine | fish, poultry, some cheese |
| Graves (blanc) | Bordeaux | soft white wine | fish, poultry |

| Wine | Region | Description | Serve with |
|---|---|---|---|
| Graves (rouge) | Bordeaux | robust red wine | meat, fowl, poultry, cheese |
| Mâconnais (Pouilly-Fuissé) | Burgundy | light, dry, white wine | fish, seafood, egg and cheese dishes |
| Médoc | Bordeaux | light red wine | meat, poultry, fowl, cheese |
| Muscadet | Loire | light, dry white wine | fish, seafood, esp. scallops |
| Muscat | Alsace | sweet white wine (also sparkling) | fish, seafood, desserts |
| Pinot | Alsace | light, fruity, white wine | fish, shellfish, cold vegetable dishes, egg and cheese dishes |
| Pomerol | Bordeaux | mellow, full-bodied red wine | meat, fowl, poultry, cheese |
| Riesling | Alsace | light, fruity, white wine | fish, shellfish, cold vegetable dishes, egg and cheese dishes |
| Saumur | Loire | dry, white wine | fish, seafood, poultry desserts |
| Sauternes (Barsac) | Bordeaux | honey-sweet white wine | meat, fowl, poultry, cheese, esp. ham |
| St-Emilion | Bordeaux | full-bodied, dark red wine | fish, seafood, meat |
| Vouvray | Loire | white or sparkling white | |

# GETTING TO KNOW PEOPLE

Remember to shake hands when meeting people. A Frenchman may feel offended if you do not. In general, Europeans don't ask many personal questions at the beginning of an acquaintance. Make contact through a neutral topic like the weather or the traffic.

## MEETING PEOPLE

| | |
|---|---|
| Do you live here? | **Habitez-vous ici?** *ah-bee-tay voo zee-ssee* |
| I am ____. | **Je suis ____.** *zhuh swee* |
| ■ from the United States | **des États-Unis** *day zay-tah zew-nee* |
| ■ from England | **de l'Angleterre** *duh lah<u>n</u>-gluh-tehr* |
| ■ from Canada | **du Canada** *dew kah-nah-dah* |
| ■ from Australia | **de l'Australie** *duh lohss-trah-lee* |
| I like France (Paris) very much. | **La France (Paris) me plaît beaucoup.** *lah frah<u>n</u>ss (pah-ree) muh pleh boh-koo* |
| I would like to go there. | **Je voudrais y aller.** *zhuh voo-dreh zee ah-lay* |
| How long will you be staying? | **Combien de temps resterez-vous ici?** *koh<u>n</u>-bya<u>n</u> duh tah<u>n</u> rehss-tray voo zee-ssee* |
| I'll stay for a few days (a week). | **Je resterai quelques jours (une semaine).** *zhuh rehss-tray kehl-kuh zhoor (ewn suh-mehn)* |
| Where are you living now? | **Où habitez-vous en ce moment?** *oo ah-bee-tay voo zah<u>n</u> suh moh-mah<u>n</u>* |

| What hotel are you at? | **À quel hôtel êtes-vous?** *ah kehl oh-tehl eht voo* |
| What do you think of ____? | **Que pensez-vous de ____?** *kuh pahn-ssay voo duh* |
| I (don't) like it very much. | **Je (ne) l'aime (pas) beaucoup.** *zhuh (nuh) lehm (pah) boh-koo* |
| I think its very ____. | **Je pense qu'il (elle) est ____.** *zhuh pahnss keel (kehl) eh* |
| ■ beautiful | **beau (belle)** *boh (behl)* |
| ■ interesting | **intéressant(e)** *an-tay-reh-ssahn(t)* |
| ■ magnificent | **magnifique** *mah-nyee-feek* |
| ■ wonderful | **formidable** *fohr-mee-dah-bluh* |

## GREETINGS AND INTRODUCTIONS

| May I introduce ____. | **Puis-je vous présenter ____.** *pweezh voo pray-zahn-tay* |
| ■ my brother | **mon frère** *mohn frehr* |
| ■ my father | **mon père** *mohn pehr* |
| ■ my friend | **mon ami(e)** *mohn nah-mee* |
| ■ my husband | **mon mari** *mohn mah-ree* |
| ■ my mother | **ma mère** *mah mehr* |
| ■ my sister | **ma soeur** *mah suhr* |
| ■ my sweetheart | **mon(ma) fiancé(e)** *mohn (mah) fee-yahn-ssay* |
| ■ my wife | **ma femme** *mah fahm* |
| How do you do (Glad to meet you). | **Enchanté(e).** *ahn-shahn-tay* |
| How do you do (The pleasure is mine). | **Moi de même.** *mwah duh mehm* |

| Allow me to introduce myself. | **Permettez-moi de me présenter.** *pehr-meh-tay mwah duh muh pray-zahn-tay* |
| My name is _____. | **Je m'appelle _____.** *zhuh mah-pehl* |
| Mine is _____. | **Et moi, je m'appelle _____.** *ay mwah zhuh mah-pehl* |
| I am _____. | **Je suis _____.** *zhuh swee* |
| ■ a teacher | **instituteur (institutrice)** *zan-sstee tew-tuhr (zan-sstee-tew-treess)* |
| ■ a doctor | **médecin** *mayd-san* |
| ■ a lawyer | **avocat(e)** *zah-voh-kah(t)* |
| ■ a businessperson | **homme (femme) d'affaires** *zohm (fahm) dah-fehr* |
| ■ a student | **étudiant(e)** *zay-tew-dyahn(t)* |

# DATING AND SOCIALIZING

May I have this dance?

**M'accordez-vous cette danse?** *mah-kohr-day voo seht dahnss*

Yes, all right. With pleasure.

**Oui, d'accord. Avec plaisir.** *wee, dah-kohr. ah-vehk pleh-zeer*

Would you like a cigarette (a drink)?

**Voudriez-vous une cigarette (une boisson)?** *voo-dree-yay voo zewn see-gah-reht (ewn bwah-ssohn)*

Do you have a light?

**Avez-vous du feu?** *ah-vay voo dew fuh*

Do you mind if I smoke?

**Ça vous dérange si je fume?** *sah voo day-rahnzh see zhuh fewm*

May I take you home?

**Puis-je vous raccompagner chez vous?** *pweezh voo rah-kohn-pah-nyay shay voo*

May I call you?

**Puis-je vous téléphoner?** *pweezh voo tay-lay-foh-nay*

What is your telephone number?

**Quel est votre numéro de téléphone?** *kehl eh voh-truh new-may-roh duh tay-lay fohn*

Here's my telephone number (address).

**Voici mon numéro de téléphone (mon adresse).** *vwah-ssee mohn new-may-roh duh tay-lay fohn (mohn nah-drehss)*

Will you write to me?

**Est-ce que vous m'écrirez?** *ehss kuh voo may-kree-ray*

Are you married?

**Êtes-vous marié(e)?** *eht voo mah-ree-ay*

Are you alone?

**Êtes-vous seul(e)?** *eht voo suhl*

Is your husband (wife) here?

**Êtes-vous ici avec votre mari (femme)?** *eht voo zee-ssee ah-vehk voh-truh mah-ree (fahm)*

| | |
|---|---|
| I'm here with my family. | **Je suis ici avec ma famille.** *zhuh swee zee-ssee ah-vehk mah fah-mee* |
| Do you have any children? | **Avez-vous des enfants?** *ah-vay voo day zahn-fahn* |
| How many? | **Combien en avez-vous?** *kohn-byan-ahn nah-vay voo* |
| How old are they? | **Quel âge ont-ils?** *kehl ahzh ohn teel* |
| I'm single. | **Je suis célibataire.** *zhuh swee say-lee-bah-tehr* |
| You must come to visit us. | **Vous devez venir nous rendre visite.** *voo duh-vay vuh-neer noo rahn-druh vee-zeet* |
| Would you like me to take a picture (snapshot) of you? | **Voudriez-vous que je vous prenne en photo?** *voo-dree-yay voo kuh zhuh voo prehn ahn foh-toh* |
| Stand here. | **Restez ici.** *rehss-tay zee-ssee* |
| Don't move. | **Ne bougez pas.** *nuh boo-zhay pah* |
| Smile. | **Souriez.** *soo-ryay* |
| That's it. | **C'est ça.** *seh sah* |
| Will you take a picture of me (us)? | **Voudriez-vous me (nous) prendre en photo?** *voo-dree-yay voo muh (noo) prahn-druh-ahn foh-toh* |
| Are you doing anything tomorrow? | **Avez-vous quelque chose à faire demain?** *ah-vay voo kehl-kuh shohz ah fehr duh-man?* |
| Are you free this evening? | **Êtes-vous libre ce soir?** *eht voo lee-bruh suh swahr* |
| Would you like to go together? | **Voudriez-vous aller ensemble?** *voo-dree-yay voo zah-lay ahn-sahn-bluh* |
| I'll wait for you in front of the hotel. | **Je vous attendrai devant l'hôtel.** *zhuh voo zah-tahn-dray duh-vahn loh-tehl* |

| I'll pick you up at your house (hotel). | **Je viendrai vous prendre chez vous (à votre hôtel).** *zhuh vyan-dray voo prahn-druh shay voo (ah voh-truh oh-tehl* |
|---|---|

## SAYING GOOD-BYE

| Nice to have met you. | **(Je suis) enchanté(e) d'avoir fait votre connaissance.** *(zhuh swee z)ahn-shahn-tay dah-vwahr feh voh-truh koh-neh-ssahnss* |
|---|---|
| The pleasure is mine. | **Le plaisir est partagé.** *luh pleh-zeer eh pahr-tah-zhay* |
| Regards to _____. | **Mon meilleur souvenir à _____.** *mohn meh-yuhr soo-vuh-neer ah* |

---

### TRAVEL TIP

When you purchase goods in a foreign country, save the receipts in case you have to prove the value of those purchases to customs agents upon returning home. Before you leave home, find out which goods you are likely to purchase that are not subject to duty and which are items you cannot bring back into the country. Consider also, especially if you plan to purchase a large number of heavy items, whether it is more advantageous to ship your purchases home or to pay airline charges for overweight.

---

# SHOPPING

## SHOPS AND STORES

It is best to start by shopping in the large department stores so that you may browse without feeling obligated to make a purchase. Most department stores are open Monday through Saturday, from 9:30 a.m. to 6:30 p.m. In Switzerland, however, stores are open from 8 a.m. to 6:30 p.m. and on Saturday from 8 to 4 p.m. Smaller stores have similar hours and many close for a lunch break between noon and 2 p.m. Most of the hairdressers are closed on Monday and the fashion boutiques on Monday morning. Sales usually take place at the beginning of January and at the end of June and the beginning of July. Most of the stores (even the department stores) remain closed on public holidays. Food stores are open on Sunday morning from 8:00 to 12:00.

In Paris the main shopping centers are located in the Palais de Congrès de Paris, the Montparnasse area, and in the Forum des Halles. Sales usually take place the first week in January and the last week of June or July. Couturier sales are in March or July.

Discounts of up to 20% are still given in many shops for purchases made in foreign currency, in the form of a refund mailed to your home address.

## GOING SHOPPING

| | |
|---|---|
| I'd like to go shopping today. | **Je voudrais aller faire des courses aujourd'hui.** *zhuh voo-dreh zah-lay fehr day koorss oh-zhoor-dwee* |
| Where can I find _____? | **Où pourrais-je trouver _____?** *oo poo-rehzh troo-vay* |
| ■ a bakery | **une boulangerie** *ewn boo-lahnzh-ree* |
| ■ a barber shop | **un coiffeur** *uhn kwah-fuhr* |

| | |
|---|---|
| ■ a beauty parlor | **un salon de beauté** *uhn sah-lohn duh boh-tay* |
| ■ a bookstore | **une librairie** *ewn lee-breh-ree* |
| ■ a butcher | **une boucherie** *ewn boosh-ree* |
| ■ a camera shop | **un magasin d'appareils-photo** *uhn mah-gah-zan dah-pah-rehy foh-toh* |
| ■ a candy store | **une confiserie** *ewn kohn-feess-ree* |
| ■ a clothing store | **un magasin de vêtements** *uhn mah-gah-zan duh veht-mahn* |
|    for children's clothes | **pour enfants** *poor ahn-fahn* |
|    men's store | **pour hommes** *poor ohm* |
|    women's boutique | **pour femmes** *poor fahm* |
| ■ a delicatessen | **une charcuterie** *ewn shahr-kew-tree* |
| ■ a department store | **un grand magasin** *uhn grahn mah-gah-zan* |
| ■ a drugstore | **une pharmacie** *ewn fahr-mah-ssee* |
| ■ a dry cleaner's | **une teinturerie** *ewn tan-tew-ruh-ree* |
| ■ a florist | **un fleuriste** *uhn fluh-reesst* |
| ■ a gift (souvenir) shop | **un magasin de souvenirs** *uhn mah-gah-zan duh soov-neer* |
| ■ a grocery store | **une épicerie** *ewn ay-peess-ree* |
| ■ a hardware store | **une quincaillerie** *ewn kahn-kahy-ree* |
| ■ a jewelry store | **une bijouterie** *ewn bee-zhoo-tree* |
| ■ a laundry | **une blanchisserie** *ewn blahn-sheess-ree* |

| | |
|---|---|
| ■ a liquor store | **un magasin de vins et spiritueux** *uhn mah-gah-zan duh van ay spee-ree-tew-uh* |
| ■ a newsstand | **un kiosque à journaux** *uhn kee-ohsk ah zhoor-noh* |
| ■ an optician | **un opticien** *uhn nohp-tee-ssyan* |
| ■ a record store | **un magasin de disques** *uhn mah-gah-zan duh deessk* |
| ■ a shoemaker | **un cordonnier** *uhn kohr-doh-nyay* |
| ■ a shoe store | **un magasin de chaussures** *uhn mah-gah-zan duh shoh-ssewr* |
| ■ a supermarket | **un supermarché** *uhn sew-pehr-mahr-shay* |
| ■ a tailor | **un tailleur** *uhn tah-yuhr* |
| ■ a tobacco shop | **un bureau de tabac** *uhn bew-roh duh tah-bah* |
| ■ a toy store | **un magasin de jouets** *uhn mah-gah-zan duh zhoo-eh* |
| ■ a travel agent | **une agence de voyages** *ewn ah-zhahnss duh vwah-yahzh* |
| ■ a watchmaker | **un horlogier** *uhn nohr-lohzh-yay* |
| ■ a wine merchant | **un négociant en vins** *uhn nay-gohss-yahn ahn van* |
| Sir. | **Monsieur.** *muh-ssyuh* |
| Young man. | **Jeune homme.** *zhuhn ohm* |
| Miss. | **Mademoiselle.** *mahd-mwah-zehl* |
| Can you help me? | **Pouvez-vous m'aider?** *poo-vay voo meh-day* |
| Where is the Lost and Found Office? | **Où est le Bureau d'Objets Trouvés?** *oo eh luh bew-roh dohb-zheh troo-vay* |

## BOOKS

Where is the best (biggest) bookstore here? **Où se trouve la meilleure (la plus grande) librairie par ici?** *oo suh troov lah meh-yuhr (lah plew grahnd) lee-breh-ree pahr ee-ssee*

What can I do for you? **On vous sert?** *ohn voo sehr*

I'm looking for a copy of _____. **Je cherche un exemplaire de _____.** *zhuh shehrsh uhn nehg-zahn-plehr duh*

The title of the bok is _____. **Le titre du livre est _____.** *luh tee-truh dew lee-vruh eh*

The author of the book is _____. **L'auteur du livre est _____.** *loh-tuhr dew lee-vruh eh*

I don't know the title (author). **Je ne sais pas le titre (le nom de l'auteur).** *zhuh nuh seh pah luh tee-truh (le nohn duh loh-tuhr)*

I'm just looking. **Je regarde tout simplement.** *zhuh ruh-gahrd too san-pluh-mahn*

Do you have books (novels) in English? **Avez-vous des livres (des romans) en anglais?** *ah-vay voo day lee-vruh (day roh-mahn) ahn nahn-gleh*

I would like _____. **Je voudrais _____.** *zhuh voo-dreh*

■ a guide book **un guide touristique** *uhn geed too-reess-teek*

■ a map of this city **un plan de la ville** *uhn plahn duh lah veel*

■ a pocket dictionary **un dictionnaire de poche** *uhn deek-ssyoh-nehr duh pohsh*

■ a French-English dictionary **un dictionnaire français-anglais** *uhn deek-ssyoh- nehr frahn-sseh ahn-gleh*

Where can I find _____? **Où puis-je trouver _____?** *oo pweezh troo-vay*

| | |
|---|---|
| ■ detective stories | **des romans policiers** *day roh-mahn poh-leess-yay* |
| ■ history books | **des livres d'histoire** *day lee-vruh deess-twahr* |
| ■ short story books | **des contes** *day kohnt* |
| I'll take these books. | **Je vais prendre ces livres.** *zhuh veh prahn-druh say lee-vruh* |
| Will you wrap them, please? | **Voulez-vous bien les emballer?** *voo-lay voo byan lay zahn-bah-lay* |

## CLOTHING

| | |
|---|---|
| Would you please show me ____? | **Veuillez me montrer ____?** *vuh-yay muh mohn-tray* |
| ■ a belt | **une ceinture** *ewn san-tewr* |
| ■ a blouse | **un chemisier** *uhn shuh-mee-zyay* |
| ■ a bra | **un soutien-gorge** *uhn soo-tyan gohrzh* |
| ■ a dress | **une robe** *ewn rohb* |
| ■ an evening gown | **une robe du soir** *ewn rohb duh swahr* |
| ■ leather (suede) gloves | **des gants en cuir (en daim)** *day gahn ahn kweer (ahn dan)* |
| ■ handkerchiefs | **des mouchoirs** *day moo-shwahr* |
| ■ a hat | **un chapeau** *uhn shah-poh* |
| ■ a jacket | **un veston** *uhn vehss-tohn* |
| ■ an overcoat | **un manteau/pardessus** *uhn mahn-toh/pahr-duh-ssew* |
| ■ panties (women) | **un slip** *uhn sleep* |
| ■ pants | **un pantalon** *uhn pahn-tah-lohn* |
| ■ pantyhose | **des collants** *day koh-lahn* |

| ■ a raincoat | **un imperméable** *uhn nan-pehr-may-ah-bluh* |
| ■ a robe | **une robe de chambre** *ewn rohb duh shahn-bruh* |
| ■ a shirt | **une chemise** *ewn shuh-meez* |
| ■ (a pair of) shoes | **une paire de chaussures** *ewn pehr duh shoh-ssewr* |
| ■ shorts (briefs) | **des caleçons** *day kahl-ssohn* |
| ■ a skirt | **une jupe** *ewn zhewp* |
| ■ a slip | **un jupon** *uhn zhew-pohn* |
| ■ slippers | **des pantoufles** *day pahn-too-fluh* |
| ■ socks | **des chaussettes** *day shoh-sseht* |
| ■ (nylon) stockings | **des bas (nylon)** *day bah (nee-lohn)* |
| ■ a suit | **un complet/un tailleur** *uhn kohn-pleh/uhn tah-yuhr* |
| ■ a sweater | **un chandail** *uhn shahn-dahy* |
| ■ a tie | **une cravate** *ewn krah-vaht* |

| | |
|---|---|
| ■ an undershirt (T-shirt) | **un sous-vêtement** *uhn soo veht-mahn* |
| ■ a wallet | **un portefeuille** *uhn pohr-tuh-fuhy* |
| Is there a special sale today? | **Y a-t-il des soldes aujourd'hui?** *ee ah teel day sohld oh-zhoor-dwee* |
| I'd like the _____ with short (long) (no) sleeves. | **Je voudrais le/la _____ à manches courtes (longues) (sans manches).** *zhuh voo-dreh luh/lah _____ ah mahnsh koort (lohng) (sahn mahnsh)* |
| Do you have anything _____? | **Avez-vous quelque chose _____?** *ah-vay voo kehl-kuh shohz* |
| ■ cheaper | **de moins cher** *duh mwan shehr* |
| ■ else | **d'autre** *doh-truh* |
| ■ larger | **de plus grand** *duh plew grahn* |
| ■ more (less) expensive | **de plus (moins) cher** *duh plew (mwan) shehr* |
| ■ longer | **de plus long** *duh plew lohn* |
| ■ of better quality | **de meilleure qualité** *duh meh-yuhr kah-lee-tay* |
| ■ shorter | **de plus court** *duh plew koor* |
| ■ smaller | **de plus petit** *duh plew puh-tee* |
| I don't like the color. | **Je n'aime pas la couleur.** *zhuh nehm pah lah koo-luhr* |
| Do you have it in _____? | **L'avez-vous en _____?** *lah-vay voo zahn* |
| ■ black | **noir** *nwahr* |
| ■ blue | **bleu** *bluh* |
| ■ brown | **brun/marron** *bruhn/mah-rohn* |
| ■ gray | **gris** *gree* |
| ■ green | **vert** *vehr* |
| ■ pink | **rose** *rohze* |

| ■ red | **rouge** *roozh* |
| ■ white | **blanc** *blahn* |
| ■ yellow | **jaune** *zhohn* |
| I want something in \_\_\_\_. | **Je voudrais quelque chose en** \_\_\_\_. *zhuh voo-dreh kehl-kuh shohz ahn* |

## CHART OF MATERIALS

| ■ chiffon | **mousseline de soie** *mooss-leen duh swah* |
| ■ corduroy | **velours côtelé** *vuh-loor koht-lay* |
| ■ cotton | **coton** *koh-tohn* |
| ■ denim | **coutil** *koo-tee* |
| ■ felt | **feutre** *fuh-truh* |
| ■ flannel | **flanelle** *flah-nehl* |
| ■ gabardine | **gabardine** *gah-bahr-deen* |
| ■ lace | **dentelle** *dahn-tehl* |
| ■ leather | **cuir** *kweer* |
| ■ linen | **lin** *lan* |
| ■ nylon | **nylon** *nee-lohn* |
| ■ permanent press | **infroissable** *an-frwah-ssah-bluh* |
| ■ polyester | **polyester** *poh-lee-ehss-tehr* |
| ■ satin | **satin** *sah-tan* |
| ■ silk | **soie** *swah* |
| ■ suede | **daim** *dan* |
| ■ terrycloth | **tissu-éponge** *tee-ssew-ay-pohnzh* |
| ■ velvet | **velours** *vuh-loor* |
| ■ wash and wear | **ne pas repasser** *nuh pah ruh-pah-ssay* |
| ■ wool | **laine** *lehn* |

| Show me something ___. | **Montrez-moi quelque chose ___.** *mohn-tray mwah kehl-kuh shohz* |
|---|---|
| ■ in a solid color | **uni** *ew-nee* |
| ■ with stripes | **à rayures** *ah rah-yewr* |
| ■ with polka dots | **à pois** *ah pwah* |
| ■ in plaid | **en tartan** *ahn tahr-tahn* |
| ■ in herringbone | **à chevrons** *ah shuh-vrohn* |
| ■ checked | **à carreaux** *ah kah-roh* |
| It doesn't fit me. | **Cela ne me va pas.** *suh-lah nuh muh vah pah* |
| It fits very well. | **Ça va à la perfection.** *sah vah ah lah pehr-fehk-ssyohn* |
| I'll take it. | **Je le/la prends.** *zhuh luh/lah prahn* |
| Will you wrap it? | **Voulez-vous l'emballer, s'il vous plaît?** *voo-lay voo lahn-bah-lay, seel voo pleh* |
| I'd like to see a pair of shoes (boots). | **Je voudrais voir une paire de chaussures (bottes).** *zhuh voo-dreh vwahr ewn pehr duh shoh-ssewr (boht)* |
| Show me the pair in the window. | **Montrez-moi la paire en vitrine.** *mohn-tray mwah lah pehr ahn vee-treen* |
| I take size ___. | **Je chausse du ___.** *zhuh shohss dew* |
| These shoes are too narrow (wide). | **Ces chaussures sont trop étroites (larges).** *say shoh-ssewr sohn troh pay-trwaht (lahrzh)* |
| They pinch me. | **Elles me serrent.** *ehl muh sehr* |
| They fit fine. | **Elles me vont très bien.** *ehl muh vohn treh byan* |
| I'll take them. | **Je vais les prendre.** *zhuh veh lay prahn-druh* |

# CONVERSION TABLES FOR CLOTHING SIZES

## WOMEN

### SHOES

| American | 4 | $4\frac{1}{2}$ | 5 | $5\frac{1}{2}$ | 6 | $6\frac{1}{2}$ | 7 | $7\frac{1}{2}$ | 8 | $8\frac{1}{2}$ | 9 | $9\frac{1}{2}$ | 10 |
|---|---|---|---|---|---|---|---|---|---|---|---|---|---|
| Continental | 35 | 35 | 36 | 36 | 37 | 37 | 38 | 38 | 39 | 39 | 40 | 40 | 41 |

### DRESSES, SUITS

| American | 8 | 10 | 12 | 14 | 16 | 18 |
|---|---|---|---|---|---|---|
| Continental | 36 | 38 | 40 | 42 | 44 | 46 |

### BLOUSES, SWEATERS

| American | 32 | 34 | 36 | 38 | 40 | 42 |
|---|---|---|---|---|---|---|
| Continental | 40 | 42 | 44 | 46 | 48 | 50 |

## MEN

### SHOES

| American | 7 | $7\frac{1}{2}$ | 8 | $8\frac{1}{2}$ | 9 | $9\frac{1}{2}$ | 10 | $10\frac{1}{2}$ | 11 | $11\frac{1}{2}$ |
|---|---|---|---|---|---|---|---|---|---|---|
| Continental | 39 | 40 | 41 | 42 | 43 | 43 | 44 | 44 | 45 | 45 |

### SUITS, COATS

| American | 34 | 36 | 38 | 40 | 42 | 44 | 46 | 48 |
|---|---|---|---|---|---|---|---|---|
| Continental | 44 | 46 | 48 | 50 | 52 | 54 | 56 | 58 |

### SHIRTS

| American | 14 | $14\frac{1}{2}$ | 15 | $15\frac{1}{2}$ | 16 | $16\frac{1}{2}$ | 17 | $17\frac{1}{2}$ |
|---|---|---|---|---|---|---|---|---|
| Continental | 36 | 37 | 38 | 39 | 40 | 41 | 42 | 43 |

| | |
|---|---|
| I also need shoe-laces. | **Il me faut aussi des lacets.** *eel muh foh toh-ssee day lah-sseh* |
| That's all I want for now. | **C'est tout pour le moment.** *seh too poor luh moh-mahn* |
| Please take my measurements. | **Veuillez prendre mes mesures.** *vuh-yay prahn-druh may muh-zewr* |
| I take size (My size is) ____. | **Je porte du (Ma taille est) ____.** *zhuh pohrt dew (mah tahy eh)* |
| ■ small | **petit (petite)** *puh-tee (puh-teet)* |
| ■ medium | **moyen (moyenne)** *mwah-yan (mwah-yehn)* |
| ■ large | **grand (grande)** *grahn (grahnd)* |
| Can I try it on? | **Puis-je l'essayer?** *pweezh leh-sseh-yay* |
| Can you alter it? | **Pouvez-vous le/la retoucher?** *poo-vay voo luh/lah ruh-too-shay* |
| Can you let it out? | **Pouvez-vous l'élargir?** *poo-vay voo lay-lahr-zheer* |
| Can I return the article? | **Puis-je rendre cet article?** *pweezh rahn-druh seht ahr-tee-kluh* |
| Do you have something hand-made? | **Avez-vous quelque chose fait à la main?** *ah-vay voo kehl-kuh shohz feh-tah-lah-man* |
| The zipper doesn't work. | **La fermeture-éclair ne marche pas.** *lah fehr muh-tewr ay-klehr nuh mahrsh pah* |

## ELECTRICAL APPLIANCES

When buying electrical items, check the voltage, which may not correspond to what you have at home. Or look for appliances with dual voltage.

| I want to buy ___. | **Je voudrais acheter ___.** *zhuh voo-dreh zahsh-tay* |
|---|---|
| ■ a battery | **une pile** *ewn peel* |
| ■ a blender | **un mixer** *uhn meek-sehr* |
| ■ an electric shaver | **un rasoir électrique** *uhn rah-zwahr ay-lehk-treek* |
| ■ a hair dryer | **un sèche-cheveux** *uhn sehsh shuh-vuh* |
| ■ a plug | **une fiche** *ewn feesh* |
| ■ a (portable) radio | **une radio (portative)** *ewn rah-dyoh pohr-tah-teev* |
| ■ an (automatic) record player | **un tourne-disques (automatique)** *uhn toorn deessk oh-toh-mah-teek* |
| ■ a cassette player/recorder | **un magnétophone à cassettes** *uhn mah-nyay-toh-fohn ah kah-sseht* |
| ■ a (color) television set | **une télévision (en couleurs)** *ewn tay-lay-vee-zyohn (ahn koo-luhr)* |
| ■ a toaster | **un grille-pain** *uhn gree pan* |
| It's out of order (broken). | **Il/elle ne marche pas. Il/elle est cassé(e).** *eel/ehl nuh mahrsh pah eel/ehl eh kah-ssay* |

## FOOD AND HOUSEHOLD ITEMS

Don't forget to bring your basket when you go to the food market. Large paper bags are not given out. The cashier does not load the basket for you; you must do that yourself. The French are more inclined to shop in specialty stores than we are, so you may want to follow their lead, buying bread in the **boulangerie,** pastries in a **patisserie** or candy in a **confiserie.**

| I'd like ___. | **Je voudrais ___.** *zhuh voo-dreh* |
|---|---|
| ■ a bar of soap | **une savonnette** *zewn sah-voh-neht* |

| | |
|---|---|
| ■ a bottle of juice | **une bouteille de jus** *zewn boo-tehy duh zhew* |
| ■ a box of cereal | **une boîte de céréale** *zewn bwaht duh say-ray-ahl* |
| ■ a can of tomato sauce | **une boîte de sauce-tomate** *zewn bwaht duh sohss toh-maht* |
| ■ a dozen eggs | **une douzaine d'oeufs** *zewn doo-zehn duh* |
| ■ a jar of coffee | **un bocal de café** *zuhn boh-kal duh kah-fay* |
| ■ a kilo (2.2 lbs.) of potatoes | **un kilo de pommes de terre** *zuhn kee-loh duh pohm duh tehr* |
| ■ a half-kilo (1.1 lbs.) of cherries | **un demi-kilo de cerises** *zuhn duh-mee kee-loh duh suh-reez* |
| ■ a liter (quart) of milk | **un litre de lait** *zuhn lee-truh duh leh* |
| ■ a package of candies | **un paquet de bonbons** *zuhn pah-keh duh bohn-bohn* |
| ■ a $\frac{1}{4}$ pound of cheese | **cent grammes de fromage** *sahn grahm duh froh-mahzh* |
| ■ a quart of milk | **un litre de lait** *uhn lee-truh duh leh* |
| ■ a roll of toilet paper | **un rouleau de papier hygiénique** *uhn roo-loh duh pah-pyay ee-zhyay-neek* |
| Can you give me 2 liters (half a gallon) of milk? | **Pouvez-vous me donner deux litres de lait?** *poo-vay voo muh doh-nay duh lee-truh duh leh* |
| I'd like a half liter of beer. | **Je voudrais un demi-litre de bière.** *zhuh voo-dreh zuhn duh-mee lee-truh duh byehr* |
| I'd like ____. | **Je voudrais ____.** *zhuh voo-dreh* |

■a kilo of oranges     **un kilo d'oranges** *zuhn kee-loh doh-rahnzh*

## METRIC WEIGHTS AND MEASURES

### Solid Measures
(approximate measurements only)

| OUNCES | GRAMS (GRAMMES) | GRAMS | OUNCES |
|---|---|---|---|
| $\frac{1}{4}$ | 7 | 10 | $\frac{1}{3}$ |
| $\frac{1}{2}$ | 14 | 100 | $3\frac{1}{2}$ |
| $\frac{3}{4}$ | 21 | 300 | $10\frac{1}{2}$ |
| 1 | 28 | 500 | 18 |
| POUNDS | KILOGRAMS (KILO) | KILOGRAMS | POUNDS |
| 1 | $\frac{1}{2}$ | 1 | $2\frac{1}{4}$ |
| 5 | $2\frac{1}{4}$ | 3 | $6\frac{1}{2}$ |
| 10 | $4\frac{1}{2}$ | 5 | 11 |
| 20 | 9 | 10 | 22 |
| 50 | 23 | 50 | 110 |
| 100 | 45 | 100 | 220 |

### Liquid Measures
(approximate measurements only)

| OUNCES | MILLILITERS (MILLILITRES) | MILLILITERS | OUNCES |
|---|---|---|---|
| 1 | 30 | 10 | $\frac{1}{3}$ |
| 6 | 175 | 50 | $1\frac{1}{2}$ |
| 12 | 350 | 100 | $3\frac{1}{2}$ |
| 16 | 475 | 150 | 5 |
| GALLONS | LITERS (LITRES) | LITERS | GALLONS |
| 1 | $3\frac{3}{4}$ | 1 | $\frac{1}{4}$ (1 quart) |
| 5 | 19 | 5 | $1\frac{1}{3}$ |
| 10 | 38 | 10 | $2\frac{1}{2}$ |

Note: Common measurements for purchasing food are a kilo or fractions thereof, 100 (cent), 200 (deux cent), and 500 (cinq cent) grams (grammes). See also NUMBERS, p. 13–17.

| a half kilo of butter | **un demi-kilo de beurre**  *zuhn duh-mee kee-loh duh buhr* |
|---|---|
| ■ 200 grams (about ½ pound) of cookies | **deux cents grammes de biscuits**  *duh sahn grahm duh beess-kwee* |
| ■ a hundred grams of bologna. | **cent grammes de mortadelle**  *sahn grahm duh mohr-tah-dehl* |
| What is this (that)? | **Qu'est-ce que c'est?**  *kehss kuh seh* |
| Is it fresh? | **Est-ce frais?**  *ehss freh* |

## THE CHARCUTERIE

A **charcuterie** is a rather special type of French delicatessen where you may buy food to take out, including various sausages and smoked meats. You will often see ordinary butcher's meat being sold in the same case as the sausage. Besides smoked meats you can find simple items like salads or paté. The **Rue de bucherie** in Paris is a street entirely filled with **charcuteries,** where you may go from one to another, selecting the items that appeal to you, for your lunch or for a picnic.

## JEWELER

| I'd like to see ____. | **Je voudrais voir ____.**  *zhuh voo-dreh vwahr* |
|---|---|
| ■ a bracelet | **un bracelet**  *uhn brahss-leh* |
| ■ a brooch | **une broche**  *ewn brohsh* |
| ■ a chain | **une chaînette**  *ewn sheh-neht* |
| ■ a charm | **un porte-bonheur**  *uhn pohrt boh-nuhr* |
| ■ some earrings | **des boucles d'oreille**  *day boo-kluh doh-rehy* |
| ■ a necklace | **un collier**  *uhn koh-lyay* |
| ■ a pin | **une épingle**  *ewn ay-pan-gluh* |

| | |
|---|---|
| ■a ring | **une bague**  *ewn bahg* |
| an engagement ring | **une bague de fiançailles**  *ewn bahg duh fee-ahn-ssahy* |
| a wedding ring | **une alliance**  *ewn ah-lee-ahnss* |
| ■a watch | **une montre**  *ewn mohn-truh* |
| ■a wristwatch (digital) | **une montre-bracelet (digitale)**  *ewn mohn-truh brahss-leh (dee-zhee-tahl)* |
| Is this _____? | **Est-ce _____?**  *ehss* |
| ■gold | **en or**  *ahn nohr* |
| ■platinum | **en platine**  *ahn plah-teen* |
| ■silver | **en argent**  *ahn nahr-zhahn* |
| ■stainless steel | **en acier inoxydable**  *ahn nah-ssyay ee-nohk-ssee-dah-bluh* |
| Is it solid gold or gold-plated? | **C'est en or massif ou en plaqué or?**  *seh-tahn-nohr mah-sseef oo ahn plah-kay ohr* |
| How many carats is it? | **Combien de carats y a-t-il?**  *kohn-byan duh kah-rah ee ah teel* |
| What is that stone? | **Quelle est cette pierre?**  *kehl eh seht pyehr* |
| I would like _____. | **Je voudrais _____.**  *zhuh voo-dreh* |
| ■an amethyst | **une améthyste**  *zewn ah-may-teesst* |
| ■an aquamarine | **une aigue-marine**  *zewn ehg mah-reen* |
| ■a diamond | **un diamant**  *zuhn dee-ah-mahn* |
| ■an emerald | **une émeraude**  *zewn aym-rohd* |
| ■ivory | **un ivoire**  *zuhn nee-vwahr* |
| ■jade | **un jade**  *zuhn zhahd* |
| ■onyx | **un onyx**  *zuhn oh-neeks* |
| ■pearls | **des perles**  *day pehrl* |

| a ruby | **un rubis** *uhn rew-bee* |
| a sapphire | **un saphir** *uhn sah-feer* |
| a topaz | **une topaze** *ewn toh-pahz* |
| turquoise | **une turquoise** *ewn tewr-kwahz* |
| I love this ring! | **J'adore cette bague.** *zhah-dohr seht bahg* |
| How much is it? | **Cela coûte combien?** *suh-lah koot kohn-byan* |

## MUSIC, RECORDS AND TAPES

| Is there a record shop around here? | **Y a-t-il un magasin de disques par ici?** *ee ah teel uhn mah-gah-zen duh deessk pahr ee-ssee* |
| Do you sell _____? | **Vendez-vous _____?** *vahn-day voo* |
| cartridges | **des cartouches** *day kahr-toosh* |
| cassettes | **des cassettes** *day kah-sseht* |
| needles | **des diamants** *day dee-ah-mahn* |
| records | **des disques** *day deessk* |
| tapes | **des bandes** *day bahnd* |
| Do you have an album of _____? | **Avez-vous un disque de _____?** *ah-vay voo uhn deessk duh* |
| 33 R.P.M. | **trente-trois tours** *trahn trwah toor* |
| 45 R.P.M. | **quarante-cinq tours** *kah-rahnt sank toor* |
| Where is the _____ section? | **Où est le rayon de/des _____?** *oo eh luh reh-yohn duh/day* |
| American music | **la musique américaine** *lah mew-zeek ah-may-ree-kehn* |
| classical music | **la musique classique** *lah mew-zeek klah-sseek* |

| | |
|---|---|
| ■ folk music | **la musique folklorique** *lah mew-zeek fohl-kloh-reek* |
| ■ latest hits | **derniers succès** *dehr-nyay sewk-sseh* |
| ■ French music | **la musique française** *lah mew-zeek frah<u>n</u>-ssehz* |
| ■ opera | **l'opéra** *loh-pay-rah* |
| ■ pop music | **la musique pop** *lah mew-zeek pohp* |

## NEWSSTAND

| | |
|---|---|
| Do you carry newspapers (magazines) in English? | **Avez-vous des journaux (magazines) en anglais?** *ah-vay voo day zhoor-noh (mah-gah-zeen) ah<u>n</u> nah<u>n</u>-gleh* |
| I'd like to buy some (picture) postcards. | **Je voudrais acheter des cartes postales (illustrées).** *zhuh voo-dreh zahsh-tay day kahrt pohss-tahl (ee-lewss-tray)* |
| Do you have stamps? | **Avez-vous des timbres?** *ah-vay voo day ta<u>n</u>-bruh* |
| How much is it? | **C'est combien?** *seh koh<u>n</u>-bya<u>n</u>* |
| I'd like _____. | **Je voudrais _____.** *zhuh voo-dreh* |
| ■ a daily | **un quotidien** *zuh<u>n</u> koh-tee-dya<u>n</u>* |
| ■ a weekly | **un hebdomadaire** *zuh<u>n</u> ehb-doh-mah-dehr* |
| ■ a monthly | **un mensuel** *zuh<u>n</u> mah<u>n</u>-ssew-ehl* |

## PHOTOGRAPHIC SUPPLIES

| | |
|---|---|
| Where is there a camera shop? | **Où y a-t-il le magasin de photos?** *oo ee-ah-teel luh mah-gah-za<u>n</u> duh foh-toh* |

| | |
|---|---|
| Do you develop film here? | **Développez-vous les films ici?** *Day-vloh-pay voo lay feelm ee-ssee* |
| How much does it cost to develop a roll? | **Combien coûte le développement d'une pellicule?** *kohn-byan koot luh day-vlohp-mahn dewn peh-lee-kewl* |
| I have two rolls. | **J'ai deux pellicules.** *zhay duh peh-lee-kewl* |
| I want _____. | **Je voudrais _____.** *zhuh voo-dreh* |
| ■ a print of each | **une épreuve de chacune** *zewn ay-pruhv duh shah-kewn* |
| ■ an enlargement | **un agrandissement** *zuhn nah-grahn-deess-mahn* |
| with a glossy finish | **sur papier brillant** *sewr pah-pyay bree-yahn* |
| with a matte finish | **sur papier mat** *sewr pah-pyay maht* |
| I want a roll of 20 (36) exposures of color (black and white) film. | **Je voudrais une pellicule de vingt (trente-six) en couleur (noir et blanc).** *zhuh voo-dreh zewn peh-lee-kewl duh van (trahn-seess) ahn koo-luhr (nwahr ay blahn)* |
| ■ for slides | **pour diapositives** *poor dee-ah-poh-zee-teev* |
| ■ a film pack, number . . . | **une cartouche, numéro . . .** *ewn kahr-toosh, new-may-roh* |
| When can I pick up the pictures? | **Quand puis-je venir chercher les photos?** *kahn pweezh vuh-neer shehr-shay lay foh-toh* |
| Do you sell cameras? | **Vendez-vous des appareils?** *vahn-day voo day zah-pah-rehy* |
| I want an expensive (inexpensive) camera. | **Je cherche un appareil cher (pas très cher).** *zhuh shehrsh uhn nah-pah-rehy shehr (pah treh shehr)* |

## SOUVENIRS

You may want to purchase specialties of certain cities or regions as gifts or as souvenirs.

### FRANCE

| | |
|---|---|
| **Alençon** | lace products |
| **Aubusson, Beauvais** | rugs |
| **Baccarat** | crystal |
| **Besançon** | watches and clocks |
| **Grasse** | perfume (Coty, Fragonard, Lanvin) |
| **Grenoble** | gloves |
| **Limoges, Sèvres** | fine porcelain |
| **Nancy** | crystal |
| **Paris** | haute couture, high style fashions at stores like Rive Gauche, Galeries Lafayette, Au Printemps, La Samaritaine |

If you are in Paris, you may be able to pick up real bargains at the Flea Market (Marché aux Puces) and, at the small book shops along the Seine, old books, magazines, or comic strips.

Don't forget the famous wines and cheeses, of course!

### BELGIUM

| | |
|---|---|
| **Ghent and Kortrijk** | linen |
| **Brussels, Brugge** | lace |
| **Antwerp** | diamonds and jewelry |
| **Val-Saint-Lambert** | crystal and glassware |
| **Dinant and Brugge** | copperware |

Everywhere in the country you can find the renowned Belgian beers, candy, and chocolate.

## SWITZERLAND

There are "Swiss-craft" shops throughout the country where you will find a large selection of handmade products from all parts of Switzerland. Typical items include: linen, embroideries, fine handkerchiefs, textiles, wood carvings, ceramics, music boxes, and multi-blade knives. Switzerland is also known for its watches, cuckoo clocks, fondue forks and pots, and, of course, the chocolates and cheese available in all sizes and shapes.

Don't forget the high quality of Swiss-printed books.

## GIFT SHOP

| | | |
|---|---|---|
| I'd like ____. | **Je voudrais ____.** | *zhuh voo-dreh* |
| ■ a pretty gift | **un joli cadeau** | *zuhn zhoh-lee kah-doh* |
| ■ a small gift | **un petit cadeau** | *zuhn puh-tee kah-doh* |
| ■ a souvenir | **un souvenir** | *zuhn soov-neer* |
| It's for . . . | **C'est pour . . .** | *seh poor* |
| Could you suggest something? | **Pourriez-vous me suggérer quelque chose?** | *poo-ree-yay voo muh sewg-zhay-ray kehl-kuh shohz* |
| Would you show me your selection of ____. | **Voudriez-vous me montrer votre choix de ____.** | *voo-dree-yay voo muh mohn-tray voh-truh shwah duh* |
| ■ blown glass | **verre soufflé** | *vehr soo-flay* |
| ■ carved objects | **objets sculptés** | *ohb-zheh skewl-tay* |
| ■ cut crystal | **cristal taillé** | *kreess-tahl tah-yay* |
| ■ dolls | **poupées** | *poo-pay* |
| ■ earthenware (pottery) | **poterie** | *poh-tree* |
| ■ fans | **éventails** | *ay-vahn-tahy* |
| ■ jewelry | **bijouterie** | *bee-zhoo-tree* |

| | | |
|---|---|---|
| ■ lace | **dentelles** *dahn-tehl* | |
| ■ leather goods | **objets en cuir** *ohb-zheh ahn kweer* | |
| ■ liqueurs | **liqueurs** *lee-kuhr* | |
| ■ musical instruments | **instruments de musique** *an-strew-mahn duh mew-zeek* | |
| ■ perfumes | **parfums** *pahr-fuhn* | |
| ■ pictures | **tableaux** *tah-bloh* | |
| ■ posters | **affiches** *ah-feesh* | |
| ■ religious articles | **articles religieux** *ahr-tee-kluh ruh-lee-zhuh* | |

I don't want to spend more than _____ francs.  **Je ne voudrais pas dépenser plus de _____ francs.** *zhuh nuh voo-dreh pah day-pahn-ssay plew duh _____ frahn*

## ANTIQUE SHOPPING

French-speaking Europe boasts a large number of antique shops where you can find old books, watches, toys, antiquities, etc.

Haggle as much as you can!

### PRINCIPAL SHOPPING AREAS FOR ANTIQUES

#### FRANCE

#### Paris

| | |
|---|---|
| Rue du Bac and Rue des Saints Pères | 7ème arrondissement |
| Marché aux Puces | 18ème arrondissement |
| Quai Voltaire | 7ème arrondissement |
| Rue Jacob and Rue Bonaparte | 6ème arrondissement |

## BELGIUM

| | |
|---|---|
| **Brussels** | le Sablon (there is also an open-air market here on Saturday and on Sunday morning) |
| **Antwerp** | Near the House of Rubens |

| | |
|---|---|
| What's the price of this old book? | **Quel est le prix de ce vieux livre?** *Kehl eh luh pree duh suh vyuh lee-vruh* |
| From what century is this item? | **De quel siècle date cet objet** *Duh kehl see-yeh-kluh daht seht ohb-zheh* |
| Where does this Roman plate come from? | **Quelle est l'origine de cette assiette romaine?** *Kehl eh loh-ree-zheen duh seht ah-ssyeht roh-mehn* |
| Does that clock work with a key? | **Cette horloge se remonte-t-elle avec une clé?** *Seht ohr-lohzh suh ruh-mohn-tehl ah-vehk ewn klay* |
| For what price will you give me the statue? | **A quel prix me laissez-vous la statue?** *Ah kehl pree muh leh-ssay voo lah stah-tew* |

## STATIONERY

| | |
|---|---|
| I want to buy ____. | **Je voudrais acheter ____.** *zhuh voo-dreh zahsh-tay* |
| ■ a ball-point pen | **un stylo à bille** *uhn stee-loh ah bee* |
| ■ a deck of cards | **un paquet de cartes** *uhn pah-keh duh kahrt* |
| ■ envelopes | **des enveloppes** *day zahn-vlohp* |
| ■ an eraser | **une gomme** *ewn gohm* |
| ■ glue | **de la colle** *duh lah kohl* |
| ■ a notebook | **un cahier** *uhn kah-yay* |
| ■ pencils | **des crayons** *day kreh-yohn* |

| | |
|---|---|
| ■ a pencil sharpener | **un taille-crayon** *uhn tahy kreh-yohn* |
| ■ a ruler | **une règle** *ewn reh-gluh* |
| ■ Scotch tape | **une bande adhésive (un scotch)** *ewn bahnd ahd-ay-zeev (uhn skohtsh)* |
| ■ some string | **de la ficelle** *duh lah fee-ssehl* |
| ■ typing paper | **du papier pour machine à écrire** *dew pah-pyay poor mah-sheen ah ay-kreer* |
| ■ wrapping paper | **du papier d'emballage** *dew pah-pyay dahn-bah-lahzh* |
| ■ a writing pad | **un bloc** *uhn blohk* |
| ■ writing paper | **du papier à lettres** *dew pah-pyay ah leh-truh* |

## TOBACCO SHOP

Tobacco, cigarettes and cigars may be purchased from a state-licensed tobacconist. Look for the sign with the red cones outside cafés and bars.

Newly promulgated laws have outlawed smoking in many public places and fines are imposed. Be careful to heed the no smoking signs: DÉFENSE DE FUMER.

| | |
|---|---|
| A pack (carton) of cigarettes, please. | **Un paquet (une cartouche) de cigarettes, s'il vous plaît.** *uhn pah-keh (ewn kahr-toosh) duh see-gah-reht, seel voo pleh* |
| ■ filtered | **avec filtre** *ah-vehk feel-truh* |
| ■ unfiltered | **sans filtre** *sahn feel-truh* |
| ■ menthol | **mentholées** *mahn-toh-lay* |
| ■ king-size | **long format** *lohn fohr-mah* |

| | |
|---|---|
| Are these cigarettes (very) strong (mild)? | **Ces cigarettes sont elles (très) fortes (douces)?** *say see-gah-reht sohn-tehl (treh) fohrt (dooss)* |
| Do you have American cigarettes? | **Avez-vous des cigarettes américaines?** *ah-vay voo day see-gah-reht ah-may-ree-kehn* |
| What brands? | **Quelles marques?** *kehl mahrk* |
| Please give me a pack of matches also. | **Donnez-moi aussi une boîte d'allumettes, s'il vous plaît.** *doh-nay mwah oh-ssee ewn bwaht dah-lew-meht, seel voo pleh* |
| Do you sell ____? | **Vendez-vous ____?** *vahn-day voo* |
| ■ chewing tobacco | **du tabac à chiquer** *dew tah-bah ah shee-kay* |
| ■ a cigarette holder | **un fume-cigarettes** *uhn fewm see-gah-reht* |
| ■ cigars | **des cigares** *day see-gahr* |
| ■ flints | **des pierres à briquet** *day pyehr ah bree-keh* |
| ■ lighter fluid | **de l'essence à briquet** *duh leh-ssahnss ah bree-keh* |
| ■ lighters | **des briquets** *day bree-keh* |
| ■ pipes | **des pipes** *day peep* |
| ■ pipe tobacco | **du tabac pour pipe** *dew tah-bah poor peep* |

## TOILETRIES

The new *drugstores* in France resemble small department stores. They sell newspapers, international magazines, books, maps, guides, small gifts, records and have fast-food restaurants for items such as ice cream, sandwiches or drinks. Many of these drugstores even have a counter where prescriptions may be filled. Perfumes and cosmetics may also be purchased at a *parfumerie*.

Do you have _____? **Avez-vous** _____? *ah-vay voo*

- bobby pins **des épingles à cheveux** *day zay-pan-gluh ah shuh-vuh*

- a brush **une brosse** *ewn brohss*

- cleansing cream **une crème démaquillante** *ewn krehm day-mah-kee-yahnt*

- a comb **un peigne** *uhn peh-nyuh*

- a deodorant **du déodorant** *dew day-oh-doh-rahn*

- (disposable) diapers **des couches disponibles** *day koosh deess-poh-nee-bluh*

- emery boards **des limes à ongles** *day leem ah ohn-gluh*

- eye liner **du traceur à paupières** *dew trah-ssuhr ah poh-pyehr*

- eyebrow pencil **le crayon pour les yeux** *luh kreh-yohn poor lay zyuh*

- eye shadow **du fard à paupières** *dew fahr ah poh-pyehr*

- hair spray **la laque** *lah lahk*

- lipstick **le rouge à lèvres** *luh roozh ah leh-vruh*

- makeup **le maquillage** *luh mah-kee-yahzh*

- mascara **le cosmétique pour les cils** *luh kohz-may-teek poor lay seel*

- a mirror **un miroir** *uhn meer-wahr*

- mouth wash **le dentifrice** *luh dahn-tee-freess*

- nail clippers **un coupe-ongles** *uhn koop ohn-gluh*

- a nail file **une lime à ongles** *ewn leem ah ohn-gluh*

| | |
|---|---|
| ■ nail polish | **du vernis à ongles** *dew vehr-nee ah ohn-gluh* |
| ■ nail polish remover | **du dissolvant** *dew dee-ssohl-vahn* |
| ■ a prophylactic | **un prophylactique** *uhn proh-fee-lahk-teek* |
| ■ a razor | **un rasoir** *uhn rah-zwahr* |
| ■ razor blades | **une lame de rasoir** *ewn lahm duh rah-zwahr* |
| ■ rouge | **du fard** *dew fahr* |
| ■ sanitary napkins | **des serviettes hygiéniques** *day sehr-vyeht ee-zhyay-neek* |
| ■ (cuticle) scissors | **des ciseaux** *day see-zoh* |
| ■ shampoo | **le shampooing** *luh shahn-pwan* |
| ■ shaving lotion | **la lotion à raser** *lah loh-ssyohn ah rah-zay* |
| ■ soap | **du savon** *dew sah-vohn* |
| ■ a sponge | **une éponge** *ewn ay-pohnzh* |
| ■ talcum powder | **le talc** *luh tahlk* |
| ■ tampons | **des tampons périodiques** *day tahn-pohn pay-ree-oh-deek* |
| ■ tissues | **des mouchoirs en papier** *day moo-shwahr ahn pah-pyay* |
| ■ toilet paper | **du papier hygiénique** *dew pah-pyay ee-zhyay-neek* |
| ■ a toothbrush | **une brosse à dents** *ewn brohss ah dahn* |
| ■ toothpaste | **de la pâte dentifrice** *duh lah paht dahn-tee-freess* |
| ■ tweezers | **une pince à épiler** *ewn panss ah ay-pee-lay* |

# PERSONAL CARE AND SERVICES

If your hotel doesn't offer these amenities, ask the desk clerk to recommend someone nearby.

## AT THE BARBER

| | |
|---|---|
| Where is there a good barber shop? | **Où y a-t-il un bon coiffeur?** *oo eeah-teel uhn bohn kwah-fuhr* |
| Do I have to wait long? | **Faut-il attendre longtemps?** *foh teel ah-tahn-druh lohn-tahn* |
| Whose turn is it? | **C'est à qui le tour?** *seh tah kee luh toor* |
| I want a shave. | **Je voudrais me faire raser.** *zhuh voo-dreh muh fehr rah-zay* |
| I want a haircut. | **Je voudrais une coupe de cheveux.** *zhuh voo-dreh zewn koop duh shuh-vuh* |
| Short in back, long in front. | **Plus courts sur la nuque, plus longs sur le dessus.** *plew koor sewr lah newk plew lohn sewr luh duh-ssew* |
| Leave it long. | **Laissez-les longs.** *leh-ssay lay lohn* |
| I want it (very) short. | **Je les veux (très) courts.** *zhuh lay vuh treh koor* |
| You can cut a little ____. | **Vous pouvez dégager un peu ____.** *voo poo-vay day-gah-zhay uhn puh* |
| ■ in back | **derrière** *deh-ryehr* |
| ■ in front | **devant** *duh-vahn* |
| ■ off the top | **dessus** *duh-ssew* |
| ■ on the sides | **les côtés** *lay koh-tay* |

| I part my hair _____. | **Je fais la raie** _____. *zhuh feh lah ray* |
| ■ on the left | **à gauche** *ah gohsh* |
| ■ on the right | **à droite** *ah drwaht* |
| ■ in the middle | **au milieu** *oh meel-yuh* |
| I comb my hair straight back. | **Je me peigne en arrière.** *zhuh muh peh-nyuh ahn nah-ryehr* |
| Cut a little bit more here. | **Coupez un peu plus ici.** *koo-pay uhn puh plew ee-ssee* |
| That's enough. | **Ça suffit.** *sah sew-fee* |
| It's fine that way. | **C'est parfait comme ça.** *seh pahr-feh kohm sah* |
| I (don't) want _____. | **Je (ne) veux (pas de)** _____. *zhuh (nuh) vuh (pah duh)* |
| ■ shampoo | **un shampooing** *uhn shan-pwan* |
| ■ tonic | **une lotion** *ewn loh-ssyohn* |
| Use the scissors only. | **Employez seulement les ciseaux.** *ahn-plwah-yay suhl-mahn lay see-zoh* |
| I would like a razor cut. | **Je voudrais une coupe au rasoir.** *zhuh voo-dreh zewn koop oh rah-zwahr* |
| You can use the machine. | **Vous pouvez employer la machine.** *voo poo-vay zahn-plwah-yay lah mah-sheen* |
| Please trim my _____. | **Rafraîchissez moi** _____. *rah-freh-sshee-ssay mwah* |
| ■ beard | **la barbe** *lah bahrb* |
| ■ moustache | **la moustache** *lah mooss-tahsh* |
| ■ sideburns | **les favoris** *lay fah-voh-ree* |
| Where's the mirror? | **Où est le miroir?** *oo eh luh meer-wahr* |

| | |
|---|---|
| I'd like to look at myself in the mirror. | **Je voudrais me regarder dans le miroir.** *zhuh voo-dreh muh ruh-gahr-day dahn luh meer-wahr* |
| How much do I owe you? | **Combien vous dois-je?** *kohn-byan voo dwahzh* |

## AT THE BEAUTY PARLOR

| | |
|---|---|
| Is there a beauty parlor (hairdresser) near the hotel? | **Y a-t-il un salon de beauté près de l'hôtel?** *ee ah teel uhn sah-lohn duh boh-tay preh duh loh-tehl* |
| I'd like to make an appointment for this afternoon (tomorrow). | **Je voudrais prendre rendez-vous pour cet après-midi (demain).** *zhuh voo-dreh prahn-druh rahn-day voo poor seht ah-preh mee-dee (duh-man)* |
| Can you give me _____? | **Pouvez-vous me donner _____?** *poo-vay voo muh doh-nay* |
| ■ a color rinse | **un shampooing colorant** *uhn shahn-pwan koh-loh-rahn* |
| ■ a facial massage | **un massage facial** *uhn mah-ssahzh fah-ssyahl* |
| ■ a haircut | **une coupe de cheveux** *ewn koop duh shuh-vuh* |
| ■ a manicure | **une manucure** *ewn mah-new-kewr* |
| ■ a permanent | **une permanente** *ewn pehr-mah-nahnt* |
| ■ a shampoo | **un shampooing** *uhn shahn-pwan* |
| ■ a tint | **des reflets** *day ruh-fleh* |
| ■ a touch up | **une retouche** *ewn ruh-toosh* |
| ■ a wash and set | **un shampooing et une mise en plis** *uhn shahn-pwan ay ewn meez ahn plee* |

| I'd like to see a color chart. | **Je voudrais voir une échelle de teintes.** *zhuh voo-dreh vwahr ewn ay-shehl duh tant* |
| I want ____. | **Je voudrais ____.** *zhuh voo-dreh* |
| ■ auburn | **auburn** *oh-buhrn* |
| ■ (light) blond | **blond (clair)** *blohn (klehr)* |
| ■ brunette | **brun** *bruhn* |
| ■ a darker color | **une teinte plus foncée** *ewn tant plew fohn-ssay* |
| ■ a lighter color | **une teinte plus claire** *ewn tant plew klehr* |
| ■ the same color | **la même couleur** *lah mehm koo-luhr* |
| Don't apply any hair-spray. | **Ne mettez pas de laque, s'il vous plaît.** *nuh meh-tay pah duh lahk seel voo pleh* |
| Not too much hair-spray. | **Pas trop de laque.** *pah troh duh lahk* |

# LAUNDRY AND DRY CLEANING

| | |
|---|---|
| Where is the nearest laundry? | **Où est la blanchisserie la plus proche?** *oo eh lah blahn-sheess-ree lah plew prohsh* |
| Where is the nearest laundromat? | **Où est la laverie automatique la plus proche?** *oo eh lah lah-vree oh-toh-mah-teek lah plew prohsh* |
| Where is the nearest dry cleaner's? | **Où est la teinturerie la plus proche?** *oo eh lah tahn-tew-ruh-ree lah plew prohsh* |
| I have a lot of (dirty) clothes to be ____. | **J'ai beaucoup de vêtements (sales) à faire ____.** *zhay boh-koo duh veht-mahn sahl ah fehr* |
| ■ dry cleaned | **nettoyer à sec** *neh-twah-yay ah sehk* |
| ■ washed | **laver** *lah-vay* |
| ■ mended | **réparer** *ray-pah-ray* |
| ■ ironed | **repasser** *ruh-pah-ssay* |
| Here's the list: ____. | **Voici la liste: ____.** *vwah-ssee lah leesst.* |
| ■ 3 shirts (men's) | **trois chemises** *trwah shuh-meez* |
| ■ 12 handkerchiefs | **douze mouchoirs** *dooz moo-shwahr* |
| ■ 6 pairs of socks | **six paires de chaussettes** *see pehr duh shoh-sseht* |
| ■ 1 blouse (nylon) | **une blouse (nylon)** *ewn blooz (nee-lohn)* |
| ■ 4 panties | **quatre slips** *kah-truh sleep* |
| ■ 2 pyjamas | **deux paires de pyjama** *duh pehr duh pee-zhah-mah* |
| ■ 2 suits | **deux complets** *duh kohn-pleh* |

| | | |
|---|---|---|
| ■ 3 ties | **trois cravates** *trwah krah-vaht* | |
| ■ 2 dresses (cotton) | **deux robes (en coton)** *duh rohb ahn koh-tohn* | |
| ■ 1 sweater (wool) | **un chandail (laine)** *uhn shahn-dahy (lehn)* | |
| ■ 1 pair of gloves | **une paire de gants** *ewn pehr duh gahn* | |
| I need them for ____. | **J'en ai besoin pour ____.** *zhahn nay buh-zwan poor* | |
| ■ tonight | **ce soir** *suh swahr* | |
| ■ tomorrow | **demain** *duh-man* | |
| ■ next week | **la semaine prochaine** *lah suh-mehn proh-shehn* | |
| ■ the day after to-morrow | **après-demain** *ah-preh duh-man* | |
| ■ at the latest | **au plus tard** *oh plew tahr* | |
| I'm leaving ____. | **Je pars ____.** *zhuh pahr* | |
| ■ soon | **bientôt** *byan-toh* | |
| ■ tomorrow | **demain** *duh-man* | |
| When will you bring it back? | **Quand est-ce que vous me le rendrez?** *kahn tehss kuh voo muh luh rahn-dray* | |
| When will it be ready? | **Quand sera-t-il prêt?** *kahn suh-rah teel preh* | |
| There's a button missing. | **Il y a un bouton qui manque.** *eel yah uhn boo-tohn kee mahnk* | |
| Can you sew it back on? | **Pouvez-vous le recoudre?** *poo-vay voo luh ruh-koo-druh* | |
| This isn't my laundry. | **Ce n'est pas ma lessive.** *suh neh pah mah lay-sseev* | |

## SHOE REPAIRS

Can you fix these shoes (boots)?

**Pouvez-vous réparer ces chaussures (bottes)?** *poo-vay voo ray-pah-ray say shoh-ssewr (boht)*

Put on (half) soles and rubber heels.

**Mettez les (demi-) semelles et les talons en caoutchouc.** *meh-tay lay duh-mee suh-mehl ay lay tah-lohn ahn kah-oo-tshoo*

I'd like to have my shoes shined (too).

**Je voudrais un cirage (aussi).** *zhuh voo-dreh zuhn see-rahzh (oh-ssee)*

**Je voudrais me faire cirer les chaussures.** *zhuh voo-dreh muh fehr see-ray lay shoh-ssewr*

When will they be ready?

**Quand seront-elles prêtes?** *kahn suh-rohn tehl preht*

I need them by Saturday (without fail).

**Il me les faut samedi (sans faute).** *eel muh lay foh sahm-dee (sahn foht)*

## WATCH REPAIRS

Can you fix this watch (alarm clock) for me?

**Pouvez-vous me réparer cette montre (ce réveil)?** *poo-vay voo muh ray-pah-ray seht mohn-truh (suh ray-vehy)*

I need _____.

**Il me faut _____.** *eel muh foh*

■ a crystal, glass

**un verre** *uhn vehr*

■ an hour hand

**une petite aiguille** *ewn puh-teet ay-gwee*

■ a minute hand

**une aiguille des minutes** *ewn ay-gwee day mee-newt*

■ a screw

**une vis** *ewn veess*

■ a second hand

**une aiguille des secondes** *ewn ay-gwee day suh-gohnd*

| | |
|---|---|
| When will it be ready? | **Quand sera-t-elle prête?** *kahn suh-rah tehl preht?* |
| May I have a receipt? | **Puis-je avoir un reçu?** *pweezh ah-vwahr uhn ruh-ssew?* |
| Can you look at it? | **Pouvez-vous l'examiner?** *poo-vay voo lehg-zah-mee-nay* |
| Can you clean it? | **Pouvez-vous la nettoyer?** *poo-vay voo lah neh-twah-yay* |
| I dropped it. | **Je l'ai laissé tomber.** *zhuh lay leh-ssay tohn-bay* |
| It doesn't run well. | **Elle ne marche pas bien.** *ehl nuh mahrsh pah byan* |
| It's fast (slow). | **Cette montre avance (retarde).** *seht mohn-truh ah-vahnss (ruh-tahrd)* |
| It's stopped. | **Elle s'est arrêtée.** *ehl seh tah-reh-tay* |
| I wind it every day. | **Je la remonte tous les jours.** *zhuh lah ruh-mohnt too lay zhoor* |

## CAMERA REPAIRS

| | |
|---|---|
| Can you fix this camera? | **Pouvez-vous réparer cet appareil?** *poo-vay voo ray-pah-ray seht ah-pah-rehy* |
| It doesn't work well. | **Il ne fonctionne pas bien.** *eel nuh fohnk-ssyohn pah byan* |
| How much will the repair cost? | **Combien coûtera la réparation?** *kohn-byan koo-trah lah ray-pah-rah-ssyohn* |
| When can I come and get it? | **Quand puis-je venir le chercher?** *kahn pweezh vuh-neer luh shehr-shay* |
| I need it as soon as possible. | **Il me le faut aussitôt que possible.** *Eel muh luh foh oh-see-toh kuh poh-ssee-bluh* |

# MEDICAL CARE

## AT THE PHARMACY

A green cross indicates a pharmacy, where you buy over-the-counter or prescription drugs. If the pharmacy is closed there will be a sign on the door to indicate which pharmacies are open in the neighborhood.

| | |
|---|---|
| Where is the nearest (all-night) pharmacy? | **Où se trouve la pharmacie de garde (de nuit) la plus proche?** *oo suh troov lah fahr-mah-ssee duh gahrd (duh nwee) lah plew prohsh* |
| At what time does the pharmacy open (close)? | **À quelle heure ouvre (ferme) la pharmacie?** *ah kehl uhr oo-vruh (fehrm) lah fahr-mah-ssee* |
| I need something for ____. | **Il me faut quelque chose pour** ____. *eel muh foh kehl-kuh shohz poor* |
| ■ a cold | **un rhume** *uhn rewm* |
| ■ constipation | **la constipation** *lah kohn-sstee-pah-ssyohn* |
| ■ a cough | **une toux** *ewn too* |
| ■ diarrhea | **la diarrhée** *lah dee-ah-ray* |
| ■ a fever | **une fièvre** *ewn fyeh-vruh* |
| ■ hay fever | **le rhume des foins** *luh rewm day fwan* |
| ■ a headache | **un mal de tête** *uhn mahl duh teht* |
| ■ insomnia | **l'insomnie** *lan-sohm-nee* |
| ■ nausea | **la nausée** *lah noh-zay* |
| ■ sunburn | **les coups de soleil** *lay koo duh soh-lehy* |
| ■ a toothache | **un mal de dents** *uhn mahl duh dahn* |

| | |
|---|---|
| ■ an upset stomach | **les indigestions** *lay-zan-dee-zhehss-tyohn* |
| Is a prescription needed for the medicine? | **Faut-il avoir une ordonnance pour ce médicament?** *foh-teel ah-vwahr ewn ohr-doh-nahnss poor suh may-dee-kah-mahn* |
| Can you fill this prescription for me now? | **Pourriez-vous me préparer cette ordonnance maintenant?** *poo-ree-yay voo muh pray-pah-ray seht ohr-doh-nahnss mant-nahn* |
| It's an emergency. | **C'est urgent.** *seh-tewr-zhahn* |
| Can I wait for it? | **Puis-je l'attendre?** *pweezh lah-tahn-druh* |
| How long will it take? | **Ça prendra combien de temps?** *sah prahn-drah kohn-byan duh tahn* |
| When can I come for it? | **Quand puis-je venir la chercher?** *kahn pweezh vuh-neer lah shehr-shay* |
| When can I come back? | **Quand puis-je revenir?** *kahn pweezh ruh-vuh-neer* |
| I would like ____. | **Je voudrais ____.** *zhuh voo-dreh* |
| ■ adhesive tape | **une bande adhésive** *zewn bahnd ahd-ay-zeev* |
| ■ alcohol | **l'alcool** *lahl-kohl* |
| ■ an antacid | **un anti-acide** *zuhn nahn-tee ah-sseed* |
| ■ an antiseptic | **un antiseptique** *zuhn nahn-tee-ssehp-teek* |
| ■ aspirins | **des aspirines** *day-zahss-pee-reen* |
| ■ bandages | **des bandes** *day bahnd* |
| ■ Band-Aids | **des bandages** *day bahn-dazh* |
| ■ corn plasters | **des emplâtres pour les cors** *day zahn-plah-truh poor lay kohr* |
| ■ (absorbent) cotton | **de l'ouate** *duh lwaht* |

| | |
|---|---|
| ■ cough drops | **des pastilles contre la toux** *day pahss-tee kohn-truh lah too* |
| ■ cough syrup | **le sirop contre la toux** *luh see-roh kohn-truh lah too* |
| ■ ear drops | **les gouttes pour les oreilles** *lay goot poor lay zoh-rehy* |
| ■ eye drops | **les gouttes pour les yeux** *lay goot poor lay zyuh* |
| ■ iodine | **de la teinture d'iode** *duh lah tan-tewr dyohd* |
| ■ a (mild) laxative | **un laxatif (léger)** *zuhn lahk-ssah-teef (lay-zhay)* |
| ■ milk of magnesia | **le lait de magnésie** *luh leh duh mah-nyay-zee* |
| ■ suppositories | **les suppositoires** *lay sew-poh-zee-twahr* |
| ■ a thermometer | **un thermomètre** *uhn tehr-moh-meh-truh* |
| ■ tranquilizers | **des tranquillisants** *day trahn-kee-lee-zahn* |
| ■ vitamins | **des vitamines** *day vee-tah-meen* |

## DOCTORS

You never know when you may need a doctor while on vacation. In Paris the U.S. Embassy (tel: 296.12.02) has a list of English-speaking doctors. There is also an American Hospital where most of the doctors speak English (tel: 637.72.00) and a British Hospital (tel: 757.24.10). In other areas and situations, the following phrases will help you:

| | |
|---|---|
| I don't feel well. | **Je ne me sens pas bien.** *zhuh nuh muh sahn pah byan* |
| I feel sick. | **Je me sens mal.** *zhuh muh sahn mahl* |

| I need a doctor. | **Il me faut un docteur.** *eel muh foh tuhn dohk-tuhr* |
|---|---|
| Do you know a doctor who speaks English? | **Connaissez-vous un docteur qui parle anglais?** *koh-neh-ssay voo uhn dohk-tuhr kee pahrl ahn-gleh* |
| Where is his office? | **Où se trouve son cabinet?** *oo suh troov sohn kah-bee-neh* |
| I'm dizzy. | **J'ai des vertiges.** *zhay day vehr-teezh* |
| I feel weak. | **Je me sens faible.** *zhuh muh sahn feh-bluh* |
| I want to sit down for a while. | **Je voudrais m'asseoir un moment.** *zhuh voo-dreh mah-sswahr uhn moh-mahn* |
| My temperature is normal (37°C). | **Ma température est normale (trente-sept degrés).** *mah tahn-pay-rah-tewr eh nohr-mahl (trahnt seht duh-gray)* |

## PARTS OF THE BODY

| head | **la tête** | *lah teht* |
|---|---|---|
| face | **la figure** | *lah fee-gewr* |
| ear | **l'oreille** | *loh-rehy* |
| eye | **l'oeil** | *luhy* |
| nose | **le nez** | *luh nay* |
| mouth | **la bouche** | *lah boosh* |
| tooth | **la dent** | *lah dahn* |
| throat | **la gorge** | *lah gohrzh* |
| neck | **le cou** | *luh koo* |
| shoulder | **l'épaule** | *lay-pohl* |
| breast | **la poitrine** | *lah pwah-treen* |

| | | |
|---|---|---|
| heart | **le coeur** | *luh kuhr* |
| arm | **le bras** | *luh brah* |
| elbow | **le coude** | *luh kood* |
| wrist | **le poignet** | *luh pwah-nyeh* |
| hand | **la main** | *lah man* |
| appendix | **l'appendice** | *lah-pan-deess* |
| hip | **la hanche** | *lah ahnsh* |
| leg | **la jambe** | *lah zhahnb* |
| knee | **le genou** | *luh zhuh-noo* |
| ankle | **la cheville** | *lah shuh-vee* |
| foot | **le pied** | *luh-pyay* |
| skin | **la peau** | *lah poh* |

## TELLING THE DOCTOR

| | | |
|---|---|---|
| I have _____. | **J'ai _____.** *zhay* | |
| ■ an abscess | **un abcès** *uhn nahb-sseh* | |
| ■ a broken bone | **une fracture** *ewn frahk-tewr* | |
| ■ a bruise | **une contusion** *ewn kohn-tew-zyohn* | |
| ■ a burn | **une brûlure** *ewn brew-lewr* | |
| ■ something in my eye | **quelque chose dans l'oeil** *kehl-kuh shohz dahn luhy* | |
| ■ the chills | **des frissons** *day free-ssohn* | |
| ■ a cold | **un rhume** *uhn rewm* | |
| a chest cold | **une bronchite** *ewn brohn-sheet* | |
| a head cold | **un rhume de cerveau** *uhn rewm duh sehr-voh* | |
| ■ cramps | **des crampes** *day krahnp* | |

| | | |
|---|---|---|
| ■ a cut | **une coupure** | *ewn koo-pewr* |
| ■ diarrhea | **la diarrhée** | *lah dee-ah-ray* |
| ■ dysentery | **la dysenterie** | *lah dee-ssah<u>n</u>-tree* |
| ■ a fever | **de la fièvre** | *duh lah fyeh-vruh* |
| ■ a fracture | **une fracture** | *ewn frahk-tewr* |
| ■ a headache | **mal à la tête** | *mahl ah lah teht* |
| ■ an infection | **une infection** | *ewn a<u>n</u>-fehk-ssyoh<u>n</u>* |
| ■ a lump | **une grosseur** | *ewn groh-ssuhr* |
| ■ a sore throat | **mal à la gorge** | *mahl ah lah gohrzh* |
| ■ a stomach ache | **mal à l'estomac** | *mahl ah lehss-toh-mah* |
| ■ swelling | **une enflure** | *ewn ah<u>n</u>-flewr* |
| ■ a wound | **une blessure** | *ewn bleh-ssewr* |
| I am constipated. | **Je suis constipé(e).** | *zhuh swee koh<u>n</u>-sstee-pay* |
| It hurts me here. | **J'ai mal ici.** | *zhay mahl ee-ssee* |
| My whole body hurts. | **Tout mon corps me fait mal.** | *too moh<u>n</u> kohr muh feh mahl* |
| My ___ hurts. | **J'ai mal ___.** | *zhay mahl* |
| ■ ankle | **à la cheville** | *ah lah shuh-vee* |
| ■ arm | **au bras** | *oh brah* |
| ■ back | **au dos** | *oh doh* |
| ■ cheek | **à la joue** | *ah lah zhoo* |
| ■ ear | **à l'oreille** | *ah loh-rehy* |
| ■ eye | **aux yeux** | *oh zyuh* |
| ■ face | **à la figure** | *ah lah fee-gewr* |
| ■ finger | **au doigt** | *oh dwah* |
| ■ foot | **au pied** | *oh pyay* |

| | |
|---|---|
| ■ glands | **aux ganglions** *oh gah<u>n</u>-glee-yoh<u>n</u>* |
| ■ head | **à la tête** *ah lah teht* |
| ■ hand | **à la main** *ah lah ma<u>n</u>* |
| ■ hip | **à la hanche** *ah lah ah<u>n</u>sh* |
| ■ leg | **à la jambe** *ah lah zhah<u>n</u>b* |
| ■ lip | **à la lèvre** *ah lah leh-vruh* |
| ■ neck | **au cou** *oh koo* |
| ■ nose | **au nez** *oh nay* |
| ■ shoulder | **à l'épaule** *ah lay-pohl* |
| ■ throat | **à la gorge** *ah lah goh<u>r</u>zh* |
| ■ thumb | **au pouce** *oh pooss* |
| ■ toe | **à l'orteil** *ah lohr-tehy* |
| ■ wrist | **au poignet** *oh pwah-nyeh* |

I've had this pain since yesterday.

**J'ai cette douleur depuis hier.**
*zhay seht doo-luhr duh-pwee yehr*

There's a (no) history of asthma (diabetes) in my family.

**Il y a (Il n'y a pas) d'asthme (de diabète) dans ma famille.** *eel yah (eel nyah pah) dahss-muh (duh dee-ah-beht) dah<u>n</u> mah fah-mee*

| | |
|---|---|
| I'm (not) allergic to antibiotics (penicillin). | **Je (ne) suis (pas) allergique aux antibiotiques.** *zhuh (nuh) swee (pah) zah-lehr-zheek oh zah_n_-tee-bee-oh-teek* |
| I have a pain in my chest around my heart. | **J'ai une douleur à la poitrine près du coeur.** *zhay ewn doo-luhr ah lah pwah-treen preh dew kuhr* |
| I had a heart attack ____ year(s) ago. | **J'ai eu une crise cardiaque il y a ____ ans.** *zhay ew ewn kreez kahr-dyahk eel yah ____ ah_n_* |
| I'm taking this medicine. | **Je prends ce médicament.** *zhuh prah_n_ suh may-dee-kah-mah_n_* |
| I'm pregnant. | **J'attends un enfant.** *zah-tah_n_ zuh_n_ nah_n_-fah_n_* |
| I feel faint. | **Je vais m'évanouir.** *zhuh veh may-vah-nweer* |
| I feel all right now. | **Je vais bien maintenant.** *zhuh veh byan ma_n_t-nah_n_* |
| I feel better. | **Je vais mieux.** *zhuh veh myuh* |
| I feel worse. | **Je me sens moins bien.** *zhuh muh sah_n_ mwan byan* |
| Do I have ____? | **Est-ce que j'ai ____?** *ehss kuh zhay* |
| ■ appendicitis | **l'appendicite** *lah-pah_n_-dee-sseet* |
| ■ the flu | **la grippe** *lah greep* |
| ■ tonsilitis | **une amygdalite** *ewn nah-meeg-dah-leet* |
| Is it serious (contagious)? | **C'est grave? (contagieux)?** *seh grahv (koh_n_-tah-zhyuh)* |
| Do I have to go to the hospital? | **Dois-je aller à l'hôpital?** *dwahzh ah-lay ah loh-pee-tahl* |
| When can I continue my trip? | **Quand pourrai-je poursuivre mon voyage?** *kah_n_ poo-rayzh poor-swee-vruh moh_n_ vwah-yahzh* |

## DOCTOR'S INSTRUCTIONS

| | | |
|---|---|---|
| Open your mouth. | **Ouvrez la bouche.** | *oo-vray lah boosh* |
| Stick out your tongue. | **Tirez la langue.** | *tee-ray lah lah<u>ng</u>* |
| Cough. | **Toussez.** | *too-ssay* |
| Breathe deeply. | **Respirez profondément.** | *rehss-pee-ray proh-foh<u>n</u>-day-mah<u>n</u>* |
| Take off your clothing (to the waist). | **Déshabillez-vous (jusqu'à la ceinture).** | *day-zah-bee-yay voo (zhewss-kah lah sa<u>n</u>-tewr)* |
| Lie down. | **Étendez-vous.** | *ay-tah<u>n</u>-day voo* |
| Stand up. | **Levez-vous.** | *luh-vay voo* |
| Get dressed. | **Habillez-vous.** | *ah-bee-yay voo* |

## PATIENT

| | | |
|---|---|---|
| Are you going to give me a prescription? | **Allez-vous me donner une ordonnance?** | *ah-lay voo muh doh-nay ewn ohr-doh-nah<u>n</u>ss* |
| How often must I take this medicine (these pills)? | **Combien de fois par jour dois-je prendre ce médicament (ces pilules)?** | *koh<u>n</u>-bya<u>n</u> duh fwah pahr zhoor dwahzh prah<u>n</u>-druh suh may-dee-kah-mah<u>n</u> (seh pee-lewl)* |
| (How long) do I have to stay in bed? | **(Combien de temps) dois-je garder le lit?** | *(koh<u>n</u>-bya<u>n</u> duh tah<u>n</u>) dwahzh gahr-day luh lee* |
| Thank you (for everything), doctor. | **Merci bien (pour tout), monsieur le docteur.** | *mehr-ssee bya<u>n</u> (poor too), muh-ssyuh luh dohk-tuhr* |
| What is your fee? | **Quels sont vos honoraires?** | *kehl soh<u>n</u> voh zoh-noh-rehr* |
| I have medical insurance. | **J'ai une assurance médicale.** | *zhay ewn ah-ssew-rah<u>n</u>ss may-dee-kahl* |

## IN THE HOSPITAL (ACCIDENTS)

| | |
|---|---|
| Help! | **Au secours!** *oh suh-koor* |
| Help me, somebody! | **Que quelqu'un m'aide, je vous en prie!** *kuh kehl-kuhn mehd zhuh voo zahn pree* |
| Get a doctor, quick! | **Vite, appelez un docteur!** *veet, ah-play uhn dohk-tuhr* |
| Call an ambulance! | **Faites venir une ambulance!** *feht vuh-neer ewn ahn-bew-lahnss* |
| Take me (him, her) to the hospital. | **Emmenez-moi (le, la) à l'hôpital.** *ahn-muh-nay mwah (luh, lah) ah loh-pee-tahl* |
| I need first aid. | **J'ai besoin de premiers soins.** *zhay buh-zwan duh pruh-myay swan* |
| I've fallen. | **Je suis tombé(e).** *zhuh swee tohn-bay* |
| I was knocked down (run over). | **On m'a renversé(e).** *ohn mah rahn-vehr-ssay* |
| I've had a heart attack. | **J'ai eu une crise cardiaque.** *zhay ew ewn kreez kahr-dyahk* |
| I burned myself. | **Je me suis brûlé(e).** *zhuh muh swee brew-lay* |
| I cut myself. | **Je me suis coupé(e).** *zhuh muh swee koo-pay* |
| I'm bleeding. | **Je saigne.** *zhuh seh-nyuh* |
| I've (He's) lost a lot of blood. | **J'ai (Il a) perdu beaucoup de sang.** *zhay (eel ah) pehr-dew boh-koo duh sahn* |
| I think the bone is broken (dislocated). | **Je crois que l'os est fracturé (déboîté).** *zhuh krwah kuh lohss eh frahk-tew-ray (day-bwah-tay)* |
| The leg is swollen. | **La jambe est enflée.** *lah zhahnb eh tahn-flay* |

| The wrist (ankle) is sprained (twisted). | **Le poignet (la cheville) est démis (démise) (tordu(e)).** *luh pwah-nyeh (lah shuh-vee) eh day-mee (day-meez) (tohr-dew)* |
|---|---|
| I can't move my elbow (knee). | **Je ne peux pas remuer le coude (le genou).** *zhuh nuh puh pah ruh-mew-ay luh kood (luh zhuh-noo)* |

## EMERGENCY PHONE NUMBERS IN PARIS
These lines are open twenty-four hours a day.

| | |
|---|---|
| Ambulance | 887.27.50 |
| Anti-Poison Squad | 205.63.29 |
| Dentist | 253.76.53 |
| Drugs | 707.85.05 |
| Police | 17 |
| Fire Department | 18 |
| SAMU (emergency ambulance) | 567.50.50 |

## AT THE DENTIST

| I have to go to the dentist. | **Il me faut aller chez le dentiste.** *eel muh foh tah-lay shay luh dahn-teesst* |
|---|---|
| Can you recommend a dentist? | **Pouvez-vous me recommander un dentiste?** *poo-vay voo muh ruh-koh-mahn-day uhn dahn-teesst* |
| I have a toothache that's driving me crazy. | **J'ai un mal de dents à tout casser. (J'ai une rage de dents.)** *zhay uhn mahl duh dahn ah too kah-ssay (zhay ewn rahzh duh dahn)* |
| I have a rotten tooth that's giving me a lot of pain. | **J'ai une dent cariée qui me fait très mal.** *zhay ewn dahn kah-ree-yay kee muh feh treh mahl* |

| | |
|---|---|
| I've lost a filling. | **J'ai perdu un plombage.** *zhay pehr-dew uhn plohn-bahzh* |
| I've broken a tooth. | **Je me suis cassé une dent.** *zhuh muh swee kah-ssay ewn dahn* |
| I can't chew. | **Je ne peux pas mâcher.** *zhuh nuh puh pah mah-shay* |
| My gums hurt me. | **Les gencives me font mal.** *lay zhahn-sseev muh fohn mahl* |
| Is there an infection? | **Y a-t-il une infection?** *ee ah-teel ewn an-fehk-ssyohn* |
| Will you have to extract the tooth? | **Faut-il extraire la dent?** *foh teel ehkss-trehr lah dahn* |
| Can you fill it _____? | **Pouvez-vous l'obturer _____?** *poo-vay voo lohb-tew-ray* |
| ■ with amalgam | **avec une amalgame** *ah-vehk ewn ah-mahl-gahm* |
| ■ with gold | **avec de l'or** *ah-vehk duh lohr* |
| ■ with silver | **avec de l'argent** *ah-vehk duh lahr-zhahn* |
| ■ for now | **pour le moment** *poor luh moh-mahn* |
| ■ temporarily | **provisoirement** *proh-vee-zwahr-mahn* |
| Can you fix _____? | **Pouvez-vous réparer _____?** *poo-vay voo ray-pah-ray* |
| ■ this bridge | **ce bridge** *suh breedzh* |
| ■ this crown | **cette couronne** *seht koo-rohn* |
| ■ this denture | **ce dentier** *suh dahn-tyay* |
| ■ these false teeth | **ces fausses dents** *say fohss dahn* |
| When should I come back? | **Quand devrais-je revenir?** *kahn duh-vrehzh ruh-vuh-neer* |

| | |
|---|---|
| What is your fee? . . . are your fees? | **Combien vous dois-je?** *kohn-byan voo dwahzh* |

## WITH THE OPTICIAN

| | |
|---|---|
| Can you repair these glasses (for me)? | **Pouvez-vous (me) réparer ces lunettes?** *poo-vay voo (muh) ray-pah-ray say lew-neht* |
| I've broken a lens (the frame). | **J'ai cassé un verre (la monture).** *zhay kah-ssay uhn vehr (lah mohn-tewr)* |
| Can you put in a new lens? | **Pouvez-vous mettre un nouveau verre?** *poo-vay voo meh-truh uhn noo-voh vehr* |
| Can you tighten the screw? | **Pouvez-vous resserrer la vis?** *poo-vay voo ruh-sseh-ray lah veess* |
| I need the glasses as soon as possible. | **Il me faut ces lunettes aussitôt que possible.** *eel muh foh say lew-neht oh-ssee-toh kuh poh-ssee-bluh* |
| I don't have any others. | **Je n'ai pas d'autre paire.** *zhuh nay pah doh-truh pehr* |
| Do you sell contact lenses? | **Vendez-vous des verres de contact?** *vahn-day voo day vehr duh kohn-tahkt* |
| I've lost a lens. | **J'ai perdu un verre.** *zhay pehr-dew uhn vehr* |
| Can you replace it right away? | **Pouvez-vous le remplacer tout de suite?** *poo-vay voo luh rahn-plah-ssay toot sweet* |
| Do you sell sun glasses? | **Vendez-vous des lunettes de soleil?** *vahn-day voo day lew-neht duh soh-lehy* |

# COMMUNICATIONS

## POST OFFICE

The letters P.T. (**Postes et Télécommunications**—for letters and telephones) identify the post offices. They are open from 8 a.m.–7 p.m., with a two hour break for lunch in many instances. The main Paris post office never closes. You may purchase stamps at post offices, at café-tabacs, or at your hotel. Look for the yellow mail box.

| | |
|---|---|
| I want to mail a letter. | **Je voudrais mettre cette lettre à la poste.** *zhuh voo-dreh meh-truh seht leh-truh ah lah pohsst* |
| Where's the post office? | **Où se trouve le bureau de poste?** *oo suh troov luh bew-roh duh pohsst* |
| Where's a letterbox? | **Où se trouve la boîte aux lettres?** *oo suh troov lah bwaht oh leh-truh* |
| What is the postage on ___ to the United States? | **Quel est l'affranchissement ___ pour les États-Unis?** *kehl eh lah-frahn-sheess-mahn poor lay zay-tah zew-nee* |
| ■ a letter | **d'une lettre** *dewn leh-truh* |
| ■ an air-mail letter | **pour une lettre envoyée par avion** *poor ewn leh-truh ahn-vwah-yay pahr ah-vyohn* |
| ■ an insured letter | **pour une lettre recommandée** *poor ewn leh-truh ruh-koh-mahn-day* |
| ■ a registered letter | **pour une lettre recommandée** *poor ewn leh-truh ruh-koh-mahn-day* |
| ■ a special delivery letter | **pour une lettre par exprès** *poor ewn leh-truh pahr ehkss-prehss* |
| ■ a package | **un colis** *zuhn koh-lee* |
| ■ a post card | **une carte postale** *zewn kahrt pohss-tahl* |

| | |
|---|---|
| When will it arrive? | **Quand arrivera-t-il (elle)?** *kah<u>n</u> tah-ree-vrah teel? (tehl)* |
| Which is the ___ window? | **Quel est le guichet ___?** *kehl eh luh gee-sheh* |
| ■ general delivery | **pour la poste restante** *poor lah pohsst rehss-tah<u>n</u>t* |
| ■ money order | **pour les mandats-poste** *poor lay mah<u>n</u>-dah pohsst* |
| ■ stamp | **pour les timbres-poste** *poor lay ta<u>n</u>-bruh pohsst* |
| ■ wholesale | **en gros** *ah<u>n</u> groh* |
| ■ retail | **en détail** *ah<u>n</u> day-tahy* |
| Are there any letters for me? | **Y a-t-il des lettres pour moi?** *ee ah-teel day leh-truh poor mwah* |
| My name is ___. | **Je m'appelle ___.** *zhuh mah-pehl* |
| I'd like ___. | **Je voudrais ___.** *zhuh voo-dreh* |
| ■ 10 post cards | **dix cartes postales** *dee kahrt pohss-tahl* |
| ■ 5 (air mail) stamps | **cinq timbres (courrier aérien)** *sa<u>n</u>k tah<u>n</u>-bruh (koo-ryay ah-ay-rya<u>n</u>)* |

## TELEGRAMS

| | |
|---|---|
| Where's the telegraph window? | **Où est le guichet pour les télégrammes?** *oo eh luh gee-sheh poor lay tay-lay-grahm* |
| How late is it open? | **Jusqu'à quelle heure est-il ouvert?** *zhewss-kah kehl uhr eh teel oo-vehr* |
| I'd like to send a telegram (night letter) to ___. | **Je voudrais envoyer un télégramme (une lettre-télégramme) à ___.** *zhuh voo-dreh zah<u>n</u>-vwah-yay uh<u>n</u> tay-lay-grahm (ewn leh-truh tay-lay-grahm) ah* |

| How much is it per word? | **Quel est le tarif par mot?** *kehl eh luh tah-reef pahr moh* |
| Where are the forms? | **Où sont les formulaires (imprimés)?** *oo sohn lay fohr-mew-lehr (an-pree-may)* |
| May I please have a form? | **Puis-je avoir un formulaire (un imprimé) s'il vous plaît?** *pweezh ah-vwahr uhn fohr-mew-lehr (uhn an-pree-may) seel voo pleh* |
| I want to send it collect. | **Je voudrais l'envoyer en P.C.V.** *zhuh voo-dreh lahn-vwah-yay ahn pay say vay* |
| When will it arrive? | **Quand arrivera-t-il?** *kahn tah-ree-vrah teel* |

## TELEPHONES

Virtually the entire French telephone system is now automatic and is hooked up to the international dialing system. Public pay phone booths can be found at the post office, in cafés and on the streets of larger cities.

To place a local call from the older phones, you must purchase a slug (**un jeton**) at the café or post office. Long distance calls must be made from the post office or from your hotel. Do the following to complete a call:

**1.** Put your "jeton" in the slot.
**2.** Lift the receiver.
**3.** Wait for the dial tone.
**4.** Dial the number.
**5.** When you hear someone answer (NOT BEFORE), push the button on the front of the phone.

If there is no answer, if the line is busy, or if the phone isn't working, hang up the receiver and the jeton will be returned to you.

The more modern phones accept coins and, unlike the old phones, you may place international and long distance calls from them. Do the following to complete a call:

1. Lift the receiver.
2. Insert the coin.
3. Wait for the dial tone.
4. Dial the number.

Telephone numbers in France consist of 6 digits and are given in pairs. Phones in Paris have 7 digits; the first 3 are read together, followed by the remaining 2 pairs.

To dial direct to the U.S. from a new public pay phone, dial: 19 + 1 + area code + number.

| | |
|---|---|
| Where is ____? | **Où y a-t-il ____?** *oo ee ah-teel* |
| ■ a public telephone | **un téléphone public** *uhn tay-lay-fohn pew-bleek* |
| ■ a telephone booth | **une cabine téléphonique** *ewn kah-been tay-lay-foh-neek* |
| ■ a telephone directory | **un annuaire téléphonique** *uhn nah-new-ehr tay-lay-foh-neek* |
| May I use your phone? | **Puis-je me servir de votre téléphone?** *pweezh muh sehr-veer duh voh-truh tay-lay-fohn* |
| I want to make a ____ to | **Je voudrais téléphoner ____** *zhuh voo-dreh tay-lay-foh-nay* |
| ■ local call | **en ville** *ahn veel* |
| ■ long distance call | **à l'extérieur** *ah lehkss-tay-ryuhr* |
| ■ person to person call | **avec préavis** *ah-vehk pray-ah-vee* |
| Can I call direct? | **Puis-je téléphoner en direct?** *pweezh tay-lay-foh-nay ahn dee-rehkt* |
| Do I need tokens for the phone? | **Faut-il des jetons pour le téléphone?** *foh teel day zhuh-tohn poor luh tay-lay-fohn* |
| Can you give me a token, please? | **Pourriez-vous me donner un jeton, s'il vous plaît?** *poo-ree-yay voo muh doh-nay uhn zhuh-tohn seel voo pleh* |

| | |
|---|---|
| How do I get the _____. | **Que fait-on pour _____?** *kuh feh-tohn poor* |
| ■ Operator? | **parler à la téléphoniste?** *pahr-lay ah lah tay-lay-foh-neesst* |
| ■ area code | **obtenir le code régional** *ohp-tuh-neer luh kohd ray-zhyohn-nahl* |
| Operator, can you get me number 23.34.56? | **Mademoiselle, pourriez vous me donner le vingt-trois, trente-quatre, cinquante-six?** *mahd-mwah-zehl poo-ree-yay voo muh doh-nay luh van-trwah trahnt kah-truh san-kahnt seess* |
| My number is _____. | **Mon numéro est _____.** *mohn new-may-roh eh* |
| May I speak to _____? | **Est-ce que je pourrais parler à _____?** *ehss kuh zhuh poo-reh pahr-lay ah* |

| | |
|---|---|
| I'd like to speak to _____. | **Je voudrais parler à _____.** *zhuh voo-dreh pahr-lay ah* |
| Is Mr. _____ in? | **Monsieur _____, est-il là?** *Muh-ssyuh _____ eh-teel lah* |
| Speaking. | **C'est _____ à l'appareil.** *seh _____ ah lah-pah-rehy* |
| Hello. | **Allô.** *ah-loh* |
| Who is calling? | **Qui est à l'appareil?** *kee eh tah lah-pah-rehy* |
| I can't hear. | **Je ne peux pas vous entendre.** *zhuh nuh puh pah voo zahn-tahn-druh* |
| Speak louder. | **Parlez plus fort.** *pahr-lay plew fohr* |
| Don't hang up. | **Ne quittez pas.** *nuh kee-tay pah* |
| This is _____. | **Ici _____.** *ee-ssee* |
| Operator, there's no answer (They don't answer). | **Mademoiselle, ça ne répond pas.** *mahd-mwah-zehl, sah nuh ray-pohn pah* |
| The line is busy. | **La ligne est occupée.** *lah lee-nyuh eh toh-kew-pay* |
| You gave me (that was) a wrong number. | **Vous m'avez donné le mauvais numéro.** *voo mah-vay doh-nay luh moh-veh new-may-roh* |
| I was cut off. | **J'ai été coupé.** *zhay ay-tay koo-pay* |
| Please dial it again. | **Veuillez recomposez le numéro.** *vuh-yay ruh-kohn-poh-zay luh new-may-roh* |
| I want to leave a message. | **Je voudrais laisser un message.** *zhuh voo-dreh leh-ssay uhn meh-ssahzh* |

# DRIVING A CAR

## ROAD SYSTEM

You may choose to drive on one of the following kinds of roads:

| | |
|---|---|
| **Autoroute** | a high-speed super freeway for long distance trips. These are toll roads. |
| **Route nationale** | a main highway used by cars going from one small town to another. |
| **Route départe-mentale** | minor highway |
| **Chemin communal** | a local road |
| **Chemin rural** | a scenic country road |

A good idea would be to purchase a French **Code de la Route** which explains driving rules and regulations. The French Government Tourist Office issues free road maps. Speed limits are high and it will take some time getting used to the French way of driving. Remember to buckle up.

## PARKING

During the day you may park at parking meters located in metropolitan areas, or you may find a spot in a "Blue Zone." To park there you must use a special parking disk (**disque**) which can be obtained free of charge at auto clubs, garages, gas stations, hotels, police stations or tourist offices. You must set the time of your arrival, and departure time will show automatically on the disk. The disk should be displayed on your windshield. Be careful; if you are caught cheating, you risk a fine. Parking at night is usually free.

## SIGNS

Familiarize yourself with the traffic signs listed below:

| | |
|---|---|
| **Accotement non stabilisé** | Soft shoulder |
| **Allumez vos phares** | Put on headlights |

| | |
|---|---|
| **Arrêt interdit** | No stopping |
| **Attention** | Caution |
| **Céder le passage** | Yield |
| **Chaussée déformée** | Poor roadway |
| **Chute de pierres** | Falling rocks |
| **Circulation interdite** | No thoroughfare |
| **Descente (Pente) dangereuse** | Steep slope (hill) |
| **Déviation** | Detour |
| **Douane** | Customs |
| **École** | School |
| **Entrée interdite** | No entrance |
| **Fin d'interdiction de \_\_\_\_** | End of \_\_\_\_ zone |
| **Interdiction de doubler** | No Passing |
| **Interdiction de stationner** | No Parking |
| **Interdit aux piétons** | No Pedestrians |
| **Piste réservée aux transports publics** | Lane for Public Transportation |
| **Ralentir (Ralentissez)** | Slow |
| **Réservé aux piétons** | Pedestrians only |
| **Sens interdit** | Wrong way |
| **Sens unique** | One Way |
| **Serrez à gauche (à droite)** | Keep left (right) |
| **Sortie d'autoroute** | Freeway (throughway) Exit |
| **Sortie de véhicules** | Vehicle Exit |

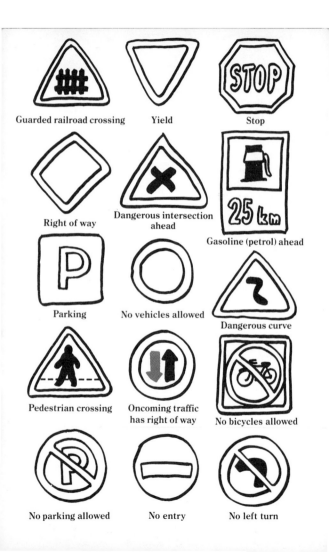

Guarded railroad crossing

Yield

Stop

Right of way

Dangerous intersection ahead

Gasoline (petrol) ahead

Parking

No vehicles allowed

Dangerous curve

Pedestrian crossing

Oncoming traffic has right of way

No bicycles allowed

No parking allowed

No entry

No left turn

No U-turn

No passing

Border crossing

Traffic signal ahead

Speed limit

Traffic circle (roundabout) ahead

Minimum speed limit

All traffic turns left

End of no passing zone

One-way street

Detour

Danger ahead

Entrance to expressway

Expressway ends

| | |
|---|---|
| **Stationnement autorisé** | Parking Permitted |
| **Stationnement interdit** | No Parking |
| **Tenez la droite (gauche)** | Keep to the right (left) |
| **Verglas** | Icy Road |
| **Virage dangereux** | Dangerous Curve |
| **Voie de dégagement** | Private Entrance |
| **Zone Bleue** | Blue Zone (parking) |

## CAR RENTALS

To drive in France you may use your driver's license. Cars may be rented or leased at airports or major railway stations. This can be quite costly since the price of gasoline abroad is prohibitive. The most economical method of renting a car is to reserve it with one of the rental agencies before you leave home.

| | |
|---|---|
| Where can I rent a car? | **Où puis-je louer une voiture?** *oo pweezh loo-ay ewn vwah-tewr* |
| ■ a motorcycle | **une motocyclette** *ewn moh-toh-see-kleht* |
| ■ a bicycle | **une bicyclette** *ewn bee-ssee-kleht* |
| ■ a scooter | **un scooter** *uhn skoo-tehr* |
| ■ a moped | **un mobilette** *uhn moh-bee-leht* |
| I want a _____. | **Je voudrais _____.** *zhuh voo-dreh* |
| ■ a small car | **une petite voiture** *zewn puh-teet vwah-tewr* |
| ■ large car | **une grande voiture** *zewn grahnd vwah-tewr* |
| ■ sports car | **une voiture de sport** *zewn vwah-tewr duh spohr* |
| I prefer automatic transmission. | **Je préfère la transmission automatique.** *zhuh pray-fehr lah trahnz-mee-ssyohn oh-toh-mah-teek* |

| How much does it cost ____? | **Quel est le tarif ____?** *kehl eh luh tah-reef* |
| ■ per day | **à la journée** *ah lah zhoor-nay* |
| ■ per week | **à la semaine** *ah lah suh-mehn* |
| ■ per kilometer | **au kilomètre** *oh kee-loh-meh-truh* |
| How much is the insurance? | **Quel est le montant de l'assurance?** *kehl eh luh mohn-tahn duh lah-ssew-rahnss* |
| Is the gas included? | **Est-ce que l'essence est comprise?** *ehss kuh leh-ssahnss eh kohn-preez* |
| Do you accept credit cards? Which ones? | **Acceptez vous des cartes de crédit? Lesquelles?** *ahk-ssehp-tay voo day kahrt duh kray-dee? Lay-kehl* |
| Here's my driver's license. | **Voici mon permis de conduire.** *vwah-ssee mohn pehr-mee duh kohn-dweer* |
| Do I have to leave a deposit? | **Dois-je verser des arrhes?** *dwahzh vehr-ssay day zahr* |
| Is there a drop-off charge? | **Faut-il payer plus en cas de non-retour ici?** *foh-teel peh-yay plews ahn kah duh nohn-ruh-toor ee-ssee* |
| I want to rent the car here and leave it in ____ (name of city). | **Je veux louer la voiture ici et la laisser à ____.** *zhuh vuh loo-ay lah vwah-tewr ee-ssee ay lah leh-ssay ah* |
| What kind of gas does it take? | **Quelle essence emploie-t-elle?** *kehl eh-ssahnss ahn-plwah-tehl* |

## ON THE ROAD

| Excuse me. | **Excusez-moi.** *ehkss-kew-zay mwah* **Pardon** *pahr-dohn* |
| Can you tell me ____? | **Pouvez-vous me dire ____?** *poo-vay voo muh deer* |

| | |
|---|---|
| Which way is it to ___? | **Comment aller à ___?** *koh-mahn ah-lay ah* |
| How do I get to ___? | **Comment puis-je aller à ___?** *koh-mahn pweezh ah-lay ah* |
| I think we're lost. | **Je crois que nous nous sommes égarés.** *zhuh krwah kuh noo noo sohm zay-gah-ray*<br>**Nous sommes sur la mauvaise route.** *noo sohm sewr lah moh-vehz root* |
| Which is the road to ___? | **Quelle est la route pour ___?** *kehl eh lah root poor* |
| Is this the road (way) to ___? | **Est-ce la route de ___?** *ehss lah root duh* |
| Where does this road go? | **Où mène cette route?** *oo mehn seht root* |
| How far is it from here to the next town? | **À quelle distance sommes-nous du prochain village?** *ah kehl deess-tahnss sohm noo dew proh-shan vee-lahzh* |
| How far away is ___? | **À quelle distance est ___?** *ah kehl deess-tahnss eh* |
| Is the next town far? | **Le prochain village, est-il loin?** *luh proh-shan vee-lahzh eh-teel lwan* |
| What's the next town called? | **Comment s'appelle le prochain village?** *koh-mahn sah-pehl luh proh-shan vee-lahzh* |
| Do you have a road map? | **Avez-vous une carte routière?** *Ah-vay voo zewn kahrt roo-tyehr* |
| Can you show it to me on the map? | **Pourriez-vous me l'indiquer sur la carte?** *poo-ree-yay voo muh lan-dee-kay sewr lah kahrt* |
| Is the road in good condition? | **Est-ce que la route est en bon état?** *ehss kuh lah root eh tahn bohn nay-tah* |

| Is this the shortest way? | **Est-ce le chemin le plus court?** *ehss luh shuh-man luh plew koor* |
| Are there any detours? | **Y a-t-il des déviations?** *ee ah-teel day day-vee-ah-ssyohn* |
| Do I go straight? | **Est-ce que je vais tout droit?** *ehss kuh zhuh veh too drwah* |
| Do I turn to the right (to the left)? | **Est-ce que je tourne à droite (à gauche)?** *ehss kuh zhuh toorn ah drwaht (ah gohsh)* |

## AT THE SERVICE STATION

Gasoline is sold by the liter in Europe, and for the traveler accustomed to gallons, it may seem confusing, especially if you want to calculate your mileage per gallon (kilometer per liter). Here are some tips on making those conversions.

| LIQUID MEASURES (APPROXIMATE) | | |
|---|---|---|
| LITERS | U.S. GALLONS | IMPERIAL GALLONS |
| 30 | 8 | $6\frac{1}{2}$ |
| 40 | $10\frac{1}{2}$ | $8\frac{3}{4}$ |
| 50 | $13\frac{1}{4}$ | 11 |
| 60 | $15\frac{1}{2}$ | 13 |
| 70 | $18\frac{1}{2}$ | $15\frac{1}{2}$ |
| 80 | 21 | $17\frac{1}{2}$ |

| DISTANCE MEASURES (APPROXIMATE) | |
|---|---|
| KILOMETERS | MILES |
| 1 | .62 |
| 5 | 3 |
| 10 | 6 |
| 20 | 12 |
| 50 | 31 |
| 100 | 62 |

| | |
|---|---|
| Where is there a gas station? | **Où y a-t-il une station-service?** *oo ee ah-teel ewn stah-ssyohn sehr-veess* |
| I need gas. | **J'ai besoin d'essence.** *zhay buh-zwan deh-ssahnss* |
| Fill'er up with ____. | **Faites-le plein, s'il vous plaît ____.** *feht-luh plan seel-voo pleh* |
| ■ diesel | **du gas-oil** *dew gahz-wahl* |
| ■ regular | **de l'ordinaire** *duh lohr-dee-nehr* |
| ■ super | **du super** *dew sew-pehr* |
| Give me ____ liters. | **Donnez m'en ____ litres, s'il vous plaît.** *doh-nay mahn ____ lee-truh, seel voo pleh* |
| I need 60 liters of gas. | **Je voudrais 60 (soixante) litres d'essence.** *zhuh voo-dreh swah-ssahnt lee-truh deh-ssahnss* |
| Please check ____. | **Veuillez vérifier ____.** *vuh-yay vay-ree-fyay* |
| ■ the battery | **la batterie** *lah bah-tree* |
| ■ the brakes | **les freins** *lay fran* |
| ■ the carburetor | **le carburateur** *luh kahr-bew-rah-tuhr* |
| ■ the oil | **le niveau de l'huile** *luh nee-voh duh lweel* |
| ■ the spark plugs | **les bougies** *lay boo-zhee* |
| ■ the tires | **les pneus** *lay pnuh* |
| ■ the tire pressure | **la pression des pneus** *lah preh-ssyohn day pnuh* |
| ■ the water | **le niveau de l'eau** *luh nee-voh duh loh* |
| Change the oil. | **Changez l'huile, s'il vous plaît.** *shahn-zhay lweel seel voo pleh* |

| Grease the car. | **Faites un graissage complet de la voiture, s'il vous plaît.** *feht zuhn greh-ssahzh kohn-pleh duh lah vwah-tewr seel voo pleh* |
| --- | --- |
| Charge the battery. | **Rechargez la batterie, s'il vous plaît.** *ruh-shahr-zhay lah bah-tree, seel voo pleh* |
| Change this tire. | **Changez ce pneu.** *shahn-zhay suh pnuh* |
| Wash the car. | **Lavez la voiture.** *Lah-vay lah vwah-tewr* |
| Where are the rest rooms? | **Où sont les toilettes?** *oo sohn lay twah-leht* |

| TIRE PRESSURE | |
| --- | --- |
| LB./SQ. IN. | KG./CM.$^2$ |
| 17 | 1.2 |
| 18 | 1.3 |
| 20 | 1.4 |
| 21 | 1.5 |
| 23 | 1.6 |
| 24 | 1.7 |
| 26 | 1.8 |
| 27 | 1.9 |
| 28 | 2.0 |
| 30 | 2.1 |
| 31 | 2.2 |
| 33 | 2.3 |
| 34 | 2.4 |
| 36 | 2.5 |
| 37 | 2.6 |
| 38 | 2.7 |
| 40 | 2.8 |

| | |
|---|---|
| It overheats. | **Elle chauffe.** *ehl shohf* |
| It doesn't start. | **Elle ne démarre pas.** *ehl nuh day-mahr pah* |
| It doesn't go. | **Elle ne marche pas.** *ehl nuh mahrsh pah* |
| I have a flat tire. | **J'ai un pneu crevé.** *zhay-uhn pnuh kruh-vay* |
| My car has broken down. | **Ma voiture est en panne.** *mah vwah-tewr eh tahn pahn* |
| The radiator is leaking. | **Le radiateur coule.** *luh rah-dee-ah-tuhr kool* |
| The battery is dead. | **La batterie ne fonctionne plus.** *lah bah-tree nuh fohnk-ssyohn plew* |
| The keys are locked inside the car. | **Les clés sont enfermées à l'intérieur de la voiture.** *lay klay sohn tahn-fehr-may ah lan-tay-ree-yuhr duh lah vwah-tewr* |
| Is there a garage near here? | **Y a-t-il un garage par ici?** *ee ah-teel uhn gah-rahzh pahr ee-ssee* |
| I need a mechanic (tow truck). | **Il me faut un mécanicien (une dépanneuse).** *eel muh foh tuhn may-kah-nee-ssyan (ewn day-pah-nuhz)* |
| Can you _____? | **Pouvez-vous _____?** *poo-vay voo* |
| ■ give me a hand | **me donner un coup de main** *muh doh-nay uhn koo duh man* |
| ■ help me | **m'aider** *meh-day* |
| ■ push me | **me pousser** *muh poo-ssay* |
| ■ tow me | **me remorquer** *muh ruh-mohr-kay* |
| I don't have any tools. | **Je n'ai pas d'outils.** *zhuh nay pas doo-tee* |

le carburateur
CARBURETOR

le radiateur
RADIATOR

la batterie
BATTERY

le phare
HEADLIGHT

l'aile
FENDER

le capot
HOOD

le pneu
TIRE

l'essuie-glace
WINDSHIELD WIPER

la poignée de porte
DOOR HANDLE

la malle arrière
TRUNK

le feu arrière
TAIL LIGHT

le pare-chocs
BUMPER

**le volant** STEERING WHEEL

**le changement de vitesse** GEAR SHIFT

**le clignotant** DIRECTIONAL SIGNAL

**la radio** RADIO

**le frein à main** PARKING BRAKE HAND BRAKE

**la pédale d'embrayage** CLUTCH PEDAL

**la pédale de frein** BRAKE PEDAL

**la pédale d'accélérateur (l'accélérateur)** GAS PEDAL

| | |
|---|---|
| Can you lend me ____? | **Pouvez-vous me prêter ____?** *poo-vay voo muh preh-tay* |
| ■ a flashlight | **une lampe de poche** *ewn lahnp duh pohsh* |
| ■ a hammer | **un marteau** *uhn mahr-toh* |
| ■ a jack | **un cric** *uhn kree* |
| ■ a monkey wrench | **une clé anglaise** *ewn klay ahn-glehz* |
| ■ pliers | **des pinces** *day panss* |
| ■ a screwdriver | **un tournevis** *uhn toorn-veess* |
| I need ____. | **J'ai besoin ____.** *zhay buh-zwan* |
| ■ a bolt | **d'un boulon** *duhn boo-lohn* |
| ■ a bulb | **d'une ampoule** *dewn ahn-pool* |
| ■ a filter | **d'un filtre** *duhn feel-truh* |
| ■ a nut | **d'un écrou** *duhn nay-kroo* |
| Can you fix the car? | **Pouvez-vous réparer la voiture?** *Poo-vay voo ray-pah-ray lah vwah-tewr* |

| | |
|---|---|
| Can you repair it temporarily? | **Pouvez-vous la réparer provisoirement?** *poo-vay voo lah ray-pah-ray proh-vee-zwahr-mahn* |
| Do you have the part? | **Avez-vous la pièce de rechange?** *ah-vay voo lah pyehss duh ruh-shahnzh* |
| I think there's something wrong with ____. | **Je crois que ____ ne fonctionne pas.** *zhuh krwah kuh ____ nuh fohnk-ssyohn pas.* |

- the directional signal — **le clignotant** *luh klee-nyoh-tahn*
- the door handle — **la poignée** *lah pwah-nyay*
- the electrical system — **l'installation électrique** *lan-stah-lah-ssyohn ay-lehk-treek*
- the fan — **le ventilateur** *luh vahn-tee-lah-tuhr*
- the fan belt — **la courroie de ventilateur** *lah koor-wah duh vahn-tee-lah-tuhr*
- the fuel pump — **la pompe à essence** *lah pohnp ah eh-ssahnss*
- the gears — **l'engrenage** *lahn-gruh-nahzh*
- the gear shift — **le changement de vitesses** *luh shahnzh-mahn duh vee-tehss*
- the headlight — **le phare** *luh fahr*
- the horn — **le klaxon** *luh klahk-ssohn*
- the ignition — **l'allumage** *lah-lew-mahzh*
- the radio — **la radio** *lah rah-dyoh*
- the starter — **le démarreur** *luh day-mah-ruhr*
- the steering wheel — **le volant** *luh voh-lahn*
- the tail light — **le feu arrière** *luh fuh ah-ryehr*
- the transmission — **la transmission** *lah trahnz-mee-ssyohn*

| | |
|---|---|
| ■ the water pump | **la pompe à eau** *lah pohnp ah oh* |
| ■ the windshield wipers | **les essuie-glaces** *lay zeh-sswee glahss* |
| Can you take a look at (check out) ____? | **Pouvez-vous regarder ____?** *poo-vay voo ruh-gahr-day* |
| ■ the brakes | **les freins** *lay fran* |
| ■ the bumper | **le pare-choc** *luh pahr-shohk* |
| ■ the exhaust | **l'échappement** *lay-shahp-mahn* |
| ■ the fender | **l'aile** *lehl* |
| ■ the gas tank | **le réservoir à essence** *luh ray-zehr-vwahr ah eh-ssahnss* |
| ■ the hood | **le capot** *luh kah-poh* |
| ■ the trunk | **la malle arrière** *lah mahl ah-ryehr* |
| What's the matter? | **Qu'est-ce qui ne va pas?** *kehss kee nuh vah pah* |
| Is it possible to (Can you) fix it today? | **Pouvez-vous la réparer aujourd'hui?** *poo-vay-voo lah ray-pah-ray oh-zhoor-dwee* |
| How long will it take? | **Combien de temps faudra-t-il?** *kohn-byan duh tahn foh-drah-teel* |
| Is everything O.K. now? | **Tout est arrangé (réparé) maintenant?** *too teh tah-rahn-zhay (ray-pah-ray) mant-nahn* |
| How much do I owe you? | **Combien vous dois-je?** *kohn-byan voo dwahzh* |

---

**TRAVEL TIP**

To avoid overcharges on long-distance telephone calls, inquire what your hotel would charge to make the call, then compare that with the cost of calling from a public phone. Usually, you can make a long-distance call from a booth located at the main post office.

# GENERAL INFORMATION

## TELLING TIME

| | | |
|---|---|---|
| What time is it? | **Quelle heure est-il?** *kehl uhr eh teel* | |
| It is ____. | **Il est ____.** *eel eh* | |
| ■ noon | **midi** *mee-dee* | |
| ■ 1:05 | **une heure cinq** *ewn-uhr sank* | |
| ■ 2:10 | **deux heures dix** *duh-zuhr deess* | |
| ■ 3:15 | **trois heures et quart** *trwah-zuhr ay kahr* | |
| ■ 4:20 | **quatre heures vingt** *kahtruh-uhr van* | |
| ■ 5:25 | **cinq heures vingt-cinq** *sank-uhr van sank* | |
| ■ 6:30 | **six heures et demie** *seez-uhr ay duh-mee* | |
| ■ 7:35 | **sept heures trente-cinq** *seht-uhr trahnt-sank* | |
| ■ 8:40 | **neuf heures moins vingt** *nuhv-uhr mwan van* | |
| ■ 9:45 | **dix heures moins le quart** *deez-uhr mwan luh kahr* | |
| ■ 10:50 | **onze heures moins dix** *ohnz uhr mwan deess* | |
| ■ 11:55 | **minuit moins cinq** *mee-nwee mwan sank* | |
| ■ 8:00 | **huit heures** *weet-uhr* | |
| ■ 2:30 | **deux heures et demie** *duhz-uhr ay duh-mee* | |
| ■ 7:15 | **sept heures et quart** *seht-uhr ay kahr* | |

## EXPRESSIONS OF TIME

| At what time ____? | À quelle heure ____? | *ah kehl-uhr____?* |
|---|---|---|
| When? | **Quand?** | *kahn?* |
| at ____ o'clock | **à ____ heures** | *ah ____ uhr* |
| at exactly noon | **à midi précis** | *ah mee-dee pray-ssee* |
| at exactly 5 o'clock | **à cinq heures précises** | *ah sank uhr pray-sseez* |
| in an hour | **dans une heure** | *dahn zewn-uhr* |
| in 2 hours | **dans deux heures** | *dahn duhz-uhr* |
| not before 2 a.m. | **pas avant deux heures du matin** | *pah zah-vahn duhz-uhr dew mah-tan* |
| after 3 p.m. | **après trois heures de l'après-midi** | *ah-preh trwah-zuhr duh lah-preh mee-dee* |
| at about 9 p.m. | **vers neuf heures du soir** | *vehr nuhv-uhr dew swahr* |
| between 8 and 9 o'clock | **entre huit et neuf heures** | *ahn-truh weet ay nuhv-uhr* |
| until 5 o'clock | **jusqu'à cinq heures** | *zhewss-kah sank uhr* |
| since what time ____? | **depuis quelle heure ____?** | *duh-pwee kehl uhr* |
| since 7 o'clock | **depuis sept heures** | *duh-pwee seht uhr* |

| | | |
|---|---|---|
| per hour | **par heure** | *pahr uhr* |
| three hours ago | **il y a trois heures** | *eel yah trwah-zuhr* |
| early | **tôt** | *toh* |
| | **de bonne heure** | *duh bohn-uhr* |
| late | **tard** | *tahr* |
| late (in arriving) | **en retard** | *ah<u>n</u> ruh-tahr* |
| on, in time | **à l'heure** | *ah luhr* |
| noon | **midi** | *mee-dee* |
| midnight | **minuit** | *mee-nwee* |
| in the morning | **le matin** | *luh mah-ta<u>n</u>* |
| in the afternoon | **l'après-midi** | *lah-preh mee-dee* |
| in the evening | **le soir** | *luh swahr* |
| at night | **la nuit** | *lah nwee* |
| second | **une seconde** | *ewn suh-goh<u>n</u>d* |
| minute | **une minute** | *ewn mee-newt* |
| hour | **une heure** | *ewn uhr* |
| a quarter of an hour | **un quart d'heure** | *uh<u>n</u> kahr duhr* |
| a half hour | **une demi-heure** | *ewn duh-mee uhr* |

Official time is based on the 24-hour clock. You will find train schedules and other such times expressed in terms of a point within the 24-hour sequence.

| | | |
|---|---|---|
| The train leaves at 15:30. | **Le train part à 15:30.** | *luh tran pahr ah kanz-uhr trahnt* |
| The time is now 21:15. | **Il est maintenant 21 heures 15.** | *eel eh mant-nahn van-tay-ewn uhr kanz* |

## DAYS OF THE WEEK

| | | |
|---|---|---|
| What day is today? | **Quel jour est-ce aujourd'hui?** | *kehl zhoor ess oh-zhoor-dwee* |
| | **Quel jour sommes-nous aujourd'hui?** | *kehl zhoor sohm noo oh-zhoor-dwee* |
| Today is ____. | **C'est aujourd'hui ____.** | *seh toh-zhoor-dwee* |
| | **Nous sommes ____** | *noo sohm* |
| Monday | **lundi** | *luhn-dee* |
| Tuesday | **mardi** | *mahr-dee* |
| Wednesday | **mercredi** | *mehr-kruh-dee* |
| Thursday | **jeudi** | *zhuh-dee* |
| Friday | **vendredi** | *vahn-druh-dee* |
| Saturday | **samedi** | *sahm-dee* |
| Sunday | **dimanche** | *dee-mahnsh* |

NOTE: In French, the names of the days and the months and seasons are written in small letters.

| | | |
|---|---|---|
| last Monday | **lundi dernier** | *luhn-dee dehr-nyay* |
| the day before | **la veille** | *lah vehy* |

| | | |
|---|---|---|
| the day before yesterday | **avant-hier** | *ah-vah<u>n</u>-tyehr* |
| yesterday | **hier** | *yehr* |
| today | **aujourd'hui** | *oh-zhoor-dwee* |
| tomorrow | **demain** | *duh-ma<u>n</u>* |
| the day after tomorrow | **après-demain** | *ah-preh-duh-ma<u>n</u>* |
| the next day | **le lendemain** | *luh lah<u>n</u>-duh-ma<u>n</u>* |
| next Monday | **lundi prochain** | *luh<u>n</u>-dee proh-sha<u>n</u>* |
| the day | **le jour** | *luh zhoor* |
| 2 days ago | **il y a deux jours** | *eel-yah duh zhoor* |
| in 2 days | **dans deux jours** | *dah<u>n</u> duh zhoor* |
| every day | **tous les jours** | *too lay zhoor* |
| day off | **(le) jour de congé** | *(luh) zhoor duh koh<u>n</u>-zhay* |
| holiday | **(le) jour de fête** | *(luh) zhoor duh feht* |
| birthday | **l'anniversaire** | *lah-nee-vehr-ssehr* |
| per day | **par jour** | *pahr zhoor* |
| during the day | **pendant la journée** | *pah<u>n</u>-dah<u>n</u> lah zhoor-nay* |
| from this day on | **dès aujourd'hui** | *deh zoh-zhoor-dwee* |
| the week | **la semaine** | *lah suh-mehn* |
| a week day | **un jour de semaine** | *uh<u>n</u> zhoor duh suh-mehn* |
| the week end | **le week-end** | *luh week-ehnd* |
| last week | **la semaine passée** | *lah suh-mehn pah-ssay* |
| this week | **cette semaine** | *seht suh-mehn* |
| next week | **la semaine prochaine** | *lah suh-mehn proh-shehn* |

| a week from today | **d'aujourd'hui en huit** | *doh-zhoor-dwee ahn weet* |
|---|---|---|
| 2 weeks from tomorrow | **de demain en quinze** | *duh duh-man ahn kanz* |
| during the week | **pendant la semaine** | *pahn-dahn lah suh-mehn* |

## MONTHS OF THE YEAR

| January | **janvier** | *zhan-vee-yay* |
|---|---|---|
| February | **février** | *fay-vree-yay* |
| March | **mars** | *mahrss* |
| April | **avril** | *ah-vreel* |
| May | **mai** | *meh* |
| June | **juin** | *zhwan* |
| July | **juillet** | *zhwee-yeh* |
| August | **août** | *oo or oot* |
| September | **septembre** | *sehp-tahn-bruh* |
| October | **octobre** | *ohk-toh-bruh* |
| November | **novembre** | *noh-vahn-bruh* |
| December | **décembre** | *day-ssahn-bruh* |
| the month | **le mois** | *luh mwah* |
| 2 months ago | **il y a deux mois** | *eel yah duh mwah* |
| last month | **le mois dernier** | *luh mwah dehr-nyay* |
| this month | **ce mois** | *suh mwah* |
| next month | **le mois prochain** | *luh mwah proh-shan* |
| during the month of | **pendant le mois de** | *pahn-dahn luh mwah duh* |

| since the month of | **depuis le mois de** | *duh-pwee luh mwah duh* |
|---|---|---|
| for the month of | **pour le mois de** | *poor luh mwah duh* |
| every month | **tous les mois** | *too lay mwah* |
| per month | **par mois** | *pahr mwah* |
| What is today's date? | **Quelle est la date d'aujourd'hui?** *kehl ay lah daht doh-zhoor-dwee?* | |
| Today is ____ . | **C'est aujourd'hui ____ .** *seht oh-zhoor-dwee* | |
| Monday, May 1 | **lundi, le premier mai** *luhn-dee luh pruh-myay meh* | |
| Tuesday, June 2 | **mardi, le deux juin** *mahr-dee luh duh zhwan* | |

NOTE: Use the ordinal number only for the first of the month.

| the year | **l'an/l'année** | *lahn/lah-nay* |
|---|---|---|
| per year | **par an** | *pahr ahn* |
| all year | **toute l'année** | *toot lah-nay* |
| every year | **chaque année** | *shahk ah-nay* |
| during the year | **pendant l'année** | *pahn-dahn lah-nay* |

## THE FOUR SEASONS

| spring | **le printemps** | *luh pran-tahn* |
|---|---|---|
| summer | **l'été** | *lay-tay* |
| autumn | **l'automne** | *loh-tohn* |
| winter | **l'hiver** | *lee-vehr* |
| in the spring | **au printemps** | *oh pran-tahn* |
| in the summer | **en été** | *ahn-nay-tay* |
| in the autumn | **en automne** | *ahn-noh-tohn* |
| in the winter | **en hiver** | *ahn nee-vehr* |

## WEATHER

| | | |
|---|---|---|
| What is the weather like? | **Quel temps fait-il?** | *kehl tahn feh-teel* |
| It is beautiful. | **Il fait beau.** | *eel feh boh* |
| It is hot. | **Il fait chaud.** | *eel feh shoh* |
| It is sunny. | **Il fait du soleil.** | *eel feh dew soh-lehy* |
| It is bad. | **Il fait mauvais.** | *eel feh moh-veh* |
| It is cold. | **Il fait froid.** | *eel feh frwah* |
| It is cool. | **Il fait frais.** | *eel feh freh* |
| It is windy. | **Il fait du vent.** | *eel feh dew vahn* |
| It is foggy. | **Il fait du brouillard.** | *eel feh dew broo-yahr* |
| It is snowing. | **Il neige.** | *eel nehzh* |
| It is raining. | **Il pleut.** | *eel pluh* |

## TEMPERATURE

The average annual daily temperatures in Paris in Fahrenheit and Centigrade are:

| MONTH | °F | °C |
|---|---|---|
| January | 42° | 5° |
| February | 45° | 7° |
| March | 54° | 12° |
| April | 61° | 16° |
| May | 68° | 20° |
| June | 73° | 23° |
| July | 77° | 25° |
| August | 75° | 23° |
| September | 70° | 21° |
| October | 61° | 16° |
| November | 50° | 10° |
| December | 44° | 6° |

| What heat! | **Quelle chaleur!** *kehl shah-luhr* |
| What cold! | **Quel froid!** *kehl frwah* |

## TEMPERATURE CONVERSIONS

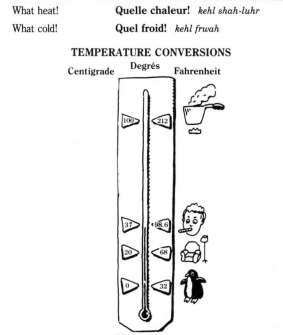

To change Fahrenheit to Centigrade: Subtract 32 and multiply by $\frac{5}{9}$.

To change Centigrade to Fahrenheit: Multiply by $\frac{9}{5}$ and add 32.

## PUBLIC HOLIDAYS AND CELEBRATIONS

| Jan. 1 | Le Jour de l'An<br>Le Nouvel An | New Year's Day |
| May 1 | La Fête du Travail | Labor Day |

| July 14 | La Fête Nationale | Bastille Day |
| Aug. 15 | L'Assomption | Assumption Day |
| Nov. 1 | La Toussaint | All Saints' Day |
| Nov. 2 | Le Jour des Morts | All Souls' Day |
| Nov. 11 | L'Armistice | Armistice Day |
| Dec. 25 | Noël | Christmas |
| February | Le Carnaval | Carnival |
| Last day of carnival | Le Mardi gras | Mardi-Gras |
| Mar/Apr | Les Rameaux | Palm Sunday |
| Mar/Apr | Le Vendredi-Saint | Good Friday |
| Mar/Apr | Pâques | Easter |
| Mar/Apr | Le Dimanche de Quasimodo | 1st Sunday after Easter |
| 40 days after Easter | L'Ascension | Ascension Thursday |
| 7 Mondays after Easter | Lundi de la Pentecôte | Whit Monday |
| May | La Fête de Jeanne d'Arc | Feast of Joan of Arc |

## COUNTRIES AND NATIONALITIES

| Where are you from? | **D'où êtes-vous?** | *doo eht voo* |
| I am from ____. | **Je suis de ____.** | *zhuh swee duh* |
| I am ____. | **Je suis ____.** | *zhuh swee* |

NOTE: The feminine form of the adjective is indicated after the masculine form. For this form remember to pronounce the last consonant.

|  | COUNTRY | NATIONALITY |
|---|---|---|
| *Africa | **l'Afrique** _lah-freek_ | **africain/e** _ah-free-kan/kehn_ |
| Asia | **l'Asie** _lah-zee_ | **asiatique** _ah-zyah-teek_ |
| Australia | **l'Australie** _loh-strah-lee_ | **australien/ne** _oh-strah-lyan/lyehn_ |
| Europe | **L'Europe** _lew-rohp_ | **européen/ne** _ew-roh-pay-an/ehn_ |
| N. America | **L'Amérique du Nord** _lah-may-reek dew nohr_ | **américain/e** _ah-may-ree-kan/ehn_ |
| S. America | **L'Amérique du Sud** _lah-may-reek dew sewd_ | **sud-américain/e** _sewd-ah-may-ree-kan/ ehn_ |
| Austria | **L'Autriche** _loh-treesh_ | **autrichien/ne** _oh-tree-shyan/shyehn_ |
| Belgium | **La Belgique** _lah behl-zheek_ | **belge** _behlzh_ |
| Canada | **Le Canada** _luh kah-nah-dah_ | **canadien/ne** _kah-nah-dyan/dyehn_ |
| China | **La Chine** _lah sheen_ | **chinois/e** _shee-nwah/nwahz_ |
| Denmark | **Le Danemark** _luh dahn-mahrk_ | **danois/e** _dah-nwah/nwahz_ |
| E. Germany | **L'Allemagne de l'Est** _lahl-mah-nyuh duh lehst_ | **allemand/e** _ahl-mahn/mahnd_ |
| England | **L'Angleterre** _lahn-gluh-tehr_ | **anglais/e** _ahn-gleh/glehz_ |

NOTE: When nationality refers to a person (noun) it is capitalized, i.e., **Un(e) Africain(e) parle français.** When the nationality is used as an adjective it begins with a lower case letter, i.e., **C'est un pays africain.**

| | COUNTRY | NATIONALITY |
|---|---|---|
| Finland | **la Finlande**<br>*lah feen-lah<u>nd</u>* | **finlandais/e**<br>*feen-lah<u>n</u>-deh/dehz* |
| France | **la France**<br>*lah Frah<u>nss</u>* | **français/e**<br>*frahn-sseh/sehz* |
| Greece | **la Grèce**<br>*lah grehss* | **grec/que**<br>*grehk* |
| Haiti | **Haïti**<br>*ahy-ee-tee* | **haïtien/ne**<br>*ahy-ee-ssya<u>n</u>/ssyehn* |
| India | **l'Inde**<br>*f. la<u>nd</u>* | **indien/ne**<br>*a<u>n</u>-dya<u>n</u>/dyehn* |
| Ireland | **l'Irlande**<br>*f. leer-lah<u>nd</u>* | **irlandais/e**<br>*eer-lah<u>n</u>-deh/dehz* |
| Israel | **Israël**<br>*m. eez-rah-ehl* | **israélite**<br>*eez-rah-ay-leet* |
| Italy | **l'Italie**<br>*f. lee-tah-lee* | **italien/ne**<br>*ee-tah-lya<u>n</u>/lyehn* |
| Japan | **le Japon**<br>*luh zhah-poh<u>n</u>* | **japonais/e**<br>*zhah-poh-neh/nehz* |
| Luxem-<br>bourg | **le Luxembourg**<br>*luh lewkss-ah<u>n</u>-boor* | **luxembourgeois/e**<br>*lewkss-ah<u>n</u>-boor-<br>zhwah/zhwahz* |
| Morocco | **le Maroc**<br>*luh mah-rohk* | **marocain/e**<br>*mah-roh-ka<u>n</u>/kehn* |
| Norway | **la Norvège**<br>*lah nohr-vehzh* | **norvégien/ne**<br>*nohr-vay-zhya<u>n</u>/<br>zhyehn* |
| Portugal | **le Portugal**<br>*luh pohr-tew-gahl* | **portugais/e**<br>*pohr-tew-geh/gehz* |
| Scotland | **l'Écosse**<br>*lay-kohs* | **écossais/e**<br>*ay-koh-sseh/ssehz* |
| Senegal | **le Sénégal**<br>*luh say-nay-gahl* | **sénégalais/e**<br>*say-nay-gah-leh/lehz* |
| Soviet<br>Union | **l'Union Soviétique**<br>*lew-nyoh<u>n</u> soh-vee-ay-<br>teek* | **Sovietique**<br>*soh-vee-ay-teek* |

| | COUNTRY | NATIONALITY |
|---|---|---|
| Spain | **l'Espagne** *f. lehss-pah-nyuh* | **espagnol/e** *ehss-pah-nyohl* |
| Sweden | **la Suède** *lah swehd* | **suédois/e** *sway-dwah/dwahz* |
| Switzer-land | **la Suisse** *lah sweess* | **suisse** *sweess* |
| Tunisia | **la Tunisie** *lah tew-nee-zee* | **Tunisien/ne** *tew-nee-zyan/zyehn* |
| U.S. | **les États-Unis** *layz ay-tah-zew-nee* | **américain/e** *ah-may-ree-kan/kehn* |
| Wales | **le pays de Galles** *luh pay-ee duh gahl* | **gallois/e** *gahl-wah/wahz* |
| W. Germany | **L'Allemagne de l'Ouest** *lahl-mah-nyuh duh lwehsst* | **allemand/e** *ahl-mahn/mahnd* |

## DIRECTIONS

| the north | **le nord** | *luh nohr* |
|---|---|---|
| the south | **le sud** | *luh sewd* |
| the east | **l'est** | *lehsst* |
| the west | **l'ouest** | *lwehsst* |

## IMPORTANT SIGNS

| **À louer** | *ah loo-ay* | For rent, hire |
|---|---|---|
| **Ascenseur** | *ah-sahn-ssuhr* | Elevator |
| **Attention** | *ah-tahn-ssyohn* | Careful |
| **À vendre** | *ah vahn-druh* | For sale |

| Dames | *dahm* | Ladies |
| **Danger** | *dah<u>n</u>-zhay* | Danger |
| **Danger de mort** | *dah<u>n</u>-zhay duh mohr* | Danger of death |
| **Défense de** | *day-fah<u>n</u>ss duh* | Do not _____ |
| **Défense d'entrer** | *day-fah<u>n</u>ss dah<u>n</u>-tray* | Do not enter |
| **Défense de cracher** | *day-fah<u>n</u>ss duh krah-shay* | No spitting |
| **Défense de fumer** | *day-fah<u>n</u>ss duh few-may* | No smoking |
| **Défense de marcher sur l'herbe** | *day-fah<u>n</u>ss duh mahr-shay sewr lehrb* | Keep off the grass |
| **Eau non potable** | *oh noh<u>n</u> poh-tah-bluh* | Don't drink the water |
| **École** | *ay-kohl* | School |
| **Entrée** | *ah<u>n</u>-tray* | Entrance |
| **Entrée interdite** | *ah<u>n</u>-tray a<u>n</u>-tehr-deet* | No Entrance |
| **Entrée libre** | *ah<u>n</u>-tray lee-bruh* | Free Admission |
| **Fermé** | *fehr-may* | Closed |
| **Fumeurs** | *few-muhr* | Smokers |
| **Hommes** | *ohm* | Men |
| **Hôpital** | *oh-pee-tahl* | Hospital |
| **Horaire** | *oh-rehr* | Schedule |
| **Toilettes** | *twah-leht* | Washroom |
| **Libre** | *lee-bruh* | Free, Unoccupied |
| **Messieurs** | *meh-ssyuh* | Gentlemen |
| **Ne pas toucher** | *nuh pah too-shay* | Don't touch |

| Non fumeurs | *nohn few-muhr* | Non smokers |
| Occupé | *oh-kew-pay* | Occupied |
| Ouvert | *oo-vehr* | Open |
| Passage souter-rain | *pah-ssahzh soo-teh-ran* | Underground passage |
| Poussez | *poo-ssay* | Push |
| Privé | *pree-vay* | Private |
| Quai/Voie | *kay/vwah* | Track, Platform |
| Renseignements | *rahn-sseh-nyuh-mahn* | Information |
| Réservé | *ray-zehr-vay* | Reserved |
| Salle d'attente | *sahl dah-tahnt* | Waiting room |
| Soldes | *sohld* | Sales |
| Sonnez | *soh-nay* | Ring |
| Sortie | *sohr-tee* | Exit |
| Sortie de se-cours | *sohr-tee duh suh-koor* | Emergency exit |
| Stationnement interdit | *stah-ssyohn-mahn an-tehr-dee* | No parking |
| Tirez | *tee-ray* | Pull |
| Toilettes | *twah-leht* | Toilets |

## COMMON ABBREVIATIONS

| ACF | **Automobile Club de France** | Automobile Club of France |
| apr. J.-C. | **après Jésus-Christ** | A.D. |
| av. J.-C. | **avant Jésus-Christ** | B.C. |

| bd. | boulevard | boulevard |
|---|---|---|
| c.-à-d. | c'est-à-dire | that is to say, i.e. |
| CEE | Communauté économique européenne (Marché commun) | European Economic Community (Common Market) |
| CGT | Compagnie générale transatlantique | French Line |
| Cie. | compagnie | Company |
| EU | États-Unis | United States |
| h. | heure(s) | hour, o'clock |
| M. | Monsieur | Mr. |
| Mlle | Mademoiselle | Miss |
| MM | Messieurs | Gentlemen |
| Mme | Madame | Mrs. |
| ONU | Organisation des Nations Unies | United Nations |
| p. | page | page |
| p. ex. | par exemple | for example |
| P et T. | Postes et Télécommunications | Post Office and Tele-communications |
| RATP | Régie Autonome des Transports Parisiens | Paris Transport Authority |
| RD | Route Départementale | local road |
| RN | Route Nationale | national road |
| SA | Société anonyme | Ltd., Inc. |
| SI | Syndicat d'initiative | Tourist Information Office |
| SNCF | Société Nationale des Chemins de Fer Français | French National Railways |
| s.v.p. | s'il vous plaît | please |

## CENTIMETERS/INCHES

It is usually unnecessary to make exact conversions from your customary inches to the metric system used in France, but to give you an approximate idea of how they compare, we give you the following guide.

**Centimètres**

**Pouces**

To convert centimeters into inches, multiply by .39.
To convert inches into centimeters, multiply by 2.54.

## METERS/FEET

1 meter (**métre**) = 39.37 inches          1 foot = 0.3 meters
                     3.28 feet             1 yard = 0.9 meters
                     1.09 yards

How tall are you in meters? See for yourself.

| FEET, INCHES | | METERS + CENTIMETERS |
|---|---|---|
| 5 | | 1.52 |
| 5 | 1 | 1.54 |
| 5 | 2 | 1.57 |
| 5 | 3 | 1.59 |
| 5 | 4 | 1.62 |

| FEET, INCHES | | METERS + CENTIMETERS |
|---|---|---|
| 5 | 5 | 1.64 |
| 5 | 6 | 1.68 |
| 5 | 7 | 1.70 |
| 5 | 8 | 1.73 |
| 5 | 9 | 1.75 |
| 5 | 10 | 1.78 |
| 5 | 11 | 1.80 |
| 6 | | 1.83 |
| 6 | 1 | 1.85 |

## WHEN YOU WEIGH YOURSELF

1 kilogram (kilo) = 2.2 pounds
1 pound = 0.45 kilograms

| KILOGRAMS | POUNDS |
|---|---|
| 40 | 88 |
| 45 | 99 |
| 50 | 110 |
| 55 | 121 |
| 60 | 132 |
| 65 | 143 |
| 70 | 154 |
| 75 | 165 |
| 80 | 176 |
| 85 | 187 |
| 90 | 198 |
| 95 | 209 |
| 100 | 220 |

## LIQUID MEASUREMENTS

1 liter = 1.06 quarts
4 liters = 1.06 gallons

For quick, approximate conversions multiply the number of gallons by 4 to get liters **(litres).** Divide the number of liters by 4 to get gallons.

## USEFUL TELEPHONE NUMBERS

| | |
|---|---|
| **Wake-up Calls** | 10, then 13 |
| **Time** | 033.84.00 |
| **Weather** | 705.97.39 |
| **Road Conditions** | 553.05.29 |
| **Traffic** | 224.22.33 |
| **News** | 4631 |
| **Railroads** | 522.94.00 |
| **Post Office** | 380.64.00 |
| **Administration** | 306.82.00 |

## A MINI-DICTIONARY FOR BUSINESS TRAVELERS

| | | |
|---|---|---|
| **amount** | le montant | *luh moh<u>n</u>-tah<u>n</u>* |
| **appraise** | évaluer | *ay-vah-lew-ay* |
| **authorize** | autoriser | *oh-toh-ree-zay* |
| **authorized edition** | l'édition autorisée (f) | *lay-dee-ssyoh<u>n</u> oh-toh-ree-zay* |
| **bill** (noun) | la facture | *lah fahk-tewr* |
| **bill of exchange** | la lettre de change | *lah leh-truh duh shah<u>n</u>zh* |

| | | |
|---|---|---|
| **bill of lading** | le connaissement | *luh koh-nehss-mahn* |
| **bill of sale** | la lettre de vente | *lah leh-truh duh vahnt* |
| **business opera-tion** | ∎ l'affaire (f) | *lah-fehr* |
| | ∎ le commerce | *luh koh-mehrss* |
| **cash** (noun) | l'argent (m.) | *lahr-zhahn* |
| **to buy for cash** | payer comptant | *peh-yay kohn-tahn* |
| **to sell for cash** | vendre au comp-tant | *vahn-druh oh kohn-tahn* |
| **to cash a check** | toucher un chèque | *too-shay uhn shehk* |
| **certified check** | le chèque assuré | *luh shehk ah-ssew-ray* |
| **chamber of com-merce** | la chambre de commerce | *lah shahn-bruh duh koh-mehrss* |
| **compensation for damage** | le dédommagement | *luh day-doh-mahzh-mahn* |
| **competition** | la concurrence | *lah kohn-kew-rahnss* |
| **competitive price** | le prix de concur-rence | *luh pree duh kohn-kew-rahnss* |
| **contract** | le contrat | *luk kohn-trah* |
| **contractual obli-gations** | les obligations du contrat | *lay-zoh-blee-gah-ssyohn dew kohn-trah* |
| **controlling inter-est** | le droit d'autorité | *luh drwah doh-toh-ree-tay* |
| **co-owner** | le co-propriétaire | *luh koh-proh-pree-ay-tehr* |
| **co-partner** | le co-associé | *luh koh-ah-ssoh-ssyay* |

| | | |
|---|---|---|
| **down payment** | ■ l'acompte (m) | *lah kohnt* |
| | ■ payer en compte | *peh-yay ahn-kohnt* |
| **due** | ■ échu | *ay-shew* |
| | ■ arrivé à l'écheance | *ah-ree-vay ah lay-shay-ahnss* |
| **enterprise** | l'entreprise (f) | *lahn-truh-preez* |
| **expedite delivery** (of letters) | expédier la livraison | *ehkss-pay-dee-ay lah lee-vreh-zohn* |
| **expedite delivery** (of goods) | expédier la distribution | *ehkss-pay-dee-ay lah deess-tree-bew-ssyohn* |
| **expenses** | les frais (m. pl.) | *lay freh* |
| **goods** | ■ les produits | *lay proh-dwee* |
| | ■ les biens (m. pl.) | *lay byan* |
| **infringement of patent rights** | l'infraction de brevet d'invention | *lan-frahk-ssyohn duh bruh-veh dan-vahn-ssyohn* |
| **insurance against all risks** | l'assurance contre tous risques | *lah-ssew-rahnss kohn-truh too reessk* |
| **international law** | le droit international | *luh drwah an-tehr-nah-ssyohn-nahl* |
| **lawful possession** | la possession légitime | *lah poh-sseh-ssyohn lay-zhee-teem* |
| **lawsuit** | le procès | *luh proh-sseh* |
| **lawyer** | l'avocat | *lah-voh-kah* |
| **letter of credit** | la lettre de crédit | *lah leh-truh duh kreh-dee* |
| **mail-order business** | l'établissement de vente par correspondance (m.) | *lay-tah-bleess-mahn duh vahnt pahr koh-rehss-pohn-dahnss* |

| | | |
|---|---|---|
| **market-value** | le cours du marché | *luh koor dew mahr-shay* |
| **manager** | le gérant | *luh zhay-rah_n_* |
| **payment** | le versement | *luh vehrss-mah_n_* |
| **partial payment** | l'acompte (m) | *lah-koh_n_t* |
| **past due** | ■ arriéré | *ahr-yay-ray* |
| | ■ en retard | *ah_n_ ruh-tahr* |
| **post office box** | la boîte postale | *lah bwaht pohss-tahl* |
| **property** | ■ la propriété | *lah proh-pree-ay-tay* |
| | ■ les biens | *lay bya_n_* |
| **purchasing agent** | l'acquéreur | *lah-kay-ruhr* |
| **to put on the American market** | mettre au marché américain | *meh-truh oh mahr-shay ah-may-ree-ka_n_* |
| **sale** | la vente | *lah vah_n_t* |
| **to sell** | vendre | *vah_n_-druh* |
| **to send** | envoyer | *ah_n_-vwah-yay* |
| **to send back** | renvoyer | *rah_n_-vwah-yay* |
| **to send C.O.D.** | envoyer payable à l'arrivée | *ah_n_-vwah-yay peh-yah-bluh ah lah-ree-vay* |
| **shipment** | l'expédition (f.) | *lehkss-pay-dee-ssyoh_n_* |
| **tax** | l'impôt (m) | *la_n_-poh* |
| **tax-exempt** | exempt d'impôts | *ehg-zah_n_ da_n_-poh* |
| **sales tax** | la taxe de luxe | *lah tahkss duh lewkss* |

| | | |
|---|---|---|
| **value added tax** | la taxe sur la valeur ajoutée | *lah tahkss sewr lah vah-luhr ah-zhoo-tay* |
| **trade** | le commerce | *luh koh-mehrss* |
| **transact business** | faire des affaires | *fehr day-zah-fehr* |
| **transfer** | transférer | *trahnss-fay-ray* |
| **transportation charges** | les frais de transport | *lay freh duh trahnss-pohr* |
| **via** | par | *pahr* |
| **yield a profit** | rendre un bénéfice | *rahn-druh uhn bay-nay-feess* |

---

### TRAVEL TIP

If you have had to change your plans and cannot use your airline ticket, you can apply for a complete refund. Treat your ticket as if it were cash, and return it to your travel agent or to the airline for your money back. Note, however, that some charter tickets are nonrefundable. If you do not use the ticket, you have lost the money, but if you take out special flight insurance, you can collect your refund for that charter ticket from the insuring company.

# QUICK GRAMMAR GUIDE

## NOUNS

**1.** All nouns in French have a gender (masculine or feminine) and a number (singular or plural).
**2.** There is no easy way to determine gender, so a noun must be learned with its identifying article and its gender memorized.
**3.** To change a singular noun to the plural, an unpronounced *S* is usually added. Add nothing if the noun ends in *S, X,* or *Z.*

## ARTICLES

Articles agree in gender and number with the nouns they modify.

| DEFINITE ARTICLES (THE) | | | |
|---|---|---|---|
| | MASC. | | FEM. |
| SING. | LE | **le livre**<br>the book | LA | **la carte**<br>the map |
| PLUR. | LES | **les livres**<br>the books | LES | **les cartes**<br>the maps |

NOTE: LE and LA become L' before a noun beginning with a vowel or an H: **l'avion, l'homme**

| INDEFINITE ARTICLES (A, AN, SOME) | | | |
|---|---|---|---|
| | MASC. | | FEM. |
| SING. | UN | **un restaurant**<br>a restaurant | UNE | **une voiture**<br>a car |
| PLUR. | DES | **des restaurants**<br>some restaurants | DES | **des voitures**<br>some cars |

| THE PARTITIVE (SOME, ANY) | | |
|---|---|---|
| **SINGULAR** | | |
| DU (de + le) + masc. sing. noun with consonant | **du pain** | some bread |
| DE LA + fem. sing. noun with consonant | **de la glace** | some ice cream |
| DE L' + masc. or fem. sing. noun with vowel or "H" | **de l'eau** | some water |
| **PLURAL** | | |
| DES (de + les) + all plural nouns | **des glaces** | some ice creams |
| **NEGATIVE** | | |
| DE is used in negative sentences | **Je n'ai pas d'argent.** | I don't have any money. |
| | **Elle n'a pas de cartes.** | She doesn't have any maps. |

NOTE: DE becomes D' before a vowel or an H.

## ADJECTIVES

**1.** Adjectives agree in number and gender with the nouns they modify.
**2.** To form the feminine of most adjectives, add E to the masculine form. If the masculine form ends in E, add nothing to get the feminine form.
**3.** To form the plural of most adjectives, add S to the singular form. If the singular form ends in S, add nothing to get the plural form.

**un livre intéressant**          **une femme intéressante**
**des livres intéressants**       **des femmes intéressantes**

**4.** Adjectives usually follow the nouns they modify. A few common exceptions that precede the noun are: **bon/bonne** good; **grand/grande** big; **jeune** young; **joli/jolie** pretty; **petit/petite** small.

**un grand appartement**

## POSSESSIVE ADJECTIVES

Possessive adjectives agree in number and gender with the object possessed, not with the possessor. They precede the noun.

| ENGLISH | MASC. SING. OR FEM. SING. WITH VOWEL | FEM. SING. WITH CONS. | ALL PLURALS |
|---|---|---|---|
| my | mon | ma | mes |
| your | ton | ta | tes |
| his/her/its | son | sa | ses |
| our | notre | notre | nos |
| your | votre | votre | vos |
| their | leur | leur | leurs |

EXAMPLES:

| **mon ami(e)** | my friend | *ami(e) starts with vowel |
|---|---|---|
| **ma chemise** | my shirt | *chemise is fem. sing. with cons. |
| **mes chemises** | my shirts | |
| **ton gant** | your glove | *gant is masc. sing. |
| **tes gants** | your gloves | |

NOTE: **sa valise** can mean his or her valise
   **son argent** can mean his or her money
   **ses parents** can mean his or her parents.

Another way to show possession is by using the preposition DE (OF) or any of its forms:

| SINGULAR | PLURAL |
|---|---|
| DU  masculine noun with consonant | DES  all nouns |
| DE LA  feminine noun with consonant | |
| DE L'  masculine or feminine noun with vowel | |
| DE  proper noun (name) | |

EXAMPLES:

| | |
|---|---|
| **la valise de Paul** | Paul's valise |
| **l'argent de la femme** | the woman's money |
| **la soupe du garçon** | the boy's soup |
| **la chemise de l'homme** | the man's shirt |
| **les cartes des touristes** | the tourists' maps |

## DEMONSTRATIVE ADJECTIVES (THIS/THAT; THESE/THOSE)

| SINGULAR | |
|---|---|
| CE  masc. noun with consonant | THIS/THAT |
| CET  masc. noun with vowel or H | THIS/THAT |
| CETTE  fem. noun | THIS/THAT |

| PLURAL | |
|---|---|
| CES  all nouns | THESE/THOSE |

EXAMPLES:

| | |
|---|---|
| **ce livre** | this/that book |
| **cet hôtel** | this/that hotel |
| **cette fille** | this/that girl |
| **cette eau** | this/that water *eau is fem. |
| **ces arbres** | these/those trees |

## PRONOUNS

*Subject* pronouns come at the beginning of the sentence before the verb.

**Je parle**          I speak

**Nous sommes**       We are

*Direct object* pronouns come before the verb except in an affirmative command* when they come after the verb.

**Il la voit.**       He sees it.

**Prenez-les!***      Take them!

*Indirect object* pronouns come before the verb except in an affirmative command* when they come after the verb.

**Elle lui parle.**   She speaks to him (to her).

**Écrivez-leur!***    Write to them.

*Object of a preposition* is a pronoun that comes after a preposition.

**Après vous.**       After you.

**Avec eux.**         With them

| SUBJECT | DIRECT OBJECT | INDIRECT OBJECT | OBJECT OF A PREPOSITION |
|---------|---------------|-----------------|-------------------------|
| **Je** I | **me** me | **me** to me | **moi** me |
| **Tu** You* | **te** you | **te** to you | **toi** you |
| **Il** He | **le** him | **lui** to him | **lui** him |
| **Elle** She | **la** her | **lui** to her | **elle** her |
| **Nous** We | **nous** us | **nous** to us | **nous** us |
| **Vous** You* | **vous** you | **vous** to you | **vous** you |
| **Ils** They m. | **les** them | **leur** to them | **eux** them |
| **Elles** They f. | **les** them | **leur** to them | **elles** them |
| **On** One | | | |

*NOTE: Use **tu** for familiar conversation with a relative, a young child or a friend. **tu** is a singular subject pronoun only.

Use **vous** to be polite and to show respect when speaking to people with whom you are not intimate. **Vous** is a singular or plural subject or object pronoun and is used when addressing a group of people.

## REGULAR VERBS

Regular verbs follow a specific pattern of conjugation (changing the verb to agree with the subject pronoun) depending upon the infinitive ending.

| PRESENT TENSE | | | |
|---|---|---|---|
| | –ER ENDING | –IR ENDING | –RE ENDING |
| SUBJECT | PARLER | FINIR | VENDRE |
| | to speak | to finish | to sell |
| **Je** | parle | finis | vends |
| **Tu** | parles | finis | vends |
| **Il/Elle** | parle | finit | vend |
| **Nous** | parlons | finissons | vendons |
| **Vous** | parlez | finissez | vendez |
| **Ils/Elles** | parlent | finissent | vendent |
| COMMANDS | Parlez! | Finissez! | Vendez! |

In order to conjugate a verb, the infinitive ending (-ER, -IR, -RE) must be removed and replaced by the appropriate ending found in the above table.

EXAMPLES:

| | | |
|---|---|---|
| **désirer** to desire, want | I desire | **Je désire** |
| **choisir** to choose | We choose | **Nous choisissons** |
| **attendre** to wait for | You wait for | **Vous attendez** |

### COMMON VERBS IN THE –ER FAMILY

| | |
|---|---|
| **admirer** to admire | **donner** to give |
| **aider** to help | **écouter** to listen to |
| **aimer** to like, to love | **entrer** to enter |
| **chercher** to look for | **fermer** to close |
| **coûter** to cost | **fumer** to smoke |
| **déjeuner** to eat lunch | **marcher** to walk |
| **demander** to ask | **montrer** to show |
| **dépenser** to spend money | **penser** to think |
| **désirer** to wish, to desire | **regarder** to look at |
| **dîner** to eat dinner | **tourner** to turn |
| | **trouver** to find |

### COMMON VERBS IN THE –IR FAMILY

| | |
|---|---|
| **choisir** | to choose |
| **grossir** | to become fat |
| **maigrir** | to become thin |

### COMMON VERBS IN THE –RE FAMILY

| | |
|---|---|
| **attendre** | to wait for |
| **descendre** | to descend, to go down |
| **entendre** | to hear |
| **répondre (à)** | to answer |

NOTE: Je + verb beginning with a vowel = J'

**Je + écoute = J'écoute**

## HELPING VERBS

The auxiliary verbs **avoir** (to have) and **être** (to be) must be memorized. They are used by themselves in the present or with other verbs to form compound tenses.

| AVOIR—to have | |
| --- | --- |
| J'ai  I have | Nous avons  We have |
| Tu as  you have | Vous avez  You have |
| Il a  he has | Ils ont  They have |
| Elle a  she has | Elles ont  They have |

| ÊTRE—to be | |
| --- | --- |
| Je suis  I am | Nous sommes  We are |
| Tu es  You are | Vous êtes  You are |
| Il est  He is | Ils sont  They are |
| Elle est  She is | Elles sont  They are |

## IRREGULAR VERBS

Irregular verbs must be memorized. Here are some common irregular verbs that you will find helpful.

| PRESENT TENSE | | | |
| --- | --- | --- | --- |
| SUBJECT | ALLER<br>to go | FAIRE<br>to make, do | POUVOIR<br>can, be able to |
| Je | vais | fais | peux |
| Tu | vas | fais | peux |
| Il/Elle | va | fait | peut |
| Nous | allons | faisons | pouvons |
| Vous | allez | faites | pouvez |
| Ils/Elles | vont | font | peuvent |
| COMMAND | Allez! | Faites! | |

| PRESENT TENSE | |
|---|---|
| **VOIR**<br>to see | **VOULOIR**<br>to wish, want |
| **vois** | **veux** |
| **vois** | **veux** |
| **voit** | **veut** |
| **voyons** | **voulons** |
| **voyez** | **voulez** |
| **voient** | **veulent** |
| Voyez! | |

The following verbs will also be helpful to you in a more limited sense.

| SUBJECT | BOIRE<br>to drink | DIRE<br>to say | ÉCRIRE<br>to write |
|---|---|---|---|
| **Je** | **bois** | **dis** | **écris** |
| **Vous** | **buvez** | **dites** | **écrivez** |
| **COMMAND** | **Buvez!** | **Dites!** | **Écrivez!** |

| SUBJECT | METTRE<br>to put (on) | OUVRIR<br>to open | RECEVOIR<br>to receive |
|---|---|---|---|
| **Je** | **mets** | **ouvre** | **reçois** |
| **Vous** | **mettez** | **ouvrez** | **recevez** |
| **COMMAND** | **Mettez!** | **Ouvrez!** | **Recevez!** |

## REFLEXIVE VERBS

Reflexive verbs show that the subject is acting upon itself. Reflexive verbs consist of a reflexive pronoun and a conjugated verb. Reflexive pronouns agree with their subjects.

| | | | |
|---|---|---|---|
| **JE** | **ME** | **NOUS** | **NOUS** |
| **TU** | **TE** | **VOUS** | **VOUS** |

| IL  SE | ILS  SE |
|--------|---------|
| ELLE  SE | ELLES  SE |

NOTE: ME, TE, and SE become M', T', and S' before a vowel or an H.

Verbs that are reflexive in French are not necessarily reflexive in English. Common reflexive verbs are:

| | |
|---|---|
| **s'appeler** | to call oneself, to be called |
| **s'asseoir** | to sit down |
| **se coucher** | to go to bed |
| **se dépêcher** | to hurry up |
| **s'habiller** | to get dressed |
| **se laver** | to wash oneself |
| **se lever** | to get up |
| **se peigner** | to comb one's hair |
| **se promener** | to go for a walk |
| **se raser** | to shave oneself |
| **se réveiller** | to wake up |

Follow this formula:

| SUBJECT | REFLEXIVE PRONOUN | VERB |
|---------|-------------------|------|
| **Je** | **m'** | **appelle** My name is (I call myself) |
| **Nous** | **nous** | **réveillons** We wake up |
| **Tu  NE** | **te** | **rases PAS** You don't shave |

NOTE: A verb is reflexive only if the subject is acting upon itself. If the subject is acting upon another person or thing, the verb is NOT reflexive.

EXAMPLE:

| | |
|---|---|
| **Je me lave.** | I wash myself. |
| **Je lave l'enfant.** | I wash the child. |
| **Je lave la voiture.** | I wash the car. |

The infinitive of a reflexive verb is always preceded by the pronoun SE.

## NEGATIVES

Form the negative by putting NE before the conjugated verb, and PAS (not) after the verb.

### OTHER NEGATIVE CONSTRUCTIONS

**NE . . . RIEN** nothing

**NE . . . JAMAIS** never

**NE . . . PERSONNE** nobody

**NE . . . PLUS** no longer

NOTE: NE becomes N' before a vowel or H.

| | |
|---|---|
| **Il parle anglais.** | **Il ne parle pas anglais.** |
| He speaks English. | He doesn't speak English. |
| **Je veux manger.** | **Je ne veux plus manger.** |
| I want to eat. | I don't want to eat any more. |
| **Elle écoute.** | **Elle n'écoute rien.** |
| She listens. | She doesn't listen to anything. |

## QUESTIONS

The two most common ways to ask a question are:

**1.** Putting EST-CE QUE *ehss-kuh* in front of a phrase.

| | |
|---|---|
| **Vous parlez anglais.** | **Est-ce que vous parlez anglais?** |

**2.** Invert the order of the subject pronoun (ONLY) and the verb.

**Vous parlez anglais.  Parlez-vous anglais?**

NOTE: a) Do NOT invert with the pronoun JE. Use EST-CE QUE.
   b) If the verb ends in a vowel and the pronoun begins with a vowel (**il** or **elle**) then **-t-** must separate the two vowels.

**Il parle anglais.**   **Parle-t-il anglais?**

**Elle a une voiture.**   **A-t-elle une voiture?**

## PREPOSITIONS

Study the list of the following prepositions. The prepositions **à** (to, at) and **de** (of, from) have contracted forms.

| | |
|---|---|
| a + le = au | de + le = du |
| à + les = aux | de + les = des |
| à la (no change) | de la (no change) |
| à l' (no change) | de l' (no change) |

EXAMPLES:
| | |
|---|---|
| to the movies | **au cinéma** |
| to the museums | **aux musées** |
| to the kitchen | **à la cuisine** |
| | |
| of the boy | **du garçon** |
| of the children | **des enfants** |
| of the year | **de l'année** |

### COMMON PREPOSITIONS

| | | |
|---|---|---|
| about | **de** | *duh* |
| according to | **selon** | *suh-lohn* |
| across | **à travers** | *ah trah-vehr* |
| after | **après** | *ah-preh* |

| among | **parmi** | *pahr-mee* |
| around | **autour de** | *oh-toor duh* |
| at | **à** | *ah* |
| at the house of | **chez** | *shay* |
| before | **avant** | *ah-vahn* |
| behind | **derrière** | *deh-ryehr* |
| between | **entre** | *ahn-truh* |
| by | **par** | *pahr* |
| down/downstairs | **en bas** | *ahn bah* |
| during | **pendant** | *pahn-dahn* |
| except | **sauf** | *sohf* |
| for | **pour** | *poor* |
| from | **de** | *duh* |
| in | **dans, en** | *dahn, ahn* |
| in front of | **devant** | *duh-vahn* |
| in order to | **pour** | *poor* |
| inside | **dedans** | *duh-dahn* |
| on | **sur** | *sewr* |
| opposite | **en face de** | *ahn fahss duh* |
| outside | **dehors** | *duh-ohr* |
| through | **à travers** | *ah trah-vehr* |
| to | **à** | *ah* |
| towards | **vers** | *vehr* |
| under | **sous** | *soo* |
| until | **jusqu'à** | *zhewss-kah* |
| up/upstairs | **en haut** | *ahn oh* |
| with | **avec** | *ah-vehk* |
| without | **sans** | *sahn* |

# ENGLISH-FRENCH DICTIONARY*

## A

**a, an** un (m.) *uhn*, une (f.) *ewn*

**able: to be able** pouvoir *poo-vwahr*

**about** à peu près *ah-puh-preh*; environ *ahn-vee-rohn*

**above** dessus *duh-ssew*

**abroad** à l'étranger *ah lay-trahn-zhay*

**according to** selon *suh-lohn*

**ache (noun)** le mal *luh mahl*; **(head)** mal de tête *mahl duh teht*; **(stomach)** mal d'estomac *mahl dehss-toh-mah*; **(tooth)** mal de dents *mahl duh dahn*

**acquaintance: make the . . . of** faire la connaissance de *fehr lah koh-neh-ssahnss duh*

**across** à travers *ah trah-vehr*

**add** ajouter *ah-zhoo-tay*

**address** une adresse *ewn ah-drehss*

**adjust** arranger *ah-rahn-zhay*

**advertisement** une réclame *ewn ray-klahm*; une annonce *ewn ah-nohnss*

**advice** l'avis (m.) *lah-vee*; le conseil *luh kohn-ssehy*

**afraid: to be afraid of** avoir peur de *ah-vwahr puhr duh*

**after** après *ah-preh*

**afternoon** l'après-midi (m.) *lah-preh mee-dee*

**again** encore une fois *ahn-kohr ewn fwah*

**against** contre *kohn-truh*

**agency** une agence *ewn ah-zhahnss*; **(travel)** une agence de voyage *ewn ah-zhahnss duh vwah-yahzh*

**ago** il y a + time *eel yah*

**agree** être d'accord *eh-truh dah-kohr*

**air conditioner** le climatiseur *luh klee-mah-tee-zuhr*

**air mail** par avion *pahr ah-vyohn*

**airplane** un avion *uhn nah-vyohn*

**airport** un aéroport *uhn nahy-roh-pohr*

**alcohol** l'alcool (m.) *lahl-kol*

**all** tout (m.), toute (f.) *too, toot*

**alley** la ruelle *lah rew-ehl*

**almond** une amande *ewn ah-mahnd*

**almost** presque *prehss-kuh*

**alone** seul(e) *suhl*

**already** déjà *day-zhah*

**also** aussi *oh-ssee*

**always** toujours *too-zhoor*

**ambulance** une ambulance *ewn ahn-bew-lahnss*

**among** parmi *pahr-mee*

**and** et *ay*

**ankle** la cheville *lah shuh-vee*

**annoy** gêner *zheh-nay*; ennuyer *ahn-nwee-yay*

**answer (noun)** la réponse *lah ray-pohnss*; **(verb)** répondre *ray-pohn-druh*

**antiseptic** un antiseptique *uhn nahn-tee-ssehp-teek*

**any** ne . . . aucun(e) *nuh . . . oh-kuhn, oh-kewn*

*Underscored letters indicate nasals.

**appendicitis** l'appendicite *lah-pah<u>n</u>-dee-sseet*

**apple** la pomme *lah pohm*

**apricot** un abricot *uh<u>n</u> nah-bree-koh*

**argument** la dispute *lah deess-pewt*

**arm** le bras *luh brah*

**around** autour de *oh-toor duh*

**arrival** l'arrivée (f.) *lah-ree-vay*

**artichoke** l'artichaut *lahr-tee-shoh*

**ashtray** le cendrier *luh ssah<u>n</u>-dree-yay*

**ask** demander *duh-mah<u>n</u>-day*

**asparagus** l'asperge (f.) *lahss-pehrzh*

**at** à *ah*

**August** août *oo*

**author** l'auteur (m.) *loh-tuhr*

**avoid** éviter *ay-vee-tay*

**awaken** réveiller *ray-veh-yay*

# B

**back (noun)** le dos *luh doh*; **in back of** derrière *deh-ryehr*

**backward** en arrière *ah<u>n</u> nah-ryehr*

**bacon** le lard *luh lahr*

**bad** mauvais(e) *moh-veh(z)*

**badly** mal *mahl*

**bag** le sac *luh sahk*

**baggage room** la consigne *lah koh<u>n</u>-ssee-nyuh*

**baked** au four *oh foor*

**baked Alaska** l'omelette norvégienne *lohm-leht nohr-vay-zhyehn*

**bakery** la boulangerie *lah boo-lah<u>n</u>-zhree*

**balcony** le balcon *luh bahl-koh<u>n</u>*

**ballet** le ballet *luh bah-leh*

**banana** la banane *lah bah-nahn*

**bandage (noun)** la bande *lah bah<u>n</u>d*

**bank** la banque *lah bah<u>n</u>k*

**bank [branch]** la succursale *lah sew-kewr-ssahl*

**bar** le bistro *luh beess-troh*

**barber** le coiffeur *luh kwah-fuhr*

**bargain (noun)** l'occasion *loh-kah-zyoh<u>n</u>*

**basket** le panier *luh pah-nyay*

**bath** le bain *luh ba<u>n</u>*

**bathe** se baigner *suh beh-nyay*

**bathing suit** le maillot de bain *luh mah-yoh duh ba<u>n</u>*

**bathrobe** la robe de chambre *lah rohb duh shah<u>n</u>-bruh*

**bathroom** la salle de bains *lah sahl duh ba<u>n</u>*

**battery** la batterie *lah bah-tree*

**be** être *eh-truh*

**beach** la plage *lah plahzh*

**bean** le haricot *luh ah-ree-koh*

**beautiful** beau (m.) *boh*, belle (f.) *behl*

**beauty parlor** le salon de beauté *luh sah-loh<u>n</u> duh boh-tay*

**because** parce que *pahrss kuh*

**become** devenir *duh-vuh-neer*

**bed** le lit *luh lee*

**bedroom** la chambre à coucher *lah shah<u>n</u>-bruh ah koo-shay*

**beef (noun)** le boeuf *luh buhf*

**beer** la bière *la byehr*

**beet** la betterave *lah beht-rahv*

**before** avant *ah-vah<u>n</u>*

**begin** commencer (à) *koh-mah<u>n</u>-ssay ah*

**behind** en arrière *ah<u>n</u> nah-ryehr*; derrière *deh-ryehr*

**believe** croire *krwahr*

**bell** la cloche *lah klohsh*

**bellboy** le chasseur *luh shah-ssuhr*

**belong** appartenir *ah-pahr-tuh-neer*

**belt** la ceinture *lah san-tewr*; **seat belt** la ceinture de sécurité *lah san-tewr duh say-kew-ree-tay*

**bench** le banc *luh bahn*

**beneath** dessous *duh-ssoo*

**berth** la couchette *lah koo-sheht*

**beside** à côté de *ah koh-tay duh*

**better (adj.)** meilleur(e) *meh-yuhr*

**better (adv.)** mieux *myuh*

**between** entre *ahn-truh*

**big** grand(e) *grahn(d)*

**bill** la facture *lah fahk-tewr*; la note *lah noht*

**birthday** l'anniversaire (m.) *lah-nee-vehr-ssehr*

**bitter** amer(ère) *ah-mehr*

**black** noir(e) *nwahr*

**blanket** la couverture *lah koo-vehr-tewr*

**blood** le sang *luh sahn*

**blouse** la blouse *lah blooz*

**blue** bleu *bluh*

**boat** le bateau *luh bah-toh*

**body** le corps *luh kohr*

**boiled** bouilli(e) *boo-yee*

**bone** l'os (m.) *lohss*

**book** le livre *luh lee-vruh*

**bookstore** la librairie *lah lee-breh-ree*

**border** la frontière *lah frohn-tyehr*

**borrow** emprunter *ahn-pruhn-tay*

**boss** le patron *luh pah-trohn*; le propriétaire *luh proh-pree-ay-tehr*

**bother** gêner *geh-nay*; ennuyer *ahn-nwee-yay*

**bottle** la bouteille *lah boo-tehy*

**box** la boîte *lah bwaht*

**box office** le bureau de location *luh bew-roh duh loh-kah-ssyohn*

**boy** le garçon *luh gahr-ssohn*

**bra** le soutien-gorge *luh soo-tyan gohrzh*

**braised** braisé *breh-zay*

**brakes** les freins (m. pl.) *lay fran*

**brand** la marque *lah mahrk*

**bread** le pain *luh pan*; **French** la baguette *lah bah-geht*; **pumpernickel** le pain bis *luh pan bee*; **rye** le pain de seigle *luh pan duh seh-gluh*; **white** le pain blanc *luh pan blahn*; **whole wheat** le pain de froment *luh pan duh froh-mahn*

**break** briser *bree-zay*; casser *kah-ssay*

**breakdown (auto)** la panne *lah pahn*; **broken down** en panne *ahn pahn*

**breakfast** le petit déjeuner *luh puh-tee day-zhuh-nay*

**bridge** le pont *luh pohn*

**bring** apporter *ah-pohr-tay*

**broiled** grillé *gree-yay*

**brother** le frère *luh frehr*

**brown** brun(e) *bruhn, brewn*; marron *mah-rohn*

**bruise (noun)** la contusion *lah kohn-tew-zyohn*

**brush (noun)** la brosse *lah brohss*; **(verb)** brosser *broh-ssay*; **toothbrush** la brosse à dents *lah brohss ah dahn*

**Brussel sprouts** les choux (m. pl.) de Bruxelles *lay shoo duh brew-ssehl*

**building** le bâtiment *luh bah-tee-mahn*

**bulb (electric)** l'ampoule (f.) *lahn-pool*

**bun (roll)** la brioche *lah bree-ohsh*

**burn (noun)** la brûlure *lah brew-lewr*; **(verb)** brûler *brew-lay*

**bus** l'autobus *loh-toh-bewss*; **bus station** la gare routière *lah gahr roo-tyehr*; **bus stop** l'arrêt de bus (m.) *lah-reh duh bewss*

**busy** occupé(e) *oh-kew-pay*

**but** mais *meh*

**butcher shop** la boucherie *lah boosh-ree*

**butter** le beurre *luh buhr*

**button** le bouton *luh boo-tohn*

**buy** acheter *ahsh-tay*

**by** par *pahr*; en *ahn*

# C

**cabbage** le chou *luh shoo*

**cake** le gâteau *luh gah-toh*

**call (verb)** appeler *ah-play*

**camera** l'appareil photographique *lah-pah-rehy foh-toh-grah-feek*

**can (verb)** pouvoir *poo-vwahr*

**candle** la bougie *lah boo-zhee*

**candy store** la confiserie *lah kohn-feess-ree*

**car** la voiture *lah vwah-tewr*

**carburetor** le carburateur *luh kahr-bew-rah-tuhr*

**card** la carte *lah kahrt*; **credit card** la carte de crédit *lah kahrt duh kray-dee*; **identification card** la carte d'identité *lah kahrt dee-dahn-tee-tay*

**care** le soin *luh swan*

**carefully** avec soin *ah-vehk swan*

**carefulness** la prudence *lah prew-dahnss*

**carrot** la carotte *lah kah-roht*

**carry** porter *pohr-tay*; **carry away** emporter *ahn-pohr-tay*

**cashier** le caissier *luh kehss-yay*

**cash register** la caisse *lah kehss*

**castle** le château *luh shah-toh*

**cat** le chat *luh shah*

**catch** attraper *ah-trah-pay*

**caution** attention *ah-tahn-ssyohn*

**ceiling** le plafond *luh plah-fohn*

**cellar** la cave *lah kahv*

**cemetery** le cimetière *luh seem-tyehr*

**chain (jewelry)** la chaînette *lah sheh-neht*

**chair** la chaise *lah shehz*

**chambermaid** la femme de chambre *lah fahm duh shahn-bruh*

**change (noun)** le changement *luh shahnzh-mahn*; **money** la monnaie *lah moh-nay*

**change (verb)** changer *shahn-zhay*: **change plane or train** faire la correspondance *fehr lah koh-rehss-pohn-dahnss*

**charge (noun)** les frais (m. pl.) *lay freh*

**charge (verb)** charger *shahr-zhay*

**charm (noun)** le porte-bonheur *luh pohrt boh-nuhr*

**cheap** bon marché *bohn mahr-shay*; **cheaper** meilleur marché *meh-yuhr mahr-shay*

**check (noun) (restaurant)** l'addition (f.) *lah-dee-ssyohn*; **(money)** le chèque *luh shehk*; **traveller's check** le chèque de voyage *luh shehk duh vwah-yahzh*; **cash a check** toucher un chèque *too-shay uhn shehk*

**check (verb)** vérifier *vay-ree-fyay*; **check bags** enregistrer *ahn-ruh-zheess-tray*

**checked (material)** à carreaux *ah kah-roh*

**cheek** la joue *lah zhoo*

**cheese** le fromage *luh froh-mahzh*

**cherry** la cerise *lah suh-reez*

**chest** la poitrine *lah pwah-treen*

**chicken** le poulet *luh poo-leh*

**chick-peas** les pois (m. pl.) chiches *lay pwah sheesh*

**chiffon** la mousseline de soie *lah mooss-leen duh swah*

**child** l'enfant (m./f.) *lah̠-fah̠*

**chin** le menton *luh mah̠-toh̠*

**choose** choisir *shwah-zeer*

**chop (noun)** la côtelette *lah koht-leht*

**church** l'église (f.) *lay-gleez*; le temple (Prot.) *luh tah̠-pluh*

**cigar** le cigare *luh see-gahr*

**cigarette** la cigarette *lah see-gah-reht*

**cigarette lighter** le briquet *luh bree-keh*

**city** la ville *la veel*

**clam** la palourde *lah pah-loord*

**clean (verb)** nettoyer *neh-twah-yay*

**clean (adj.)** propre *proh-pruh*; **dry cleaner's** la teinturerie *lah tan̠-tew-ruh-ree*

**clock** la pendule *lah pah̠-dewl*; l'horloge (f.) *lohr-lohzh*; **alarm clock** le réveil *luh ray-vehy*

**close (verb)** fermer *fehr-may*

**closet** l'armoire (f.) *lahr-mwahr*

**clothes** les habits (m. pl.) *lay zah-bee*; les vêtements (m. pl.) *lay veht-mah̠*

**coast** la côte *lah koht*

**coat** le manteau *luh mah̠-toh*; **coat check** le vestiaire *luh vehss-tyehr*

**coconut** la noix de coco *lah nwah duh koh-koh*

**coffee** le café *luh kah-fay*; **black** le café noir *luh kah-fay nwahr*; **with cream** le café crème *luh kah-fay krehm*; **iced** le café glacé *luh kah-fay glah-ssay*; **with milk** le café au lait *luh kah-fay oh leh*; **espresso** le café express *luh kah-fay ehkss-prehss*

**cold (noun) (weather)** le froid *frwah*; **(verb) to be cold (weather)** faire froid *fehr frwah*; **to be cold (person)** avoir froid *ah-vwahr frwah*

**cold (noun) (respiratory)** le rhume *luh rewm*; **chest cold** le rhume de poitrine *luh rewm duh pwah-treen*; **head cold** le rhume de cerveau *luh rewm duh sehr-voh*

**cold cuts** la charcuterie *lah shahr-kew-tree*

**collar** le col *luh kohl*

**color** la couleur *lah koo-luhr*

**comb** le peigne *luh peh-nyuh*

**come** venir *vuh-neer*; **come back** revenir *ruh-vuh-neer*

**company** la compagnie *lah koh̠-pah-nyee*

**complaint** la plainte *lah plan̠t*

**concert** le concert *luh koh̠-ssehr*; **concert hall** la salle de concert *lah sahl duh koh̠-ssehr*

**conductor** le contrôleur *luh koh̠-troh-luhr*

**confectionery store** la confiserie *lah koh̠-feess-ree*

**congratulations** félicitations *fay-lee-ssee-tah-ssoyh̠*

**connect** relier *ruh-lee-yay*

**contact lense** le verre de contact *luh vehr duh koh̠-tahk̠t*

**contagious** contagieux(ieuse) *koh̠-tah-zhuh(z)*

**contain** contenir *koh̠-tuh-neer*

**contents** le contenu *luh koh̠t-new*

**cook (noun)** le cuisinier *luh kwee-zee-nyay*

**cooked** cuit(e) *kwee(t)*

**cookie** le biscuit *luh beess-kwee*

**cooking** la cuisine *lah kwee-zeen*

**corduroy** le velours côtelé *luh vuh-loor koht-lay*

**corkscrew** le tire-bouchon *luh teer boo-shoh̠*

**corn** le maïs *luh mah-eess*

**corner** le coin *luh kwan̠*

**cost** coûter *koo-tay*

**costly** coûteux(euse) *koo-tuh(z)*

**cotton** le coton *luh koh-tohn*;
  **absorbent cotton** l'ouate (f.)
  *lwaht*

**cough (noun)** la toux *lah too*;
  **cough drops** les pastilles
  contre la toux *lay pahss-teey
  kohn-truh lah too*; **cough syrup**
  le sirop contre la toux *luh see-roh
  kohn-truh lah too*

**cough (verb)** tousser *too-ssay*

**count (verb)** compter *kohn-tay*

**country (nation)** le pays *luh
  pay-ee*; la campagne *lah
  kahn-pah-nyuh*

**countryside** le paysage *luh
  pay-ee-zhahzh*

**courtyard** la cour *lah koor*

**cover (verb)** couvrir *koo-vreer*

**cover charge** le couvert *luh
  koo-vehr*

**crab** le crabe *luh krahb*

**cramp** la crampe *lah krahnp*

**cream** la crème *lah krehm*;
  **whipped cream** la crème
  fouettée *lah krehm foo-eh-tay*

**cross (verb)** traverser
  *trah-vehr-ssay*

**crust** la croûte *lah kroot*

**cry** pleurer *pluh-ray*

**cucumber** le concombre *luh
  kohn-kohn-bruh*

**cup** la tasse *lah tahss*

**custard** le flan *luh flahn*

**customer** le client *luh klee-ahn*

**customs** la douane *lah dwahn*

**customs official** le douanier *luh
  dwah-nyay*

**cut** couper *koo-pay*

# D

**daily** quotidien(ne) *koh-tee-dyan
  (yehn)*

**dance (noun)** la danse *lah dahnss*

**dance (verb)** danser *dahn-ssay*

**dark (color)** foncé(e) *fohn-ssay*

**date** la date *lah daht*

**date (fruit)** la datte *lah daht*

**daughter** la fille *lah fee*

**day** le jour *luh zhoor*; **day before
  yesterday** avant-hier *ah-vahn
  tyehr*; **day after tomorrow**
  après-demain *ah-preh-duh-man*

**dear** cher, chère *shehr*

**deceive** tromper *trohn-pay*

**decide** décider *day-ssee-day*

**declare** déclarer *day-klah-ray*

**delay** le retard *luh ruh-tahr*

**delicatessen** la charcuterie *lah
  shahr-kew-tree*

**deliver** livrer *lee-vray*

**denim** le coutil *luh koo-tee*

**deodorant** le déodorant *luh
  day-oh-doh-rahn*

**department (in store)** le rayon
  *luh ray-ohn*

**deserve** mériter *may-ree-tay*

**desire** désirer *day-zee-ray*

**detective story** le roman policier
  *luh roh-mahn poh-lee-ssyay*

**diaper** la couche *lah koosh*

**dictionary** le dictionnaire *luh
  deek-ssyoh-nehr*

**different** différent(e) *dee-fay-rahn(t)*

**difficult** difficile *dee-fee-sseel*

**diminish** diminuer *dee-mee-new-ay*

**dine** dîner *dee-nay*

**dining car** le wagon-restaurant *luh
  vah-gohn rehss-toh-rahn*

**dining room** la salle à manger *lah
  sahl ah mahn-zhay*

**dirty** sale *sahl*

**disappointed** déçu(e) *day-ssew*

**discotheque** la disco(thèque) *lah
  deess-koh(tehk)*

**dish (of food)** le plat *luh plah*;
  **plate** l'assiette *lah-ssyeht*

**distance** le trajet *luh trah-zheh*

**district** le quartier *luh kahr-tyay*

**do** faire *fehr*

**doctor** le docteur *luh dohk-tuhr*; le médecin *luh mayd-ssan*

**dog** le chien *luh shyan*

**door** la porte *lah pohrt*

**down: to go down** descendre *day-ssahn-druh*

**downstairs** en bas *ahn bah*

**dozen** la douzaine *lah doo-zehn*

**dress (noun)** la robe *lah rohb*

**dress (verb)** s'habiller *sah-bee-yay*

**drink (noun)** la boisson *lah bwah-ssohn*; la consommation *lah kohn-ssoh-mah-ssyohn*; **soft drink** la boisson non-alcoolisée *lah bwah-ssohn nohn nahl-koh-lee-zay*

**drink (verb)** boire *bwahr*

**drinkable** potable *poh-tab-bluh*; **undrinkable** non potable *nohn poh-tah-bluhdrive*

**drive** conduire *kohn-dweer*

**drunk** ivre *ee-vruh*; soûl(e) *soo*

**dry (adj.)** sec, sèche *sehk, sehsh*

**dry (verb)** sécher *say-shay*

**duck** le canard *luh kah-nahr*

**during** pendant *pahn-dahn*

# E

**each** chaque *shahk*

**each one** chacun(e) *shah-kuhn (kewn)*

**ear** l'oreille (f.) *loh-rehy*

**early** tôt *toh*; de bonne heure *duh bohn-uhr*

**earn** gagner *gah-nyay*

**earring** la boucle d'oreille *lah boo-kluh doh-rehy*

**east** l'est *lehsst*

**easy** facile *fah-sseel*

**eat** manger *mahn-zhay*

**egg** l'oeuf *luhf*, **eggs** les oeufs *lay zuhf*; **fried** au plat *oh plah*; **hard-boiled** durs *dewr*; **soft-boiled** mollets *moh-leh*; **sunny-side up** poêlés *pwah-lay*; **scrambled** brouillés *broo-yay*

**eggplant** l'aubergine (f.) *loh-behr-zheen*

**eight** huit *weet*

**eighteen** dix-huit *deez weet*

**eighty** quatre-vingts *kah-truh van*

**elbow** le coude *luh kood*

**elevator** l'ascenseur (m.) *lah-ssahn-ssuhr*

**eleven** onze *ohnz*

**elsewhere** ailleurs *ah-yuhr*

**emergency** le cas urgent *luh kah zewr-zhahn*; **in case of emergency** en cas d'urgence *ahn kah dewr-zhahnss*

**empty** vide *veed*

**end (noun)** la fin *lah fan*

**end (verb)** finir *fee-neer*

**endorse** endosser *ahn-doh-ssay*

**English** anglais (m.) *ahn-gleh*

**enough** assez (de) *ah-ssay duh*

**enter** entrer *ahn-tray*

**entire** entier(ière) *ahn-tyay (yehr)*

**entrance** l'entrée (f.) *lahn-tray*

**envelope** l'enveloppe (f.) *lahn-vlohp*

**eraser** la gomme *lah gohm*

**especially** surtout *sewr-too*

**evening** la soirée *lah swah-ray*

**evening gown** la robe de soir *lah rohb duh swahr*

**every** tout(e) *too(t)*; chaque *shahk*; **everybody** tout le monde *too luh mohnd*; **every day** tous les jours *too lay zhoor*; **everywhere** partout *pahr-too*

**example** l'exemple (m.)
*lehg-zahn-pluh*; **for example**
par exemple *pahr ehg-zahn-pluh*

**excellent** excellent(e)
*ehkss-eh-lahn(t)*

**exchange** échanger *ay-shahn-zhay*;
**exchange office** le bureau de
change *luh bew-roh duh shahnzh*;
**exchange rate** le cours de
change *luh koor duh shahnzh*

**excursion** l'excursion (f.)
*lehkss-kewr-zyohn*

**excuse (verb)** pardonner
*pahr-doh-nay*; **excuse me**
pardon *pahr-dohn*; excusez-moi
*ehkss-kew-zay mwah*

**exhausted** épuisé(e) *ay-pwee-zay*

**exit** la sortie *lah sohr-tee*

**expense** les frais (m. pl.) *lay freh*

**expensive** cher, chère *shehr*

**express** express *ehkss-prehss*

**eye** l'oeil (m.) *luhy*; **eyes** les
yeux (m. pl.) *lay zyuh*

**eyebrow** le sourcil *luh soor-ssee*

**eyeglasses** les lunettes (f. pl.) *lay
lew-neht*

**eyelash** le cil *luh seel*

**eyelid** la paupière *lah poh-pyehr*

# F

**face (noun)** la figure *lah fee-gewr*;
le visage *luh vee-zazh*

**facing** en face de *ahn fahss duh*

**factory** l'usine (f.) *lew-zeen*

**fall** tomber *tohn-bay*; **fall sick**
tomber malade *tohn-bay mah-lahd*

**fair (market)** la foire *lah fwahr*

**false** faux, fausse *foh, fohss*

**family** la famille *lah fah-meey*

**fan** le ventilateur *luh
vahn-tee-lah-tuhr*

**far (from)** loin de *lwan duh*

**farm** la ferme *lah fehrm*

**fat** gros(se) *groh(ss)*

**faucet** le robinet *luh roh-bee-neh*

**fast** rapide *rah-peed*; vite *veet*

**father** le père *luh pehr*

**fear** la peur *lah puhr*; **to be afraid**
avoir peur *ah-vwahr puhr*

**February** février *fay-vree-yay*

**feel** (se) sentir *(suh) sahn-teer*

**felt** le feutre *luh fuh-truh*

**festival** la fête *lah feht*

**fever** la fièvre *lah fyeh-vruh*; **hay
fever** le rhume des foins *luh
rewm day fwan*

**few** peu de *puh duh*; **a few**
quelques *kehl-kuh*

**field** le champ *luh shahn*

**fifteen** quinze *kanz*

**fifty** cinquante *san-kahnt*

**fig** la figue *lah feeg*

**figure (body)** la taille *lah tahy*

**fill (out)** remplir *rahn-pleer*

**film** le film *luh feelm*; la pellicule
*lah peh-lee-kewl*

**finger** le doigt *luh dwah*

**finish** finir *fee-neer*; terminer
*tehr-mee-nay*

**fire** le feu *luh fuh*; l'incendie (m.)
*lan-ssahn-dee*

**first** premier(ière) *pruh-myay
(yehr)*; **at first** d'abord
*dah-bohr*; **first aid** le premier
secours *luh pruh-myay suh-koor*

**fish (noun)** le poisson *luh
pwah-ssohn*

**fish (verb)** pêcher *peh-shay*

**five** cinq *sank*

**flannel** la flanelle *lah flah-nehl*

**flashlight** la lampe de poche *lah
lahnp duh pohsh*

**flat** plat(te) *plah(t)*

**flavor** le parfum *luh pahr-fuhn*

**flight** le vol *luh vohl*

**floor** le plancher *luh plahn-shay*; (story) l'étage (m.) *lay-tahzh*

**florist** le fleuriste *luh fluh-reest*

**flounder** la sole *lah sohl*

**flower** la fleur *lah fluhr*

**fly (verb)** voler *voh-lay*

**follow** suivre *swee-vruh*; **following** suivant(e) *swee-vahn(t)*

**food** les aliments (m. pl.) *lay zah-lee-mahn*; la nourriture *lah noo-ree-tewr*

**foot** le pied *luh pyay*

**for** pour *poor*

**forbid** interdire *an-tehr-deer*; défendre *day-fahn-druh*; **forbidden** interdit(e) *an-tehr-dee(t)*; défendu(e) *day-fahn-dew*; **it is forbidden to** défense de *day-fahnss duh*

**forehead** le front *luh frohn*

**foreign** étranger(ère) *ay-trahn-zhay (zhehr)*

**forest** la forêt *lah foh-reh*

**forget** oublier *oo-blee-yay*

**fork** la fourchette *lah foor-sheht*

**form (noun)** la fiche *lah feesh*; la formule *lah fohr-mewl*

**former** ancien(ne) *ahn-ssyan(n)*

**forty** quarante *kah-rahnt*

**forward (adv.)** en avant *ahn nah-vahn*

**fountain** la fontaine *lah fohn-tehn*

**four** quatre *kah-truh*

**fourteen** quatorze *kah-tohrz*

**free** libre *lee-bruh*; **for free** gratuit(e) *grah-twee(t)*; **free of charge (adv.)** gratuitement *grah-tweet-mahn*

**French** le français (m.) *luh frahn-sseh*

**fresh** frais, fraîche *freh, frehsh*

**Friday** vendredi *vahn-druh-dee*

**fried** frit(e) *free(t)*

**friend** ami(e) *ah-mee*

**frog's legs** les cuisses (f. pl.) de grenouille *lay kweess duh gruh-nuhy*

**front: in front of** devant *duh-vahn*

**fruit** le fruit *luh frwee*

**fruit salad** la macédoine de fruits *lah mah-ssay-dwahn duh frwee*

**function (verb)** fonctionner *fohnk-ssyoh-nay*

**furnished** meublé(e) *muh-blay*

# G

**gabardine** la gabardine *lah gah-bahr-deen*

**game** le jeu *luh zhuh*; la partie *lah pahr-tee*

**game (meat)** le gibier *luh zhee-byay*

**garden** le jardin *luh zhahr-dan*

**garlic** l'ail (m.) *lahy*

**gas** l'essence (f.) *leh-ssahnss*

**gas station** le poste d'essence *luh pohsst deh-ssahnss*; la station-service *lah stah-ssyohn sehr-veess*

**gas tank** le réservoir à essence *luh ray-zehr-vwahr ah eh-ssahnss*

**get up** se lever *suh luh-vay*

**gift** le cadeau *luh kah-doh*

**girl** la fille *lah fee*

**give** donner *doh-nay*

**gladly** volontiers *voh-lohn-tyay*

**glass** le verre *luh vehr*

**glove** le gant *luh gahn*

**glue** la colle *lah kohl*

**go** aller *ah-lay*; **go down** descendre *day-ssahn-druh*; **go home** rentrer *rahn-tray*; **go in** entrer *ahn-tray*; **go out** sortir *sohr-teer*; **go shopping** faire des emplettes *fehr day zahn-pleht*; **go to bed** se coucher *suh koo-shay*; **go up** monter *mohn-tay*

**gold** l'or (m.) *lohr*

**good** bon(ne) *bohn, bohn*

**goose** l'oie (f.) *lwah*

**grape** le raisin *luh reh-zan*

**grapefruit** le pamplemousse *luh pahn-pluh-mooss*

**grass** l'herbe (f.) *lehrb*

**grave (adj.)** sérieux(ieuse) *say-ree-uh(z)*; grave *grahv*

**gray** gris(e) *gree(z)*

**green** vert(e) *vehr(t)*

**greet** saluer *sah-lew-ay*

**grilled** grillé(e) *gree-yay*

**grocery store** l'épicerie (f.) *lay-peess-ree*

**ground** le terrain *luh teh-ran*; la terre *lah tehr*; **camp ground** le terrain de camping *luh teh-ran duh kahn-peeng*; **golf course** le terrain de golf *luh teh-ran duh gohlf*; **playing field** le terrain de sport *luh teh-ran duh spohr*; **on the ground** par terre *pahr tehr*

**ground floor** le rez-de-chaussée *luh rayd shoh-ssay*

**guava** la goyave *lah goh-yahv*

**guide** le guide *luh geed*; **tourist guide** le guide touristique *luh geed too-reess-teek*

**gums (mouth)** les gencives (f.) *lay zhahn-sseev*

# H

**hair** les cheveux (m. pl.) *lay shuh-vuh*

**haircut** la coupe de cheveux *lah koop duh shuh-vuh*

**hair dryer** le sèche-cheveux *luh sehsh shuh-vuh*

**hair spray** la laque *lah lahk*

**half (noun)** la moitié *lah mwah-tyay*

**half (adj.)** demi(e) *duh-mee*

**ham** le jambon *luh zhahn-bohn*

**hamburger** le hamburger *luh ahn-boor-gehr*

**hand** la main *lah man*

**handkerchief** le mouchoir *luh moo-shwahr*

**handmade** fait à la main *feh Tah lah man*

**handsome** beau (m.), belle (f.) *boh, behl*

**hanger** le cintre *luh san-truh*

**hang up** accrocher *ah-kroh-sshay*

**happy** heureux(euse) *uh-ruh(z)*

**hardware store** la quincaillerie *lah kahn-kahy-ree*

**have** avoir *ah-vwahr*; **have just** venir de *vuh-neer duh*; **have to** avoir à *ah-vwahr ah*; devoir *duh-vwahr*

**he** il *eel*

**head** la tête *lah teht*

**headlight** le phare *luh fahr*

**health** la santé *lah sahn-tay*

**hear** entendre *ahn-tahn-druh*

**heart** le coeur *luh kuhr*

**heat (noun)** la chaleur *lah\shah-luhr*

**heat (verb)** chauffer *shoh-fay*

**heating** le chauffage *luh shoh-fahzh*

**heel** le talon *luh tah-lohn*

**height** la hauteur (f.) *lah oh-tuhr*

**hello** bonjour *bohn-zhoor*

**help (noun)** le secours *luh suh-koor*; **help!** au secours! *oh suh-koor*

**help (verb)** aider *eh-day*

**here** ici *ee-ssee*

**here is, are** voici *vwah-ssee*

**herring** les harengs (m. pl.) *lay ah-rahn*; **smoked herring** les harengs fumés *lay ah-rahn few-may*

**high** haut(e) *oh(t)*

**high school** le lycée *luh lee-ssay*

**highway** l'autoroute (f.) *loh-toh-root*

**hip** la hanche *lah ahnsh*

**hire** louer *loo-ay*

**hit** frapper *frah-pay*

**hold** tenir *tuh-neer*

**hole** le trou *luh troo*

**holiday** la fête *lah feht*

**hope (verb)** espérer *ehss-pay-ray*

**horn** le klaxon *luh klahk-ssohn*

**horse** le cheval *luh shuh-vahl*; les chevaux (pl.) *lay shuh-voh*

**horseradish** le raifort *luh reh-fohr*

**hospital** l'hôpital (m.) *loh-pee-tahl*

**host** l'hôte (m.) *loht*

**hostel (youth)** l'auberge (f.) de jeunesse *loh-behrzh duh zhuh-nehss*

**hostess** l'hôtesse (f.) *loh-tehss*

**hot** chaud *shoh*; **be hot (person)** avoir chaud *ah-vwahr shoh*; **be hot (weather)** faire chaud *fehr shoh*

**hotel** l'hôtel (m.) *loh-tehl*

**hour** l'heure (f.) *luhr*

**house** la maison *lah meh-zohn*; **at the house of** chez *shay*; **boardinghouse** la pension *lah pahn-ssyohn*

**house porter** le concierge *luh kohn-ssyehrzh*

**how** comment *koh-mahn*; **how far** à quelle distance *ah kehl deess-tahnss*; **how long** depuis quand *duh-pwee kahn*

**how many, much** combien *kohn-byan*

**hundred** cent *sahn*

**hunger** la faim *lah fan*; **to be hungry** avoir faim *ah-vwahr fan*

**hurry** se dépêcher *suh day-peh-shay*; **be in a hurry** être pressé *eh-truh preh-ssay*

**husband** le mari *luh mah-ree*

# I

**I** je *zhuh*

**ice** la glace *lah glahss*; **ice cream** la glace *lah glahss*; **ice cubes** les glaçons (m. pl.) *lay glah-ssohn*; **ice water** l'eau (f.) glacée *loh glah-ssay*

**if** si *see*

**ill** malade *mah-lahd*

**illness** la maladie *lah mah-lah-dee*

**immediately** immédiatement *ee-may-dyaht-mahn*

**important** important(e) *an-pohr-tahn(t)*

**impossible** impossible *an-poh-ssee-bluh*

**improbable** invraisemblable *an-vreh-sahn-blah-bluh*

**in** dans *dahn*; en *ahn*

**incapable** incapable *an-kah-pah-bluh*

**included** compris(e) *kohn-pree(z)*

**indefinite** imprécis(e) *an-pray-ssee(z)*

**infection** l'infection (f.) *lan-fehk-ssyohn*

**information** les renseignements *lay rahn-seh-nyuh-mahn*

**inn** l'auberge (f.) *loh-behrzh*

**inside** dedans *duh-dahn*

**insomnia** l'insomnie (f.) *lan-ssohm-nee*

**in spite of** malgré *mahl-gray*

**instead of** au lieu de *oh lyuh duh*

**insufficient** insuffisant(e) *an-ssew-fee-zahn(t)*

**insurance** l'assurance (f.) *lah-ssew-rahnss*

**insure** assurer *ah-ssew-ray*

**intelligent** intelligent(e) *an-teh-lee-zhahn(t)*

**interesting** intéressant(e)
*an-tay-reh-ssahn(t)*

**interpret** interpréter
*an-tehr-pray-tay*

**interpreter** l'interprète (m.)
*an-tehr-preht*

**intersection** le croisement *luh
krwahz-mahn*

**introduce** présenter *pray-zahn-tay*

**invite** inviter *an-vee-tay*

**invoice** la facture *lah fahk-tewr*

**iron (noun)** le fer *luh fehr*

**iron (verb)** repasser *ruh-pah-ssay*

**island** l'île (f.) *leel*

**itinerary** l'itinéraire *lee-tee-nay-rehr*

# J

**jack (auto)** le cric *luh kree*

**jacket** le veston *luh vehss-tohn*

**jam (marmalade)** la confiture *lah
kohn-fee-tewr*

**January** janvier *zhahn-vyay*

**jar** la jarre *lah zhahr*

**jaw** la mâchoire *lah mah-shwahr*

**jewel** le bijou *luh bee-zhoo*

**jeweler** le bijoutier *luh
bee-zhoo-tyay*

**jewelry shop** la bijouterie *lah
bee-zhoo-tree*

**joke** la plaisanterie *lah
pleh-zahn-tree*

**journey** le voyage *luh vwah-yahzh*;
le trajet *luh trah-zheh*

**judge (noun)** le juge *luh zhewzh*

**judge (verb)** juger *zhew-zhay*

**juice** le jus *luh zhew*

**July** juillet *zhwee-yeh*

**June** juin *zhwan*

**just: have just** venir de *vuh-neer
duh*

# K

**keep** garder *gahr-day*

**ketchup** le ketchup *luh keht-shuhp*

**key** la clef *lah klay*

**kiss** embrasser *ahn-brah-ssay*

**kitchen** la cuisine *lah kwee-zeen*

**knee** le genou *luh zhuh-noo*

**knife** le couteau *luh koo-toh*

**knock** frapper *frah-pay*

**know (facts)** savoir *sah-vwahr*;
**(people)** connaître *koh-neh-truh*

# L

**label** l'étiquette (f.) *lay-tee-keht*

**lace** la dentelle *lah dahn-tehl*

**lack (noun)** le manque *luh mahnk*

**lack (verb)** manquer *mahn-kay*

**lake** le lac *luh lahk*

**lamb** l'agneau *lah-nyoh*

**lamp** la lampe *lah lahnp*

**land (noun)** la terre *lah tehr*

**land (verb) (plane)** atterrir
*ah-teh-reer*; débarquer *day-bahr-kay*

**landing** l'atterrissage (m.)
*lah-teh-ree-ssahzh*; le
débarquement *luh
day-bahrk-mahn*

**lane** la ruelle *lah rew-ehl*

**language** la langue *lah lahng*

**last (adj.)** dernier(ière)
*dehr-nyay(nyehr)*

**last (verb)** durer *dew-ray*

**late** tard *tahr*; **(to be) late** (être)
en retard *ahn ruh-tahr*

**laugh** rire *reer*

**launderette** la laverie automatique
*lah lah-vree oh-toh-mah-teek*

**laundering** le blanchissage *luh
blahn-shee-ssahzh*

**laundry** la blanchisserie *lah blahn-sheess-ree*

**learn** apprendre *ah-prahn-druh*

**least: at least** au moins *oh mwan*

**leather** le cuir *luh kweer*

**leave (behind)** laisser *leh-ssay*

**leave (depart)** partir *pahr-teer;* **to go out** sortir *sohr-teer;* **to leave + (place or person)** quitter *kee-tay*

**left** gauche *gohsh;* **to the left** à gauche *ah gohsh*

**leg** la jambe *lah zhahnb*

**lemon** le citron *luh see-trohn*

**lemonade** la citronnade *lah see-troh-nahd*

**lend** prêter *preh-tay*

**less** moins *mwan*

**letter** la lettre *lah leh-truh*

**lettuce** la laitue *lah leh-tew*

**library** la bibliothèque *lah bee-blee-oh-tehk*

**life** la vie *lah vee*

**life preserver** la ceinture de sauvetage *lah san-tewr duh sohv-tahzh*

**light (noun)** la lumière *lah lew-myehr*

**light (color)** clair(e) *klehr*

**light (weight)** léger(ère) *lay-zhay(zhehr)*

**light (verb)** allumer *ah-lew-may*

**lighter** le briquet *luh bree-keh*

**like (prep.)** comme *kohm*

**like (verb)** aimer *eh-may*

**lime** la limette *lah lee-meht*

**line** la ligne *lah lee-nyuh;* la voie *lah vwah*

**line (of people)** la queue *lah kuh;* **form a line** faire la queue *fehr lah kuh*

**linen (cloth)** le lin *luh lan*

**lip** la lèvre *lah leh-vruh*

**lipstick** le rouge à lèvres *luh roozh ah leh-vruh*

**list** la liste *lah leesst*

**listen** écouter *ay-koo-tay*

**little (adj.)** petit(e) *puh-tee(t);* **(adv.)** peu (de) *puh (duh)*

**live** vivre *vee-vruh*

**live in** demeurer *duh-muh-ray;* habiter *ah-bee-tay*

**liver** le foie *luh fwah*

**lobster** le homard *luh oh-mahr*

**lock (noun)** la serrure *lah seh-rewr*

**lodging** le logis *luh loh-zhee*

**long** long, longue *lohn, lohng*

**look at** regarder *ruh-gahr-day*

**look for** chercher *shehr-shay*

**lose** perdre *pehr-druh*

**loss** la perte *lah pehrt*

**lost: get lost** s'égarer *say-gah-ray*

**lot** beaucoup de *boh-koo duh*

**loudspeaker** le haut-parleur *luh oh pahr-luhr*

**love (noun)** l'amour (m.) *lah-moor*

**love (verb)** aimer *eh-may*

**low** bas(se) *bah(ss)*

**luck** la chance *lah shahnss;* **Good luck!** Bonne chance! *bohn shahnss*

**lunch (noun)** le déjeuner *luh day-zhuh-nay*

**lunch (verb)** déjeuner *day-zhuh-nay*

**lung** le poumon *luh poo-mohn*

**luxurious** luxueux(euse) *lewk-ssew-uh(uhz)*

**luxury** le luxe *luh lewkss*

# M

**magazine** le magazine *luh mah-gah-zeen*

**mail** le courrier *luh koo-ryay*

**mailbox** la boîte à lettres *lah bwaht ah leh-truh*

**mailman** le facteur *luh fahk-tuhr*

**make** faire *fehr*

**man** l'homme (m.) *lohm*

**manager** le gérant *luh zhay-rahn*

**mango** la mangue *lah mahng*

**many** beaucoup de *boh-koo duh*; **too many** trop de *troh duh*

**map** la carte *lah kahrt*; **road map** la carte routière *lah kahrt roo-tyehr*

**March** mars *mahrss*

**margarine** la margarine *lah mahr-gah-reen*

**market** le marché *luh mahr-shay*

**marvelous** merveilleux(euse) *mehr-veh-yuh(z)*

**match (noun)** l'allumette (f.) *lah-lew-meht*

**material** le tissu *luh tee-ssew*

**matter (noun)** l'affaire (f.) *lah-fehr*; **it doesn't matter** n'importe *nan-pohrt*; **What's the matter?** Qu'est-ce qu'il y a? *Kehss keel yah*

**May** mai *meh*

**may (verb)** pouvoir *poo-vwahr*

**maybe** peut-être *puh-teh-truh*

**mayonnaise** la mayonnaise *lah may-yoh-nehz*

**meal** le repas *luh ruh-pah*

**mean (verb)** vouloir dire *voo-lwahr deer*; signifier *see-nee-fyay*

**mean (adj.)** méchant(e) *may-shahn(t)*

**meaning** la signification *lah see-nee-fee-kah-ssyohn*

**measure (noun)** la mesure *lah muh-zewr*

**measure (verb)** mesurer *muh-zew-ray*

**meat** la viande *lah vee-ahnd*

**meatballs** les boulettes *lay boo-leht*

**mechanic** le mécanicien *luh may-kah-nee-ssyan*

**medicine** la médecine *lah mayd-sseen*

**medium (cooking)** à point *ah pwan*

**meet** rencontrer *rahn-kohn-tray*

**meeting** le rendez-vous *luh rahn-day-voo*

**melon** le melon *luh muh-lohn*

**merchandise** la marchandise *lah mahr-shahn-deez*

**merchant** le marchand *luh mahr-shahn*

**mezzanine** le parterre *luh pahr-tehr*

**middle** le milieu *luh meel-yuh*; **in the middle of** au milieu de *oh meel-yuh duh*

**midnight** minuit *mee-nwee*

**milk** le lait *luh leh*

**milk shake** le frappé *luh frah-pay*

**million** le million *luh mee-lyohn*

**minute** la minute *lah mee-newt*

**mirror** le miroir *luh mee-rwahr*; la glace *lah glahss*

**miss (verb)** manquer *mahn-kay*

**miss** mademoiselle *mahd-mwah-zehl*

**mistake** la faute *lah foht*; l'erreur (f.) *leh-ruhr*; **make a mistake** se tromper *suh trohn-pay*

**mister** monsieur *muh-ssyuh*

**misunderstanding** le malentendu *luh mahl-ahn-tahn-dew*

**modify** modifier *moh-dee-fyay*

**Monday** lundi *luhn-dee*

**money** l'argent (m.) *lahr-zhahn*

**money (coins)** la monnaie *lah moh-nay*

**month** le mois *luh mwah*

**monthly** mensuel(le) *mahn-sswehl*

**morning** le matin *luh mah-taņ*

**mosque** la mosquée *lah mohss-kay*

**mother** la mère *lah mehr*

**motor** le moteur *luh moh-tuhr*

**mountain** la montagne *lah mohņ-tah-nyuh*

**mouth** la bouche *lah boosh*

**mouthwash** le dentifrice *luh dahņ-tee-freess*

**movies** le cinéma *luh see-nay-mah*

**Mr.** monsieur *muh-ssyuh*

**Mrs.** madame *mah-dahm*

**museum** le musée *luh mew-zay*

**mushroom** le champignon *luh shahņ-pee-nyohņ*

**music** la musique *lah mew-zeek*

**mussels** les moules (f. pl.) *lay mool*

**mustard** la moutarde *lah moo-tahrd*

**mutton leg** le gigot *luh zhee-goh*

# N

**nail** l'ongle *lohņ-gluh*

**nail file** la lime à ongles *lah leem ah ohņ-gluh*

**name** le nom *luh nohņ;* **family (last) name** le nom de famille *luh nohņ duh fah-mee;* **first name** le prénom *luh pray-nohņ;* **last name** le surnom *luh sewr-nohņ;* **My name is** Je m'appelle *Zhuh mah-pehl*

**napkin** la serviette *lah sehr-vyeht;* **sanitary napkin** la serviette hygiénique *lah sehr-vyeht ee-zhyay-neek*

**nationality** la nationalité *lah nah-ssyohņ-nah-lee-tay*

**nausea** la nausée *lah noh-zay*

**near (to)** près de *preh duh*

**nearby** proche *prohsh*

**nearly** presque *prehss-kuh*

**necessary** nécessaire *nay-sseh-ssehr;* **it is necessary** il est nécessaire *eel eh nay-sseh-ssehr;* il faut *eel foh*

**neck** le cou *luh koo*

**necklace** le collier *luh koh-lyay*

**need (verb)** avoir besoin de *ah-vwahr buhz-waņ duh*

**needle** l'aiguille (f.) *lay-gwee*

**neighbor** le voisin *luh vwah-saņ;* la voisine *lah vwah-zeen*

**never** jamais *zhah-meh;* ne . . . jamais *nuh . . . zhah-meh*

**new** nouveau (m.), nouvelle (f.) *noo-voh, noo-vehl*

**newspaper** le journal *luh zhoor-nahl*

**next** prochain(e) *proh-shaņ(shehn)*

**night** la nuit *lah nwee*

**night club** la boîte de nuit *lah bwaht duh nwee*

**nine** neuf *nuhf*

**nineteen** dix-neuf *deez nuhf*

**ninety** quatre-vingt-dix *kah-truh vaņ deess*

**no** non *nohņ*

**noisy** le bruit *luh brwee*

**no longer** ne . . . plus *nuh . . . plew*

**none** ne . . . aucun(e) *nuh . . . oh-kuhņ(kewn)*

**nonsmokers** nonfumeurs *nohņ few-muhr*

**noon** midi *mee-dee*

**north** le nord *luh nohr*

**nose** le nez *luh nay*

**not** ne . . . pas *nuh . . . pah*

**not any** ne . . . aucun(e) *nuh . . . oh-kuhņ(kewn)*

**notebook** le cahier *luh kah-yay*

**nothing** ne . . . rien *nuh . . . ryaņ*

**notice (noun)** l'avis (m.) *lah-vee*

**notice (verb)** remarquer *ruh-mahr-kay*

**novel** le roman *luh roh-mah_n_*

**novelty** la nouveauté *lah noo-voh-tay*

**now** maintenant *ma_n_t-nah_n_*

**number** le numéro *luh new-may-roh*

**number (quantity)** le nombre *luh noh_n_-bruh*

**nurse** l'infirmière (f.) *la_n_-feer-myehr*

**nut** la noix *lah nwah*

**nylon** le nylon *luh nee-loh_n_*

# O

**observe** observer *ohb-zehr-vay*

**obtain** obtenir *ohp-tuh-neer*

**ocean** l'océan (m.) *loh-ssay-ah_n_*

**of** de *duh*

**of course** bien entendu *bya_n_ nah_n_-tah_n_-dew*

**offer** offrir *oh-freer*

**office** le bureau *luh bew-roh*; **box office** le bureau de location *luh bew-roh duh loh-kah-ssyoh_n_*; **exchange office** le bureau de change *luh bew-roh duh shah_n_zh*; **post office** le bureau de poste *luh bew-roh duh pohsst*

**often** souvent *soo-vah_n_*

**oil** l'huile (f.) *lweel*

**O.K.** d'accord *dah-kohr*

**old** vieux (m.), vieille (f.) *vyuh, vyay*; **How old are you?** Quel âge avez-vous? *kehl ahzh ah-vay voo?*

**old-fashioned** démodé(e) *day-moh-day*

**olive** l'olive (f.) *loh-leev*

**olive oil** l'huile d'olive *lweel doh-leev*

**omelet** l'omelette (f.) *lohm-leht*

**on** sur *sewr*

**one** un (m.), une (f.) *uh_n_, ewn*

**onion** l'oignon (m.) *loh-nyoh_n_*

**only** ne . . . que *nuh . . . kuh*; seulement *suhl-mah_n_*

**only (adj.)** seul(e) *suhl*; unique *ew-neek*

**open (verb)** ouvrir *oo-vreer*

**open (adj.)** ouvert(e) *oo-vehr(t)*

**opera** l'opéra (m.) *loh-pay-rah*

**operator** la téléphoniste *lah tay-lay-foh-neesst*

**opportunity** l'occasion (f.) *loh-kah-zyoh_n_*

**opposite (noun)** le contraire *luh koh_n_-trehr*

**opposite (prep.)** en face de *ah_n_ fahss duh*

**optician** l'opticien (m.) *lohp-tee-ssya_n_*

**or** ou *oo*

**orange** l'orange (f.) *loh-rah_n_zh*

**orangeade** l'orangeade (f.) *loh-rah_n_zh-ahd*

**orchestra** l'orchestre (m.) *lohr-kehss-truh*

**order (noun)** la commande *lah koh-mah_n_d*

**order (verb)** commander *koh-mah_n_-day*

**other** autre *oh-truh*

**outside** dehors *duh-ohr*

**over** dessus *duh-ssew*

**overcoat** le manteau *luh mah_n_-toh*; le pardessus *luh pahr-duh-ssew*

**overseas** outre-mer *oo-truh mehr*

**owe** devoir *duh-vwahr*

**own** posséder *poh-ssay-day*

**owner** le propriétaire *luh proh-pree-ay-tehr*

**oyster** l'huître (f.) *lwee-truh*

# P

**package** le paquet *luh pah-keh*; le colis *luh koh-lee*

**pad (writing)** le bloc *luh blohk*

**pain** la douleur *lah doo-luhr*

**painting** le tableau *luh tah-bloh*

**pair** la paire *lah pehr*

**palace** le palais *luh pah-leh*

**panties** la culotte *lah kew-loht*

**pants** le pantalon *luh pahn-tah-lohn*

**panty hose** les collants (m. pl.) *lay koh-lahn*

**paper** le papier *luh pah-pyay*; **toilet** le papier hygiénique *luh pah-pyay ee-zhyay-neek*; **typing** le papier à machine *luh pah-pyay ah mah-sheen*; **wrapping** le papier d'emballage *luh pah-pyay dahn-bah-lahzh*; **writing** le papier à lettres *luh pah-pyay ah leh-truh*

**park (noun)** le parc *luh pahrk*

**park (verb)** garer *gah-ray*; stationner *stah-ssyoh-nay*

**part** la partie *lah pahr-tee*

**pass (verb)** passer *pah-ssay*

**pastry** la pâtisserie *lah pah-teess-ree*

**pay** payer *peh-yay*

**pear** la poire *lah pwahr*

**peas** les pois (m. pl.) *lay pwah*

**pedestrian** le piéton *luh pyay-tohn*

**pen** la plume *lah plewm*; **ball-point** le stylo à bille *luh stee-loh ah bee*

**penalty** l'amende (f.) *lah-mahnd*

**pencil** le crayon *luh kreh-yohn*; **pencil sharpener** le taille-crayon *luh tahy kreh-yohn*

**people** les gens *lay zhahn* [adj. before (f.); adj. after (m.)]

**people (nation)** le peuple *luh puh-pluh*

**pepper** le poivre *luh pwah-vruh*

**perfect** parfait(e) *pahr-feh(t)*

**performance** la représentation *lah ruh-pray-zahn-tah-ssyohn*

**perfume** le parfum *luh pahr-fuhn*

**perhaps** peut-être *puh-teh-truh*

**permanent** permanent(e) *pehr-mah-nahn(t)*

**permanent press** infroissable *an-frwah-ssah-bluh*

**permit (noun)** le permis *luh pehr-mee*

**permit (verb)** permettre *pehr-meh-truh*; **permitted** permis *pehr-mee*

**person** la personne *lah pehr-ssohn*

**persuade** persuader *pehr-sswah-day*

**pharmacy** la pharmacie *lah fahr-mah-ssee*

**photograph (noun)** la photo *lah foh-toh*

**photograph (verb)** photographier *foh-toh-grah-fyay*

**pickle** le cornichon *luh kohr-nee-shohn*

**picture (art)** le tableau *luh tah-bloh*

**pie** la tarte *lah tahrt*

**piece** le morceau *luh mohr-ssoh*

**pill** la pilule *lah pee-lewl*

**pillow** l'oreiller (m.) *loh-reh-yay*

**pin** l'épingle (f.) *lay pan-gluh*

**pineapple** l'ananas (m.) *lah-nah-nah*

**pink** rose *rohz*

**pipe (smoking)** la pipe *lah peep*; **pipe tobacco** le tabac pour pipe *luh tah-bah poor peep*

**pitcher** la cruche *lah krewsh*

**place (noun)** l'endroit (m.) *lahn-drwah*; le lieu *luh lyuh*

**plaid** le tartan *luh tahr-tahn*

**plan** le plan *luh plahn*; **plan of the city** le plan de ville *luh plahn duh veel*

**plate** l'assiette (f.) *lah-ssyeht*

**platform** le quai *luh kay*

**platinum** le platine *luh plah-teen*

**play (noun)** la pièce *lah pyehss*

**play (verb)** jouer *zhoo-ay*; **play (a game)** jouer à *zhoo-ay ah*; **play (an instrument)** jouer de *zhoo-ay duh*

**please** s'il vous plaît *seel voo pleh*

**pleasure** le plaisir *luh pleh-zeer*

**plum** la prune *lah prewn*

**pocket** la poche *lah pohsh*

**pocketbook** le sac *luh sahk*

**policeman** l'agent (m.) de police *lah-zhahn duh poh-leess*; le gendarme *luh zhahn-dahrm*

**police station** le commissariat *luh koh-mee-ssah-ryah*

**polka-dotted** à pois *ah pwah*

**polyester** synthétique *san-tay-teek*

**poor** pauvre *poh-vruh*

**pork** le porc *luh pohr*

**portable** portatif(tive) *pohr-tah-teef(teev)*

**porter** le porteur *luh pohr-tuhr*

**possess** posséder *poh-ssay-day*

**postcard** la carte postale *lah kahrt pohss-tahl*

**poster** l'affiche (f.) *lah-feesh*

**postman** le facteur *luh fahk-tuhr*

**post office** la poste *lah pohsst*; le bureau de poste *luh bew-roh duh pohsst*

**postpone** remettre *ruh-meh-truh*

**potato** la pomme de terre *lah pohm duh tehr*

**pottery** la poterie *lah poh-tree*

**pound (meas.)** la livre *lah lee-vruh*

**practice (noun)** l'usage (m.) *lew-zahzh*

**prefer** préférer *pray-fay-ray*; aimer mieux *eh-may myuh*

**prepare** préparer *pray-pah-ray*

**prescription** l'ordonnance (f.) *lohr-doh-nahnss*

**pretty** joli(e) *zhoh-lee*

**price** le prix *luh pree*

**private** privé(e) *pree-vay*

**prize** le prix *luh pree*

**profession** la profession *lah proh-feh-ssyohn*

**prohibit** interdire *an-tehr-deer*; **prohibited** interdit(e) *an-tehr-dee(t)*

**promise (verb)** promettre *proh-meh-truh*

**promise (noun)** la promesse *lah proh-mehss*

**pronounce** prononcer *proh-nohn-ssay*

**property** la propriété *lah proh-pree-ay-tay*

**protect** protéger *proh-tay-zhay*

**protest (verb)** protester *proh-tehss-tay*

**prune** le pruneau *luh prew-noh*

**public** public(ique) *pew-bleek*

**pull** tirer *tee-ray*

**purchase (noun)** l'achat (m.) *lah-shah*

**purple** violet *vee-oh-leht*

**purse** le porte-monnaie *luh pohrt moh-nay*

**push** pousser *poo-ssay*

**put** mettre *meh-truh*; **to put on** mettre *meh-truh*; **put back** remettre *ruh-meh-truh*

**pyjamas** le pyjama *luh pee-zhah-mah*

# Q

**quality** la qualité *lah kah-lee-tay*

**quantity** la quantité *lah kahn-tee-tay*

**quarter** le quart *luh-kahr*

**question** la question *lah kehss-tyohn*

**quickly** vite *veet*; rapidement *rah-peed-mahn*

**quickness** la vitesse *lah vee-tehss*

# R

**rabbit** le lapin *luh lah-pan*

**radio** la radio *lah rah-dyoh*

**radish** le radis *luh rah-dee*

**railroad** le chemin de fer *luh shuh-man duh fehr*

**railroad station** la gare *lah gahr*

**rain** la pluie *lah plwee*

**raincoat** l'imperméable (m.) *lan-pehr-may-ah-bluh*

**rare** rare *rahr*

**rare (meat)** saignant *seh-nyahn*

**raspberry** la framboise *lah frahn-bwahz*

**rate** le tarif *luh tah-reef*

**rate of exchange** le cours du change *luh koor dew shahnzh*

**rather** plutôt *plew-toh*

**raw** cru(e) *krew*

**razor** le rasoir *luh rah-zwahr*

**read** lire *leer*

**ready** prêt(e) *preh(t)*

**really** vraiment *vreh-mahn*

**reason** la raison *lah reh-zohn*

**reasonable** raisonnable *reh-zoh-nah-bluh*

**receipt** le reçu *luh ruh-ssew*

**receive** recevoir *ruh-ssuh-vwahr*

**recently** récemment *ray-sseh-mahn*

**recommend** recommander *ruh-koh-mahn-day*

**record** le disque *luh deessk*

**recover (health)** se remettre *sul ruh-meh-truh*

**recuperate** récupérer *ray-kew-pay-ray*

**red** rouge *roozh*

**reduction** le rabais *luh rah-beh*

**refreshments** les rafraîchissements (m. pl.) *lay rah-freh-sheess-mahn*

**refund** rembourser *rahn-boor-ssay*

**refuse (verb)** refuser *ruh-few-zay*

**regret** regretter *ruh-greh-tay*

**regular** régulier(ière) *ray-gew-lyay(yehr)*

**regularly** régulièrement *ray-gew-lyehr-mahn*

**reimburse** rembourser *rahn-boor-ssay*

**remain** rester *rehss-tay*

**remedy** le remède *luh ruh-mehd*

**remember** se rappeler *suh rah-play*; se souvenir de *suh soo-vuh-neer duh*

**rent (noun)** le loyer *luh lwah-yay*

**rent (verb)** louer *loo-ay*

**repair (verb)** réparer *ray-pah-ray*

**repeat** répéter *ray-pay-tay*

**replace** remplacer *rahn-plah-ssay*

**resemble** ressembler à *ruh-ssahn-blay ah*

**reservation** la réservation *lay ray-zehr-vah-ssyohn*

**reserve** réserver *ray-zehr-vay*

**resolve** résoudre *ray-zoo-druh*

**responsible** responsable *rehss-pohn-ssah-bluh*

**rest (noun)** le repos *luh ruh-poh*

**rest (verb)** se reposer *suh ruh-poh-zay*

**restaurant** le restaurant *luh rehss-toh-rahn*

**result** le résultat *luh ray-zewl-tah*

**retain** retenir *ruh-tuh-neer*

**return** retourner *ruh-toor-nay*; **return (give back)** rendre *rahn-druh*

**reward (noun)** la récompense *lah ray-kohn-pahnss*

**reward (verb)** récompenser *ray-kohn-pahn-ssay*

**rice** le riz *luh ree*

**right: to be right** avoir raison *ah-vwahr reh-zohn*

**right (direction)** droit *drwah*; **to the right** à droite *ah drwaht*

**ring (noun)** la bague *lah bahg*

**ring (verb)** sonner *soh-nay*

**river** le fleuve *luh fluhv*; la rivière *lah ree-vyehr*

**road** le chemin *luh shuh-man*

**roast (adj.)** rôti(e) *roh-tee*

**roll** le petit pain *luh puh-tee pan*

**roof** le toit *luh twah*

**room** la pièce *lah pyehss*; la salle *lah sahl*; la chambre *lah shahn-bruh*; **single room** une chambre à un lit *ewn shahn-bruh ah uhn lee*; **double room** une chambre à deux lits *ewn shahn-bruh ah duh lee*

**round** rond(e) *rohn(d)*

**route** la route *lah root*

**row (noun)** le rang *luh rahn*

**rubber** le caoutchouc *luh kah-oo-tshoo*; **rubbers** les caoutchoucs *lay kah-oo-tshoo*

**rug** le tapis *luh tah-pee*

**rule** la règle *lah reh-gluh*

**ruler** la règle *lah reh-gluh*

**run** courir *koo-reer*

**runway** la piste *lah peesst*

# S

**sad** triste *treesst*

**safe (strongbox)** le coffre-fort *luh koh-fruh fohr*

**sale** la vente *lah vahnt*; **for sale** en vente *ahn vahnt*

**sale (bargain)** les soldes (m. pl.) *lay sohld*

**salesman** le vendeur *luh vahn-duhr*

**saleswoman** la vendeuse *lah vahn-duhz*

**salmon** le saumon *luh soh-mohn*

**salt** le sel *luh sehl*

**salted** salé *sah-lay*

**sand** le sable *luh sah-bluh*

**same** même *mehm*

**sample** l'échantillon (m.) *lay-shahn-tee-yohn*

**sardine** la sardine *lah sahr-deen*

**satin** le satin *luh sah-tan*

**satisfied** satisfait(e) *sah-teess-feh(t)*

**Saturday** samedi *sahm-dee*

**sauerkraut** la choucroute *lah shoo-kroot*

**sausage** la saucisse *lah soh-sseess*

**say** dire *deer*

**scarf** l'écharpe (f.) *lay-shahrp*

**schedule** l'horaire (m.) *loh-rehr*

**school** l'école (f.) *lay-kohl*

**scissors** les ciseaux (m. pl.) *lay see-zoh*

**scrambled** brouillé(e) *broo-yay*

**sea** la mer *lah mehr*

**seafood** les fruits (m. pl.) de mer *lay frwee duh mehr*

**season** la saison *lah seh-zohn*

**seasoned** assaisonné *ah-sseh-zoh-nay*

**seat** la place *lah plahss*; le siège *luh syehzh*

**secondhand** usagé *ew-zah-zhay*

**secondhand goods** la marchandise d'occasion *lah mahr-shahn-deez doh-kah-zyohn*

**security** la sécurité *lah say-kew-ree-tay*

**see** voir *vwahr*

**seem** sembler *sahn-blay*; avoir l'air de *ah-vwahr lehr duh*

**sell** vendre *vahn-druh*

**send** envoyer *ahn-vwah-yay*; **send for** faire venir *fehr vuh-neer*; **send back** renvoyer *rahn-vwah-yay*

**sentence** la phrase *lah frahz*

**serious** sérieux(ieuse) *say-ryuh(z)*; grave *grahv*

**serve** servir *sehr-veer*

**service** le service *luh sehr-veess*

**service station** la station service *lah stah-ssyohn sehr-veess*

**settle** régler *ray-glay*; **settle an affair** régler une affaire *ray-glay ewn ah-fehr*

**seven** sept *seht*

**seventeen** dix-sept *dee seht*

**seventy** soixante-dix *swah-ssahnt deess*

**several** plusieurs *plew-zyuhr*

**sew** coudre *koo-druh*

**shade** l'ombre (f.) *lohn-bruh*

**share** partager *pahr-tah-zhay*

**shark** le requin *luh ruh-kan*

**shave (verb)** raser *rah-zay*

**shawl** le châle *luh shahl*

**she** elle *ehl*

**sheet** la feuille *lah fuhy*

**shelf** le rayon *luh reh-yohn*

**shellfish** le coquillage *luh koh-kee-yahzh*

**sherbet** le sorbet *luh sohr-beh*

**shine (verb)** cirer *see-ray*

**shirt** la chemise *lah shuh-meez*

**shoe** le soulier *luh soo-lyay*; la chaussure *lah shoh-ssewr*

**shoelaces** les lacets (m. pl.) *lay lah-sseh*

**shoemaker** le cordonnier *luh kohr-doh-nyay*

**shop (noun)** la boutique *lah boo-teek*

**shop (verb)** faire des achats *fehr day zah-shah*; faire des emplettes *fehr day zahn-pleht*

**shop window** la vitrine *lah vee-treen*

**shore (bank)** la rive *lah reev*

**short** court(e) *koor(t)*

**shorts (briefs)** le caleçon *luh kahl-ssohn*

**short story** le conte *luh kohnt*

**shoulder** l'épaule (f.) *lay-pohl*

**show (verb)** montrer *mohn-tray*

**show (noun)** le spectacle *luh spehk-tah-kluh*

**shower** la douche *lah doosh*

**shrimp** la crevette *lah kruh-veht*

**sick** malade *mah-lahd*

**sickness** la maladie *lah mah-lah-dee*

**side** le côté *luh koh-tay*

**sidewalk** le trottoir *luh troh-twahr*

**sightseeing** le tourisme *luh too-reess-muh*

**sign (noun)** l'enseigne (f.) *lahn-sseh-nyuh*

**sign (verb)** signer *see-nyay*

**silk** la soie *lah swah*

**silver** l'argent (m.) *lahr-zhahn*

**since** depuis *duh-pwee*

**since when** depuis quand *duh-pwee kahn*

**sing** chanter *shahn-tay*

**single (unmarried)** célibataire *say-lee-bah-tehr*

**sir** monsieur *muh-ssyuh*

**sister** la soeur *lah suhr*

**sit** s'asseoir *sah-sswahr*

**six** six *seess*

**sixteen** seize *sehz*

**sixty** soixante *swah-ssahnt*

**size** la taille *lah tahy*

**ski** le ski *luh skee*; **water skis** les skis nautiques *lay skee-noh-teek*

**ski lift** le téléski *luh tay-lay-sskee*

**ski slope** la piste de ski *lah peesst duh skee*

**skin** la peau *lah poh*

**skirt** la jupe *lah zhewp*

**sky** le ciel *luh syehl*

**skyscraper** le gratte-ciel *luh graht syehl*

**sleep (verb)** dormir *dohr-meer*

**sleep, sleepiness** le sommeil *luh soh-mehy*; **to be sleepy** avoir sommeil *ah-vwahr soh-mehy*; **sleeping car** le wagon-lit *luh vah-gohn lee*; **sleeping pill** le somnifère *luh sohm-nee-fehr*

**sleeve** la manche *lah mahnsh*

**slice** la tranche *lah trahnsh*

**slide (pictures)** la diapositive *lah dee-ah-poh-zee-teev*

**slip (clothing)** la combinaison *lah kohn-bee-neh-zohn*; le jupon *luh zhew-pohn*

**slippers** les pantoufles (f. pl.) *lay pahn-too-fluh*

**slow (adj.)** lent(e) *lahn(t)*

**slowly (adv.)** lentement *lahnt-mahn*

**small** petit(e) *puh-tee(t)*

**smoke** fumer *few-may*

**smoker** le fumeur *luh few-muhr*

**snail** l'escargot (m.) *lehss-kahr-goh*

**snow (noun)** la neige *lah nehzh*

**snow (verb)** neiger *neh-zhay*

**so** alors *ah-lohr*

**soap** le savon *luh sah-vohn*; **a bar of soap** la savonnette *lah sah-voh-neht*

**socket** la prise de courant *lah preez duh koo-rahn*

**socks** les chaussettes (f. pl.) *lay shoh-sseht*

**soda** le soda *luh soh-dah*

**soft** doux, douce *doo(ss)*

**softly** doucement *dooss-mahn*

**sole (fish)** la sole *lah sohl*

**solid (colored)** uni (e) *ew-nee*

**some** quelques *kehl-kuh*

**some** du *dew*; de la *duh lah*; de l' *duhl*; des *day*

**someone** quelqu'un *kehl-kuhn*

**something** quelque chose *kehl-kuh shohz*

**sometimes** quelquefois *kehl-kuh fwah*

**somewhere** quelque part *kehl-kuh pahr*

**son** le fils *luh feess*

**song** la chanson *lah shahn-ssohn*

**soon** bientôt *byan-toh*; **see you soon** à bientôt *ah byan-toh*

**sore throat** le mal de gorge *luh mahl duh gohrzh*

**sorry: to be sorry** être désolé(e) *eh-truh day-zoh-lay*; regretter *ruh-greh-tay*

**soup** la soupe *lah soop*; le potage *luh poh-tahzh*

**south** le sud *luh sewd*

**space** l'espace (m.) *lehss-pahss*

**speak** parler *pahr-lay*

**speed** la vitesse *lah vee-tehss*

**spell** épeler *ay-play*

**spend (money)** dépenser *day-pahn-ssay*

**spend (time)** passer *pah-ssay*

**spinach** les épinards (m. pl.) *lay zay-pee-nahr*

**spoon** la cuiller *lah kwee-yehr*; **teaspoon** la cuiller à café *lah kwee-yehr ah kah-fay*; **tablespoon** la cuiller à soupe *lah kwee-yehr ah soop*; **teaspoonful** la cuillerée à café *lah kwee-yuh-ray ah kah-fay*; **tablespoonful** la cuillerée à soupe *lah kwee-yuh-ray ah soop*

**spouse** l'époux (m.), l'épouse (f.) *lay-poo, lay-pooz*

**spring** le printemps *luh pran-tahn*

**square (adj.)** carré(e) *kah-ray*

**square (public)** la place *lah plahss*

**stadium** le stade *luh stahd*

**stain** la tache *lah tahsh*

**staircase** l'escalier (m.) *lehss-kah-lyay*

**stamp** le timbre *luh tan-bruh*

**stand (noun)** le kiosque *luh kee-ohssk*; **newsstand** le kiosque à journaux *luh kee-ohssk ah zhoor-noh*

**state** l'état (m.) *lay-tah*

**station** la gare *lah gahr*

**stay, sojourn** le séjour *luh say-zhoor*

**stay (verb)** rester *rehss-tay*

**stay at** loger *loh-zhay*

**steak** le bifteck *luh beef-tehk*

**steal** voler *voh-lay*

**steering wheel** le volant *luh voh-lahn*

**stew** le ragoût *luh rah-goo*

**stewardess** l'hôtesse de l'air *loh-tehss duh lehr*

**still** encore *ahn-kohr*

**stockings** les bas (m. pl.) *lay bah*

**stock market** la bourse *lah boorss*

**stomach** l'estomac (m.) *lehss-toh-mah*; le ventre *luh van-truh*

**stone** la pierre *lah pyehr*

**stop (noun)** l'arrêt (m.) *lah-reh*

**stop (verb)** arrêter *ah-reh-tay*

**stop light** le feu *luh fuh*

**store** le magasin *luh mah-gah-zan*; **book** la librairie *lah lee-breh-ree*; **camera** le magasin de photographie *luh mah-gah-zan duh foh-toh-grah-fee*; **clothing** le magasin de vêtements *luh mah-gah-zan duh veht-mahn*; **department** le grand magasin *luh grahn mah-gah-zan*; **drug** la pharmacie *lah fahr-mah-ssee*; **grocery** l'épicerie (f.) *lay-peess-ree*; **hardware** la

quincaillerie *lah kahn-kahy-ree*; **jewelry** la bijouterie *lah bee-zhoo-tree*; **liquor** le magasin de spiritueux *luh mah-gah-zan duh spee-ree-tew-uh*; **record** le magasin de disques *luh mah-gah-zan duh deessk*; **shoe** le magasin de chaussures *luh mah-gah-zan duh shoh-ssewr*; **tobacco** le bureau de tabac *luh bew-roh duh tah-bah*; **toy** le magasin de jouets *luh mah-gah-zan duh zhoo-eh*

**storm** la tempête *lah tan-peht*; l'orage (m.) *loh-rahzh*

**story** l'histoire (f.) *leess-twahr*

**straw** la paille *lah pahy*

**strawberry** la fraise *lah frehz*

**stream** la rivière *lah ree-vyehr*

**street** la rue *lah rew*

**string** la ficelle *lah fee-ssehl*

**string beans** les haricots (m. pl.) verts *lay ah-ree-koh vehr*

**stripe** la rayure *lah rah-yewr*; **striped** à rayures *ah rah-yewr*

**strong** fort(e) *fohr(t)*

**stuffed** farci(e) *fahr-ssee*

**style** la mode *lah mohd*; **in style** à la mode *ah lah mohd*

**subtitles** les sous-titres (m. pl.) *lay soo-tee-truh*

**suburb** la banlieue *lah bahn-lyuh*; le faubourg *luh foh-boor*

**subway** le métro *luh may-troh*

**suede** le daim *luh dan*

**sugar** le sucre *luh sew-kruh*

**suit (man's)** le complet *luh kohn-pleh*; **(woman's)** le tailleur *luh tah-yuhr*

**suitcase** la valise *lah vah-leez*

**sum total** le montant *luh mohn-tahn*

**summer** l'été (m.) *lay-tay*

**sun** le soleil *luh soh-lehy*

**sunburn** les coups (m. pl.) de soleil *lay kood soh-lehy*

**Sunday** dimanche *dee-mahnsh*

**sunglasses** les lunettes (f. pl.) de soleil *lay lew-neht duh soh-lehy*

**suntan lotion** la lotion à bronzer *lah loh-ssyohn ah brohn-zay*

**supermarket** le supermarché *luh sew-pehr-mahr-shay*

**supper** le dîner *luh dee-nay*; le souper *luh soo-pay*; **to have supper** dîner *dee-nay*; souper *soo-pay*

**sure** sûr(e) *sewr*

**surfboard** la planche de surf *lah plahnsh duh sewrf*

**surgeon** le chirurgien *luh sheer-ewr-zhyan*

**sweater** le chandail *luh shahn-dahy*

**sweet** doux, douce *doo, dooss*

**swim** nager *nah-zhay*

**swimming pool** la piscine *lah pee-sseen*

**synagogue** la synagogue *lah see-nah-gohg*

**synthetic** synthétique *san-tay-teek*

# T

**table** la table *lah tah-bluh*

**tablet (pill)** le comprimé *luh kohn-pree-may*

**tailor** le tailleur *luh tah-yuhr*

**take** prendre *prahn-druh*

**take off (clothing)** ôter *oh-tay*; enlever *ahn-luh-vay*

**tampon** le tampon périodique *luh tahn-pohn pay-ree-oh-deek*

**tangerine** la mandarine *lah mahn-dah-reen*

**taste (noun)** le goût *luh goo*

**taste (verb)** goûter *goo-tay*

**taxi** le taxi *luh tahk-ssee*

**tea** le thé *luh tay*; **iced** le thé glacé *luh tay glah-ssay*; **with lemon** au citron *oh see-trohn*; **with milk** au lait *oh leh*; **with sugar** sucré *sew-kray*

**team** l'équipe (f.) *lay-keep*

**telegram** le télégramme *luh tay-lay-grahm*

**telephone** le téléphone *luh tay-lay-fohn*; **telephone book** l'annuaire (m.) *lah-new-ehr*; **telephone booth** la cabine téléphonique *lah kah-been tay-lay-foh-neek*; **telephone call** le coup de téléphone *luh koo duh tay-lay-fohn*; **to call** donner un coup de téléphone *doh-nay uhn koo duh tay-lay-fohn*

**television** la télévision *lah tay-lay-vee-zyohn*

**tell** raconter *rah-kohn-tay*

**temporary** provisoire *proh-veez-wahr*

**ten** dix *deess*

**tent** la tente *lah tahnt*

**terrific** formidable *fohr-mee-dah-bluh*

**terrycloth** le tissu-éponge *luh tee-ssew ay-pohnzh*

**thank** remercier *ruh-mehr-ssyay*

**thanks to** grâce à *grahss ah*

**thank-you** merci *mehr-ssee*

**that** ça *sah*; cela *suh-lah*

**the** le(m.), la (f.), les (m./f. pl.) *luh, lah, lay*

**there** là *lah*; **over there** là-bas *lah bah*

**there is, are** il y a *eel yah*; voilà *vwah-lah*

**they** ils (m. pl.) *eel*, elles (f. pl.) *ehl*

**thief** le voleur *luh voh-luhr*

**thin** mince *manss*

**thing** la chose *lah shohz*

**think** penser *pahn-ssay*

**thirst** la soif *lah swahf*; **be thirsty** avoir soif *ah-vwahr swahf*

**thirteen** treize *trehz*

**thirty** trente *trahnt*

**this** ceci *suh-ssee*

**thousand** mille *meel*

**three** trois *trwah*

**throat** la gorge *lah gohrzh*

**through** à travers *ah trah-vehr*

**thumb** le pouce *luh pooss*

**Thursday** jeudi *zhuh-dee*

**ticket** le billet *luh bee-yeh*; **entrance ticket** le billet d'entrée *luh bee-yeh dahn-tray*

**ticket collector** le contrôleur *luh kohn-troh-luhr*

**ticket window** le guichet *luh gee-sheh*

**tie (neck)** la cravate *lah krah-vaht*

**time** l'heure (f.) *luhr*; le temps *luh tahn*; **at what time?** à quelle heure? *ah kehl uhr*; **on time** à l'heure *ah luhr*

**time (in a series)** la fois *la fwah*; **one time** une fois *ewn fwah*; **two times** deux fois *duh fwah*

**timetable** l'horaire (m.) *loh-rehr*; l'indicateur (m.) *lan-dee-kah-tuhr*

**tip (end)** le bout *luh boo*

**tip (gratuity)** le pourboire *luh poor-bwahr*

**tire (car)** le pneu *luh pnuh*

**tire (verb)** fatiguer *fah-tee-gay*

**tired** fatigué(e) *fah-tee-gay*

**tiring** fatigant(e) *fah-tee-gahn(t)*

**tissue** le mouchoir en papier *luh moo-shwahr ahn pah-pyay*

**title** le titre *luh tee-truh*

**to** à *ah*

**toast** le pain grillé *luh pan gree-yay*

**tobacco** le tabac *luh tah-bah*

**today** aujourd'hui *oh-zhoor-dwee*

**toe** l'orteil (m.) *lohr-tehy*

**together** ensemble *ahn-ssahn-bluh*

**toilet** la toilette *lah twah-leht*

**token** le jeton *luh zhuh-tohn*

**tolerate** supporter *sew-pohr-tay*

**tomato** la tomate *lah toh-maht*

**tomorrow** demain *duh-man*

**tonsilitis** l'amygdalite (f.) *lah-meeg-dah-leet*

**tooth** la dent *lah dahn*; **toothache** le mal de dent *luh mahl duh dahn*

**toothpaste** la pâte dentifrice *lah paht dahn-tee-freess*

**toothpick** le cure-dent *luh kewr dahn*

**touch** toucher *too-shay*

**tourist** le touriste *luh too-reesst*

**tourist office** le syndicat d'initiative *luh san-dee-kah dee-nee-ssyah-teev*

**towards** vers *vehr*

**towel** la serviette *lah sehr-vyeht*

**tower** la tour *lah toor*

**town hall** la mairie *lah meh-ree*

**track** la voie *lah vwah*

**traffic** la circulation *lah seer-kew-lah-ssyohn*

**traffic light** le feu *luh fuh*

**train** le train *luh tran*

**translate** traduire *trah-dweer*

**travel (verb)** voyager *vwah-yah-zhay*

**travel agency** l'agence (f.) de voyage *lah-zhahnss duh vwah-yahzh*

**treatment** le traitement *luh treht-mahn*

**tree** l'arbre (m.) *lahr-bruh*

**trick (verb)** tromper *trohn-pay*

**trip** le voyage *luh vwah-yahzh*; l'excursion (f.) *lehkss-kewr-zyohn*; **business trip** le voyage d'affaires *luh vwah-yahzh dah-fehr*

**trouble** la difficulté *lah dee-fee-kewl-tay*

**trout** la truite *lah trweet*

**truck** le camion *luh kah-myohn*

**true** vrai(e) *vreh*

**trunk** la malle *lah mahl;* **car trunk** la malle arrière *lah mahl ah-ryehr*

**truth** la vérité *lah vay-ree-tay*

**try (to)** essayer (de) *eh-sseh-yay duh*

**try (on)** essayer *eh-sseh-yay*

**Tuesday** mardi *mahr-dee*

**tuna fish** le thon *luh tohn*

**turkey** la dinde *lah dand*

**turn (noun)** le tour *luh toor*

**turn (verb)** tourner *toor-nay*

**twelve** douze *dooz*

**twenty** vingt *van*

**two** deux *duh*

# U

**ugly** laid(e) *leh(d)*

**umbrella** le parapluie *luh pah-rah-plwee*

**unbearable** insupportable *an-ssew-pohr-tah-bluh*

**unbelievable** incroyable *an-krwah-yah-bluh*

**undecided** indécis(e) *an-day-ssee(z)*

**under** sous *soo;* dessous *duh-ssoo*

**undershirt** le maillot de corps *luh mah-yoh duh kohr*

**understand** comprendre *kohn-prahn-druh*

**underwear** les sous-vêtements (m. pl.) *lay soo veht-mahn*

**unfair** injuste *an-zhewsst*

**unhappy** malheureux(euse) *mahl-uh-ruh(z)*

**unimportant** insignifiant(e) *an-ssee-nee-fee-ahn(t)*

**United States** les États-Unis *lay zay-tah zew-nee*

**until** jusqu'à *zhewss-kah*

**up, upstairs** en haut *ahn oh*

**urgent** urgent(e) *ewr-zhahn(t);* **urgently** (d'urgence) *dewr-zhahnss*

**us** nous *noo*

**use (verb)** utiliser *ew-tee-lee-zay;* employer *ahn-plwah-yay*

**use (noun)** l'emploi (m.) *lahn-plwah*

**used up** épuisé(e) *ay-pwee-zay*

**useful** utile *ew-teel*

**useless** inutile *een-ew-teel*

# V

**vacation** les vacances (f. pl.) *lay vah-kahnss*

**valid** valable *vah-lah-bluh*

**value** la valeur *lah vah-luhr*

**varied** varié(e) *vah-ree-yay*

**veal** le veau *luh voh*

**vegetable** le légume *luh lay-gewm*

**velvet** le velours *luh vuh-loor*

**very** très *treh*

**vest** le gilet *luh zhee-leh*

**vicinity** les environs (m. pl.) *lay zahn-vee-rohn*

**view** la vue *lah vew*

**village** le village *luh vee-lahzh*

**vinegar** le vinaigre *luh vee-neh-gruh*

**vitamin** la vitamine *lah vee-tah-meen*

# W

**waist** la taille *lah tahy*

**waiter** le garçon *luh gahr-ssohn*

**wait for** attendre *ah-tahn-druh*

**waiting room** la salle d'attente *lah sahl dah-tahnt*

**waitress** la serveuse *lah sehr-vuhz*

**walk (noun)** la promenade *lah prohm-nahd*; **to take a walk** faire une promenade *fehr ewn prohm-nahd*

**walk (verb)** marcher *mahr-shay*

**wall** le mur *luh mewr*

**wallet** le portefeuille *luh pohr-tuh-fuhy*

**want** désirer *day-zee-ray*; vouloir *voo-lwahr*; avoir envie de *ah-vwahr ahn-vee duh*

**war** la guerre *lah gehr*

**warm** chaud *shoh*

**wash** laver *lah-vay*; **wash oneself** se laver *suh lah-vay*

**wash and wear** ne pas repasser *nuh pah ruh-pah-ssay*

**washroom** le lavabo *luh lah-vah-boh*

**watch (noun)** la montre *lah mohn-truh*

**watch (verb); (look at)** regarder *ruh-gahr-day*; **(supervise)** surveiller *sewr-veh-yay*

**watchmaker's shop** l'horlogerie (f.) *lohr-lohzh-ree*

**waterfall** la cascade *lah kahss-kahd*

**water** l'eau *loh*

**watermelon** la pastèque *lah pahss-tehk*

**way** le moyen *luh mwah-yan*; la façon *lah fah-ssohn*

**weak** faible *feh-bluh*

**wear** porter *pohr-tay*

**weather** le temps *luh tahn*

**Wednesday** mercredi *mehr-kruh-dee*

**week** la semaine *lah suh-mehn*

**weigh** peser *puh-zay*

**weight** le poids *luh pwah*

**welcome: you're welcome** de rien *duh ryan*; il n'y a pas de quoi *eel nyah pah duh kwah*

**well** bien *byan*

**well-done (cooking)** bien cuit *byan kwee*

**west** l'ouest (m.) *lwehsst*

**wet** mouillé(e) *moo-yay*

**what** que, quoi *kuh, kwah*

**when** quand *kahn*

**where** où *oo*

**which** quel(le) *kehl*

**white** blanc(he) *blahn(sh)*

**who** qui *kee*

**whole** entier(ière) *ahn-tyay (ahn-tyehr)*

**why** pourquoi *poor-kwah*

**wife** la femme *lah fahm*

**willingly** volontiers *voh-lohn-tyay*

**win** gagner *gah-nyay*

**wind** le vent *luh vahn*

**window** la fenêtre *lah fuh-neh-truh*; **ticket window** le guichet *luh gee-sheh*

**window display** l'étalage (m.) *lay-tah-lahzh*

**windshield wipers** les essuie-glaces (m.) *lay zeh-sswee glahss*

**wine** le vin *luh van*; **red** rouge *roozh*; **rosé** rosé *roh-zay*; **sparkling** mousseux *moo-ssuh*; **white** blanc *blahn*

**wine merchant** le négociant en vins *luh nay-gohss-yahn ahn van*

**wine waiter** le sommelier *luh soh-muh-lyay*

**winter** l'hiver (m.) *lee-vehr*

**wish (verb)** désirer *day-zee-ray*; vouloir *voo-lwahr*; avoir envie de *ah-vwahr ahn-vee duh*

**wish (someone something)** souhaiter *sweh-tay*

**with** avec *ah-vehk*

**without** sans *sahn*

**woman** la femme *lah fahm*

**wood(s)** le(s) bois *luh (lay) bwah*

**wool** la laine *lah lehn*

**word** le mot *luh moh*

**work (noun)** le travail *luh trah-vahy*

**work (verb)** travailler *trah-vah-yay*; **function** fonctionner *fohnk-ssyoh-nay*; marcher *mahr-shay*

**workshop** l'atelier (m.) *lah-tuh-lyay*

**world** le monde *luh mohnd*

**worn out (things)** usé(e) *ew-zay*; **(people)** épuisé(e) *ay-pwee-zay*

**wound (noun)** la blessure *lah bleh-ssewr*

**wound (verb)** blesser *bleh-ssay*

**wounded** blessé *bleh-ssay*

**wrapper** l'enveloppe (f.) *lahn-vlohp*

**wrap up** emballer *ahn-bah-lay*; envelopper *ahn-vloh-pay*

**wrist** le poignet *luh pwah-nyeh*

**write** écrire *ay-kreer*

**wrong: to be wrong** avoir tort *ah-vwahr tohr*

# X

**X-ray** la radio *lah rah-dyoh*

# Y

**year** l'an (m.) *lahn*, l'année (f.) *lah-nay*

**yellow** jaune *zhohn*

**yes** oui *wee*

**yesterday** hier *yehr*

**yet** encore *ahn-kohr*

**yogurt** le yaourt *luh yah-oort*

**you** tu *tew*; vous *voo*

**young** jeune *zhuhn*

# Z

**zero** zéro *zay-roh*

**zipper** la fermeture éclair *lah fehr-muh-tewr ay-klehr*

**zone** la zone *lah zohn*

**zoo** le zoo *luh zoh*; le jardin zoologique *luh zhahr-dan zoh-oh-loh-zheek*

# FRENCH-ENGLISH DICTIONARY

## A

**à** to, at; **à peu près** about, approximately; **à prix fixe** fixed price meal; **à travers** across, through

**abricot (m.)** apricot

**accord (m.)** agreement; **d'accord** agreed, O.K.

**accrocher** to hang up

**achat (m.)** purchase

**acheter** to buy

**addition (f.)** check, restaurant bill

**adresse (f.)** address

**affaire (f.)** matter, concern

**affiche (f.)** poster

**agence (f.)** agency, bureau; **une agence de voyage** travel agency

**agent (de police) (m.)** policeman

**agneau (m.)** lamb

**aider** to help

**aiguille (f.)** needle

**ail (m.)** garlic

**ailleurs** elsewhere

**aimer** to like, love; **aimer mieux** to prefer

**ajouter** to add

**alcool (m.)** alcohol

**aliments (m.pl.)** food

**aller** to go; **aller à** to fit

**allumer** to light

**allumette (f.)** match

**alors** then

**amande (f.)** almond

**ambulance (f.)** ambulance

**amende (f.)** fine, penalty

**amer, amère** bitter

**ami(e) (m./f.)** friend

**amour (m.)** love (noun)

**ampoule (f.)** bulb (electric)

**amygdalite (f.)** tonsilitis

**an (m.)** year

**ananas (m.)** pineapple

**ancien(ne)** former, old

**anglais (m.)** English

**année (f.)** year

**anniversaire (m.)** birthday

**annonce (f.)** advertisement

**annuaire (m.)** telephone book

**antiseptique (m.)** antiseptic

**août** August

**appareil de photo (m.)** camera

**appartenir** to belong

**appeler** to call; **s'appeler** to be called, named

**appendicite (f.)** appendicitis

**apporter** to bring

**apprendre** to learn

**après** after; **après-demain** day after tomorrow; **après-midi** afternoon

**arbre (m.)** tree

**argent (m.)** money, silver

**armoire (f.)** closet

**arranger** to adjust

**arrêt (m.)** a stop; **arrêt obligatoire** regular bus stop

**arrêter** to stop

**arrière** back; **en arrière** backward, behind

**arrivée (f.)** arrival

**artichaut (m.)** artichoke

**ascenseur (m.)** elevator

**asperge (f.)** asparagus

**assaisonné(e)** seasoned

**asseoir (s' . . .)** to sit down;
**asseyez-vous** sit down

**assez (de)** enough

**assiette (f.)** plate

**assurance (f.)** insurance

**assurer (faire assurer)** to insure

**atelier (m.)** workshop, studio

**attendre** to wait for

**attention** caution

**atterrir** to land (plane)

**atterrissage (m.)** landing (plane)

**attraper** to catch

**au** to the; **au lieu de** instead of;
**au milieu de** in the middle of;
**au moins** at least; **au secours**
help

**auberge (f.)** inn; **auberge de
jeunesse** youth hostel

**aubergine (f.)** eggplant

**aucun(e)** any; **ne (verb) aucun(e)**
not any

**aujourd'hui** today

**aussi** also, too

**auteur (m.)** author

**autoroute (f.)** highway

**autour de** around

**autre** other

**aux** to the

**avant (de, que)** before;
**avant-hier** day before
yesterday; **en avant** forward,
ahead

**avec** with

**avion (m.)** airplane; **par avion**
air mail, by plane

**avis (m.)** notice

**avocat (m.)** lawyer

**avoir** to have; **avoir l'air de** to
seem to; **avoir besoin de** to
need; **avoir chaud** to be hot;

**avoir envie de** to want to;
**avoir faim** to be hungry; **avoir
froid** to be cold; **avoir peur de**
to be afraid of; **avoir raison** to
be right; **avoir soif** to be
thirsty; **avoir sommeil** to be
sleepy; **avoir tort** to be wrong

# B

**bague (f.)** ring

**baguette (f.)** French bread

**baigner (se . . .)** to bathe

**bain (m.)** bath

**balcon (m.)** balcony

**ballet (m.)** ballet

**banane (f.)** banana

**banc (m.)** bench

**bande (f.)** bandage

**banlieue (f.)** suburb

**banque (f.)** bank

**bas (m. pl.)** stockings

**bas (se)** low; **en bas** downstairs

**bateau (m.)** boat

**bâtiment (m.)** building

**batterie (f.)** battery (car)

**beau (m.)** beautiful

**beaucoup (de)** many, much, a lot,
a great deal of

**belle (f.)** beautiful

**besoin (m.)** need; **avoir besoin
de** to need

**betterave (f.)** beet

**beurre (m.)** butter

**bibliothèque (f.)** library

**bien** well; **bien entendu** of
course

**bientôt** soon; **à bientôt** see you
soon

**bière (f.)** beer

**bifteck (m.)** steak

**bijou (m.)** jewel

**bijouterie (f.)** jewelry shop

**bijoutier (m.)** jeweler

**billet (m.)** ticket; **billet d'entrée** admission ticket

**biscuit (m.)** cookie

**bistro (m.)** bar, tavern, saloon

**blanc(he)** white

**blanchissage (m.)** laundering, washing

**blanchisserie (f.)** laundry

**blessé(e)** wounded

**blesser** to wound, hurt

**blessure (f.)** wound

**bleu(e)** blue

**bloc (m.)** writing pad

**blouse (f.)** blouse

**boeuf (m.)** beef, ox

**boire** to drink

**bois (m.)** wood; **bois (m. pl.)** woods

**boisson (f.)** drink; **une boisson non-alcoolisée** soft drink

**boîte (f.)** box; **boîte aux lettres** mailbox; **boîte de nuit** nightclub

**bon(ne)** good

**bonjour** hello

**bon marché** cheap

**bouche (f.)** mouth

**boucherie (f.)** butcher shop

**boucle (f.)** curl; **boucles d'oreille** earrings

**bougie (f.)** candle, spark plug

**bouilli(e)** boiled

**boulangerie (f.)** bakery

**boulette (f.)** meatball

**bourse (f.)** stock market

**bout (m.)** tip, point, end

**bouteille (f.)** bottle

**boutique (f.)** shop

**bouton (m.)** button

**braisé(e)** braised

**bras (m.)** arm

**brioche (f.)** breakfast bun

**briquet (m.)** cigarette lighter

**briser** to break

**brosse (f.)** brush; **brosse à dents** toothbrush

**brosser (se . . .)** to brush

**brouillé(e)** scrambled; **les oeufs brouillés** scrambled eggs

**bruit (m.)** noise

**brûler** to burn

**brûlure (f.)** a burn

**brun(e)** brown

**bureau (m.)** office, desk; **bureau de location** theater box office; **bureau d'objets trouvés** lost and found; **bureau de poste** post office; **bureau de renseignements** information desk; **bureau de tabac** tobacconist shop

# C

**ça** that; **ça ne fait rien** it doesn't matter

**cabine téléphonique (f.)** telephone booth

**cadeau (m.)** gift, present

**café (m.)** coffee, cafe; **café au lait** coffee with milk; **café crème** coffee with cream; **café express** espresso; **café glacé** iced coffee; **café noir** black coffee

**cahier (m.)** notebook

**caisse (f.)** cash register

**caissier (m.)** cashier

**caleçon (m.)** men's shorts, undergarments

**camion (m.)** truck

**campagne (f.)** country (outside city)

**canard (m.)** duck

**caoutchouc (m.)** rubber; **caoutchoucs (m. pl.)** rubbers

**carburateur (m.)** carburetor

**carotte (f.)** carrot

**carré(e)** square

**carreaux (à carreaux)** checked (material)

**carrefour (m.)** crossroad

**carte (f.)** map, card; **cartes à jouer** playing cards; **carte de crédit** credit card; **carte postale** post card; **carte routière** road map

**cas (m.)** case; **en cas d'urgence** in case of emergency

**cascade (f.)** waterfall

**casser** to break; **casser la croûte** to get a bite to eat

**cave (f.)** cellar

**ceci** this, it

**ceinture (f.)** belt; **ceinture de sauvetage** life preserver; **ceinture de sécurité** seat belt

**célibataire** single (unmarried)

**cendrier (m.)** ashtray

**cent** one hundred

**cerise (f.)** cherry

**chacun(e)** each one

**chaînette (f.)** chain (jewelry)

**chaise (f.)** chair

**châle (m.)** shawl

**chaleur (f.)** heat

**chambre (f.)** room; **chambre à coucher** bedroom; **chambre à un lit** single room; **chambre à deux lits** double room

**champignon (m.)** mushroom

**champ (m.)** field

**chance (f.)** luck; **Bonne chance!** Good luck!

**chandail (m.)** sweater

**changement (m.)** change

**changer** to change

**chanson (f.)** song

**chanter** to sing

**chaque** each

**charcuterie (f.)** cold cuts, delicatessen

**chasseur (m.)** bellboy, bellhop

**chat (m.)** cat

**château (m.)** castle

**chaud** hot; **avoir chaud** to be hot (person); **faire chaud** to be hot (weather)

**chauffage (m.)** heating

**chauffer** to heat

**chaussettes (f.)** socks

**chaussures (f.)** shoes

**chemin (m.)** road, way

**chemin de fer (m.)** railway, railroad

**chemise (f.)** shirt

**chèque (m.)** check; **toucher un chèque** to cash a check

**cher, chère** dear, expensive

**chercher** to look for

**cheval (m.) (pl. chevaux)** horse

**cheveux (m. pl.)** hair

**cheville (f.)** ankle

**chez** at the house (shop, business) of

**chien (m.)** dog

**chirurgien (m.)** surgeon

**choisir** to choose

**chose (f.)** thing

**chou (m.)** cabbage

**choucroute (f.)** sauerkraut

**choux de Bruxelles (m. pl.)** Brussel sprouts

**ciel (m.)** sky

**cigare (m.)** cigar

**cigarette (f.)** cigarette

**cil (m.)** eyelash

**cimetière (m.)** cemetery

**cinéma (m.)** movies
**cinq** five
**cinquante** fifty
**cintre (m.)** hanger
**circulation (f.)** traffic
**cirer** to shine, wax
**ciseaux (m. pl.)** scissors
**citron (m.)** lemon
**citronnade (f.)** lemonade
**clair(e)** clear, light (color)
**clef (f.)** key
**client (m.)** customer
**climatiseur (m.)** air conditioner
**cloche (f.)** bell
**coco (m.)** coconut
**coeur (m.)** heart
**coffre-fort (m.)** safe, strong-box
**coiffeur (m.)** barber
**coin (m.)** corner
**col (m.)** collar
**colis (m.)** package, parcel
**collants (m. pl.)** panty hose
**colle (f.)** glue
**collier (m.)** necklace
**combien (de)** how much, how many
**combinaison (f.)** slip (clothing)
**commande (f.)** order
**commander** to order
**comme** like, as
**commencer** to begin
**comment** how
**commissariat (m.)** police station
**compagnie (f.)** company
**complet (m.)** suit (man's)
**comprendre** to understand
**comprimé (m.)** tablet
**compris(e)** included
**compter** to count
**concert (m.)** concert; **la salle de concert** concert hall

**concierge (m. or f.)** house porter, caretaker, doorman
**concombre (m.)** cucumber
**conduire** to drive, take a person somewhere
**confiserie (f.)** confectionery store
**confiture (f.)** jam, marmalade
**connaître** to know, be acquainted with
**conseil (m.)** advice
**consigne (f.)** baggage checkroom
**consommation (f.)** drink
**contagieux (ieuse)** contagious
**conte (m.)** short story
**contenir** to contain
**contenu (m.)** contents
**contraire (m.)** opposite
**contre** against
**contrôleur (m.)** ticket collector
**contusion (f.)** bruise
**coquillage (m.)** shellfish
**cordonnier (m.)** shoemaker
**cornichon (m.)** pickle
**corps (m.)** body
**costume (m.)** suit (woman's)
**côte (f.)** coast
**côté (m.)** side; **à côté de** beside, next to
**côtelette (f.)** cutlet, chop
**coton (m.)** cotton
**cou (m.)** neck
**couche (f.)** diaper
**couchette (f.)** berth
**coude (m.)** elbow
**coudre** to sew
**couleur (f.)** color
**coup de téléphone (m.)** phone call
**coupe de cheveux (f.)** haircut
**coupe de glace (f.)** sundae
**couper** to cut
**cour (f.)** courtyard

courir  to run

courrier (m.)  mail

cours du change (m.)  exchange rate

court(e)  short

couteau (m.)  knife

coûter  to cost

coûteux (euse)  costly

couvert (m.)  cover charge

couverture (f.)  blanket

couvrir  to cover

crabe (m.)  crab

crampe (f.)  cramp

cravate (f.)  tie

crayon (m.)  pencil

crème (f.)  cream; la crème anglaise  custard; la crème fouettée  whipped cream

crêpe (f.)  thin French pancakes

crevette (f.)  shrimp

cric (m.)  jack (auto)

croire  to believe

croisement (m.)  intersection

croissant (m.)  crescent-shaped breakfast pastry

croûte (f.)  crust; casser la croûte  to get a bite to eat

cru(e)  raw, uncooked

cruche (f.)  pitcher

cuiller (f.)  spoon; cuiller à soupe tablespoon; cuiller à café  teaspoon

cuillerée (f.)  spoonful; cuillerée à soupe  tablespoonful; cuillerée à café  teaspoonful

cuir (m.)  leather

cuisine (f.)  cooking, kitchen

cuisinier (m.)  the cook

cuisse (f.)  thigh; les cuisses de grenouille  frog's legs

cuit(e)  cooked

cure-dent (m.)  toothpick

# D

d'abord  at first

d'accord  agreed, O.K.

daim (m.)  suede

dans  in

danse (f.)  the dance

danser  to dance

date (f.)  date

datte (f.)  date (fruit)

de  of; de bonne heure  early

débarquement (m.)  landing (boat)

débarquer  to land (boat)

décider  to decide

déclarer  to declare

déçu(e)  disappointed

dedans  inside

défendre  to forbid; défense de cracher  no spitting; défense d'entrée  no entry; défense de fumer  no smoking

défendu(e)  forbidden

dehors  outside

déjà  already

déjeuner (m.)  lunch

déjeuner  to eat lunch

demain  tomorrow

demander  to ask (for)

demeurer  to live, reside

demi(e)  half

démodé(e)  old-fashioned

dent (f.)  tooth; mal (m.) de dent toothache

dentelle (f.)  lace

dentifrice (m.)  mouthwash; la pâte dentifrice  toothpaste

déodorant (m.)  deodorant

dépêcher (se . . .)  to hurry up; dépêchez-vous  hurry up

dépenser  to spend money

déranger  to bother

**dernier(ière)** last

**derrière** behind

**des** some

**descendre** to go down, get off

**désirer** to desire, wish, want

**désolé(e)** sorry; **être désolé(e)** to be sorry

**dessous** under, beneath

**dessus** over, above

**deux** two

**devant** in front of

**devenir** to become

**devoir** to owe, have to, ought to

**diapositive (f.)** slide (photo)

**dictionnaire (m.)** dictionary; **dictionnaire de poche** pocket dictionary

**Dieu** God

**différent(e)** different

**difficile** difficult

**dimanche** Sunday

**diminuer** to diminish

**dinde (f.)** turkey

**dîner (m.)** dinner

**dîner** to dine

**dire** to say

**discothèque (f.)** discotheque

**dispute (f.)** dispute, argument

**disque (m.)** record

**dix** ten

**dix-huit** eighteen

**dix-neuf** nineteen

**dix-sept** seventeen

**docteur (m.)** doctor

**doigt (m.)** finger

**donner** to give

**dormir** to sleep

**dos (m.)** back

**douane (f.)** customs

**douanier (m.)** custom's official

**doucement** softly

**douche (f.)** shower

**douleur (f.)** pain

**doux, douce** sweet, mild, soft

**douzaine (f.)** dozen

**douze** twelve

**droit (m.)** right; **à droite** to the right

**du** some

**durer** to last

# E

**eau (f.)** water; **eau courante** running water; **eau chaude** hot water; **eau froide** cold water; **eau glacée** ice water; **eau minérale** mineral water

**échanger** to exchange

**échantillon (m.)** sample

**écharpe (f.)** scarf

**école (f.)** school

**écouter** to listen to

**écrire** to write

**égarer (s' . . .)** to lose one's way, to get lost

**église (f.)** church

**elle** she

**elles** they

**emballer** to wrap up

**embrasser** to kiss

**emploi (m.)** employ, use

**employer** to use

**emporter** to carry, take away

**emprunter** to borrow

**en** in; **en arrière** behind; **en avant** ahead; **en bas** downstairs; **en ce moment** right now; **en face de** opposite, facing; **en retard** late; **en voiture** all aboard

**encore** yet, still; **encore une fois** again

**endosser** to endorse

**endroit (m.)** place

**enfant (m./f.)** child

**ennuyer** to annoy, bother

**enregistrer** to check bags

**enseigne (f.)** sign

**ensemble** together

**entendre** to hear

**entier (entière)** entire, whole

**entre** between

**entrée (f.)** entrance

**entrer** to enter

**enveloppe (f.)** envelope, wrapper, cover

**envelopper** to wrap up

**environ** about

**environs (m. pl.)** vicinity

**envoyer** to send

**épaule (f.)** shoulder

**épeler** to spell

**épicerie (f.)** grocery store

**épinards (m. pl.)** spinach

**épingle (f.)** pin

**époux (épouse)** spouse

**épuisé(e)** exhausted, used up

**équipe (f.)** team

**escalier (m.)** stairs

**escargot (m.)** snail

**espace (m.)** space

**espérer** to hope

**essayer (de)** to try (to)

**essence (f.)** gas; **le réservoir à essence** gas tank

**essuie-glaces (m. pl.)** windshield wipers

**est (m.)** east

**estomac (m.)** stomach

**et** and

**étage (m.)** story, floor

**étalage (m.)** window display

**état (m.)** state

**États-Unis (m. pl.)** United States

**été (m.)** summer

**étiquette (f.)** label

**étranger(ère)** foreign; **à l'étranger** abroad

**être** to be; **être d'accord** to agree; **être de retour** to be back; **être en difficulté** to be in trouble

**éviter** to avoid

**excellent(e)** excellent

**excursion (f.)** excursion, trip

**exemple (m.)** example; **par exemple** for example

**express (m.)** express

# F

**facile** easy

**façon (f.)** way, style, fashion

**facteur (m.)** mailman

**facture (f.)** bill, invoice

**faible** weak

**faim (f.)** hunger; **avoir faim** to be hungry

**faire** to make, do; **faire beau** to be beautiful weather; **faire chaud** to be hot weather; **faire des achats** to go shopping; **faire des emplettes** to go shopping; **faire du soleil** to be sunny; **faire du vent** to be windy; **faire froid** to be cold weather; **faire la connaissance de** to make the acquaintance of; **faire la correspondance** to change trains or planes; **faire la queue** to form a line; **faire une promenade** to take a walk; **faire venir** to send for

**fait(e) à la main** handmade

**famille (f.)** family

**farci(e)** stuffed

**fatigant(e)** tiring
**fatigué(e)** tired
**fatiguer** to tire
**faubourg (m.)** suburb
**faut: il faut** it is necessary
**faute (f.)** mistake, error
**faux, fausse** false
**félicitations (f.)** congratulations
**femme (f.)** woman, wife; **femme de chambre** chambermaid
**fenêtre (f.)** window
**fer (m.)** iron
**ferme (f.)** farm
**fermer** to close
**fermeture éclair (f.)** zipper
**fête (f.)** festival, feast, holiday
**feu (m.)** fire, traffic light
**feuille (f.)** sheet, leaf
**feutre (m.)** felt
**février** February
**ficelle (f.)** string
**fiche (f.)** form
**fièvre (f.)** fever
**figue (f.)** fig
**figure (f.)** face
**fille (f.)** girl, daughter
**film (m.)** film
**fils (m.)** son
**fin (f.)** end
**finir** to finish, end
**flan (m.)** custard
**flanelle (f.)** flannel
**fleur (f.)** flower
**fleuriste (m.)** florist
**fleuve (m.)** river
**foie (m.)** liver
**foire (f.)** fair, market
**fois (f.)** time in a series; **une fois** one time, once; **deux fois** two times, twice
**foncé(e)** dark (color)

**fonctionner** to function, work
**fontaine (f.)** fountain
**forêt (f.)** forest
**formidable** terrific
**formule (f.)** form
**fort(e)** strong
**fourchette (f.)** fork
**frais, fraîche** fresh
**frais (m. pl.)** expense, charge, cost
**fraise (f.)** strawberry
**framboise (f.)** raspberry
**français (m.)** French
**frappé (m.)** milk shake
**frapper** to knock, hit, strike
**freins (m. pl.)** brakes
**frère (m.)** brother
**frit(e)** fried
**froid (m.)** cold; **avoir froid** to be cold (person); **faire froid** to be cold (weather)
**fromage (m.)** cheese
**front (m.)** forehead
**frontière (f.)** border
**fruit (m.)** fruit
**fruits de mer (m. pl.)** seafood
**fumer** to smoke
**fumeur (m.)** smoker, smoking compartment

# G

**gabardine (f.)** gabardine
**gagner** to earn, win
**gant (m.)** glove
**garçon (m.)** boy, waiter
**garder** to keep
**gare (f.)** station
**garer** to park a car
**gare routière (f.)** bus station
**gâteau (m.)** cake

**gauche** left; **à gauche** to the left
**gencives (f. pl.)** gums
**gendarme (m.)** policeman
**gêner** to bother, annoy
**genou (m.)** knee
**gens (m./f. pl.)** people
**gérant (m.)** manager
**gibier (m.)** game (meat)
**gigot (m.)** leg of mutton
**gilet (m.)** vest
**glace (f.)** ice, ice cream
**glacé(e)** iced
**glaçon (m.)** ice cube
**gomme (f.)** eraser
**gorge (f.)** throat; **avoir mal à la gorge** to have a sore throat
**goût (m.)** taste
**goûter** to taste
**goyave (f.)** guava
**grâce à** thanks to
**grand(e)** big
**gratte-ciel (m.)** skyscraper
**gratuit(e) (adj.)** free
**gratuitement (adv.)** free of charge
**grave** grave, serious
**grillé(e)** grilled, broiled
**gris(e)** gray
**gros(se)** fat
**guerre (f.)** war
**guichet (m.)** ticket window
**guide (m.)** guide; **guide touristique** tourist guide

# H

**habiller (s' . . . )** to dress oneself
**habiter** to live in
**habits (m. pl.)** clothes
**hamburger (m.)** hamburger
**hanche (f.)** hip

**hareng (m.)** herring; **hareng fumé** smoked herring
**haricot (m.)** bean
**haricots verts (m. pl.)** string beans
**haut(e)** high
**hauteur (f.)** height, elevation
**haut-parleur (m.)** loudspeaker
**herbe (f.)** grass
**heure (f.)** hour; **à l'heure** on time; **de bonne heure** early
**heureux(euse)** happy
**hier** yesterday
**histoire (f.)** story
**hiver (m.)** winter
**homard (m.)** lobster
**homme (m.)** man
**hôpital (m.)** hospital
**horaire (m.)** schedule, timetable
**horloge (f.)** clock
**horlogerie (f.)** watchmaker's shop
**hôte (m.)** host
**hôtel (m.)** hotel
**hôtesse (f.)** hostess
**huile (f.)** oil; **l'huile d'olive** olive oil
**huit** eight
**huître (f.)** oyster

# I

**ici** here
**il** he
**île (f.)** island
**ils** they
**il y a** there is, are; **il y a + time** ago
**immédiatement** immediately
**imperméable (m.)** raincoat
**important(e)** important
**impossible** impossible

imprécis(e) indefinite
incapable incapable
incendie (m.) fire
incroyable unbelievable
indécis(e) undecided
infection (f.) infection
infirmière (f.) nurse
infroissable permanent press
injuste unfair
insignifiant(e) unimportant
insomnie (f.) insomnia
insuffisant(e) insufficient
insupportable unbearable
intelligent(e) intelligent
interdire to prohibit, forbid
interdit(e) prohibited, forbidden
intéressant(e) interesting
interprète (m./f.) interpreter
interpréter to interpret
inutile useless
inviter to invite
invraisemblable improbable, unlikely
itinéraire (m.) itinerary, route
ivre drunk

jeune young
joli(e) pretty
joue (f.) cheek
jouer to play; jouer à to play a game, sport; jouer de to play a musical instrument
jour (m.) day
journal (m.) newspaper
juge (m.) judge
juger to judge
juillet July
juin June
jupe (f.) skirt
jupon (m.) slip
jus (m.) juice
jusqu'à until

# K

ketchup (m.) ketchup
kiosque (m.) stand; le kiosque à journaux newsstand
klaxon (m.) horn

# J

jamais never; ne . . . jamais never
jambe (f.) leg
jambon (m.) ham
janvier January
jardin (m.) garden
jarre (f.) jar
jaune yellow
je I
jeton (m.) token
jeu (m.) game
jeudi Thursday

# L

là there; là-bas over there
lac (m.) lake
lacet (m.) lace (shoe)
laid(e) ugly
laine (f.) wool
laisser to let, leave behind
lait (m.) milk
laitue (f.) lettuce
lampe (f.) lamp; la lampe de poche flashlight
langue (f.) language, tongue
lapin (m.) rabbit

laque (f.) hairspray
lard (m.) bacon
lavabo (m.) washroom
laver to wash; se laver to wash oneself
laverie automatique (f.) launderette
léger(ère) light (weight)
légume (m.) vegetable
lent(e) slow
lentement slowly
lettre (f.) letter
lever: se lever to get up
lèvre (f.) lip; rouge à lèvres (m.) lipstick
librairie (f.) bookstore
libre free
ligne (f.) line
limette (f.) lime
lin (m.) linen (material)
lire to read
liste (f.) list
lit (m.) bed
livre (m.) book
livre (f.) pound (weight)
livrer to deliver
loger to stay at
logis (m.) lodging
loin far; loin de far from
long(ue) long
lotion (f.) lotion; la lotion à bronzer suntan lotion
louer to rent, hire
loyer (m.) the rent
lumière (f.) light
lundi Monday
lunettes (f. pl.) eye glasses; les lunettes de soleil sunglasses
luxe (m.) luxury
luxueux(euse) luxurious
lycée (m.) high school

# M

macédoine de fruits (f.) fruit salad
mâchoire (f.) jaw
madame Mrs.
mademoiselle Miss
magasin (m.) store; de chaussures shoe store; de disques record store; un grand magasin department store; de jouets toy store; de photographie camera store; de souvenirs gift shop; de spiritueux liquor store; de vêtements clothing store
magazine (m.) magazine
mai May
maillot (m.) de bain bathing suit; de corps undershirt
main (f.) hand
maintenant now
mairie (f.) town hall
mais but
maïs (m.) corn
maison (f.) house; à la maison at home
mal (m.) ache; mal de dents toothache; mal d'estomac stomachache; mal de gorge sore throat; mal de tête headache
malade sick
maladie (f.) sickness, illness
malentendu (m.) misunderstanding
malgré in spite of
malheureux(euse) unhappy
malle (f.) trunk; malle arrière auto trunk

**manche (f.)** sleeve
**mandarine (f.)** tangerine
**manger** to eat
**mangue (f.)** mango
**manque (m.)** lack
**manquer** to lack, miss
**manteau (m.)** overcoat
**marchand (m.)** merchant
**marchandise (f.)** merchandise
**marché (m.)** market
**marcher** to walk
**mardi** Tuesday
**margarine (f.)** margarine
**mari (m.)** husband
**marque (f.)** brand (of product)
**marron** brown
**marron (m.)** chestnut
**mars** March
**matin (m.)** morning
**mauvais(e)** bad
**mayonnaise (m.)** mayonnaise
**mécanicien (m.)** mechanic
**médecin (m.)** doctor
**médecine (f.)** medicine
**meilleur(e)** better (adj.)
**melon (m.)** melon
**même** same; **le/la même** the same
**menton (m.)** chin
**mer (f.)** sea; **au bord de la mer** at the seashore
**merci** thank-you
**mercredi** Wednesday
**mère (f.)** mother
**mériter** to deserve
**merveilleux(euse)** marvelous
**mesure (f.)** measurement
**mesurer** to measure
**métro (m.)** subway
**mettre** to put, put on

**meublé(e)** furnished
**midi** noon
**mieux** better (adv.)
**milieu (m.)** middle; **au milieu de** in the middle of
**mille** thousand
**million (m.)** million; **un million de + noun** a million
**mince** thin
**minuit** midnight
**minute (f.)** minute
**miroir (m.)** mirror
**mode (f.)** style; **à la mode** stylish, in style
**modifier** to modify, change
**moins** less
**mois (m.)** month
**moitié (f.)** half
**monde (m.)** world; **tout le monde** everybody.
**monnaie (f.)** coin money, change
**monsieur (m.)** mister, Mr., sir
**montagne (f.)** mountain
**montant (m.)** sum total
**monter** to go up
**montre (f.)** watch
**montrer** to show
**morceau (m.)** piece
**mosquée (f.)** mosque
**mot (m.)** word
**moteur (m.)** motor
**mouchoir (m.)** handkerchief; **le mouchoir en papier** tissue
**mouillé(e)** wet
**moule (f.)** mussel
**mousseline de soie (f.)** chiffon
**moutarde (f.)** mustard
**moyen (m.)** way
**mur (m.)** wall
**musée (m.)** museum
**musique (f.)** music

# N

**nager** to swim
**nationalité (f.)** nationality
**nausée (f.)** nausea
**ne; ne . . . aucun(e)** not . . . any;
  **ne . . . jamais** never; **ne . . .
  pas** not; **ne . . . plus** no
  longer, not . . . any more;
  **ne . . . que** only; **ne . . .
  rien** nothing
**nécessaire** necessary
**neige (f.)** snow
**neiger** to snow
**nettoyer** to clean
**nettoyer à sec** to dry clean
**neuf** nine
**nez (m.)** nose
**noir(e)** black
**noix (f.)** nut
**nom (m.)** name; **nom de famille**
  family name; **prénom (m.)** first
  name; **surnom (m.)** last name,
  nickname
**nombre (m.)** number (quantity)
**non** no
**non-fumeurs** non-smoking
**nord (m.)** north
**note (f.)** bill (hotel)
**nourriture (f.)** food
**nous** us
**nouveau (m.)** new
**nouveauté (f.)** novelty
**nouvelle (f.)** new
**nuit (f.)** night
**numéro (m.)** number; **le numéro
  de téléphone** telephone number
**nylon (m.)** nylon

# O

**observer** to observe
**obtenir** to obtain

**occasion (f.)** opportunity, bargain;
  **marchandise d'occasion (f.)**
  secondhand (used) goods; **une
  véritable occasion** a genuine
  bargain
**occupé(e)** busy
**océan (m.)** ocean
**oeil (m.)** eye; (pl.) **les yeux**
  eyes
**oeuf (m.)** egg; **au plat** fried;
  **brouillé** scrambled; **dur**
  hard-boiled; **frit** fried; **mollet**
  soft-boiled; **poêlé** sunny-side up
**offrir** to offer
**oie (f.)** goose
**oignon (m.)** onion
**olive (f.)** olive; **l'huile (f.) d'olive**
  olive oil
**ombre (f.)** shade (tree)
**omelette (f.)** omelet; **l'omelette
  norvégienne** baked Alaska
**omnibus (m.)** local bus
**ongle (m.)** nail (finger); **la lime à
  ongle** nail file
**onze** eleven
**opéra (m.)** opera, opera hall
**opticien (m.)** optician
**or (m.)** gold; **en or** of gold
**orage (m.)** storm
**orange (f.)** orange
**orangeade (f.)** orangeade
**orchestre (m.)** orchestra
**ordonnance (f.)** prescription
**oreille (f.)** ear; **boucle (f.)
  d'oreille** earring
**oreiller (m.)** pillow
**orteil (m.)** toe
**os (m.)** bone
**ôter** to take off, remove
**ou** or
**où** where
**ouate (f.)** absorbent cotton
**oublier** to forget

**ouest (m.)** west
**oui** yes
**outre-mer** overseas
**ouvert(e)** open (adj.)
**ouvrir** to open

# P

**paille (f.)** straw (material)
**pain (m.)** bread; **baguette (f.)** French bread; **pain blanc** white bread; **pain bis** pumpernickel; **pain de froment** whole wheat; **pain grillé** toast; **pain de seigle** rye bread; **petit pain** roll
**paire (f.)** pair
**palais (m.)** palace
**palourde (f.)** clam
**pamplemousse (m.)** grapefruit
**panier (m.)** basket
**panne (f.)** breakdown, mishap; **en panne** broken down
**pantalon (m.)** pants
**pantoufle (f.)** slipper
**papier (m.)** paper; **papier à lettres** note paper; **papier à machine** typing paper; **papier d'emballage** wrapping paper; **papier hygiénique** toilet paper
**paquet (m.)** package
**par** by; per; **par avion** air mail, by plane; **par exemple** for example; **par ici** this way; **par jour** per day
**parapluie (m.)** umbrella
**parc (m.)** park
**parce que** because
**pardessus (m.)** overcoat
**pardon** excuse me
**pardonner** to excuse
**parfait(e)** perfect
**parfum (m.)** perfume, flavor

**parler** to speak
**parmi** among
**partager** to share
**parterre (m.)** mezzanine
**partie (f.)** part
**partir** to leave
**partout** everywhere
**pastèque (f.)** watermelon
**pâte (f.)** paste; **la pâte dentifrice** toothpaste
**pâtisserie (f.)** pastry, pastry shop
**patron (m.)** boss
**pauvre** poor
**payer** to pay
**pays (m.)** country (nation)
**paysage (m.)** countryside
**peau (f.)** skin
**pêche (f.)** peach; fishing
**pêcher** to fish
**peigne (m.)** comb
**pellicule (f.)** roll of film
**pendant** during
**pendule (f.)** clock
**penser** to think
**pension (f.)** boardinghouse
**perdre** to lose
**père (m.)** father
**permanent(e)** permanent
**permettre** to permit; **permis** permitted
**permis (m.)** permit
**personne (f.)** person
**persuader** to persuade
**perte (f.)** loss
**peser** to weigh
**petit(e)** small
**petit déjeuner (m.)** breakfast
**peu (adv.)** little, not much
**peuple (m.)** people (nation)
**peur (f.)** fear; **avoir peur de** to be afraid of

**peut-être** maybe, perhaps

**phare (m.)** headlight

**pharmacie (f.)** pharmacy

**photo (f.)** photograph

**photographier** to photograph

**phrase (f.)** sentence

**pièce (f.)** room, play

**pied (m.)** foot; **à pied** on foot

**pierre (f.)** stone

**piéton (m.)** pedestrian

**pilule (f.)** pill

**pipe (f.)** pipe; **le tabac pour pipe** pipe tobacco

**piscine (f.)** swimming pool

**piste (f.)** runway; **piste de ski** ski slope

**place (f.)** square (public); seat in conveyance

**plafond (m.)** ceiling

**plage (f.)** beach

**plainte (f.)** complaint

**plaisanterie (f.)** joke

**plaisir (m.)** pleasure

**plan (m.)** plan; **plan de ville** street map of city; **plan à vue d'oiseau** bird's-eye view of the city

**planche de surf (f.)** surfboard

**plancher (m.)** floor

**plat (m.)** dish of food

**plat(e)** flat

**platine (m.)** platinum

**pleurer** to cry

**pluie (f.)** rain

**plume (f.)** pen

**plusieurs** several

**plutôt** rather

**pneu (m.)** tire; **pneu crevé** flat tire

**poche (f.)** pocket; **livre de poche** paperback

**poids (m.)** weight

**poignet (m.)** wrist

**poire (f.)** pear

**pois (m.)** pea; **pois chiches (m. pl.)** chick-peas; **à pois** polka-dotted

**poisson (m.)** fish

**poitrine (f.)** chest

**poivre (m.)** pepper

**pomme (f.)** apple

**pomme de terre (f.)** potato

**pont (m.)** bridge

**porc (m.)** pork

**portatif(ive)** portable

**porte (f.)** door

**porte-bonheur (m.)** charm

**portefeuille (m.)** wallet

**porte-monnaie (m.)** purse

**porter** to carry, wear

**porteur (m.)** porter

**posséder** to possess, own

**poste (f.)** post office; **poste aérienne** air mail

**poste (m.)** station; **poste d'essence** gas station

**potable** drinkable; **eau potable** drinking water

**potage (m.)** soup

**poterie (f.)** pottery

**pouce (m.)** thumb

**poulet (m.)** chicken

**poumon (m.)** lung

**pour** for, in order to

**pourboire (m.)** tip (gratuity)

**pourquoi** why

**pousser** to push

**pouvoir** to be able to, can

**préférer** to prefer

**premier(ière)** first; **premier secours (m.)** first aid

**prendre** to take

**prénom (m.)** first name

**préparer** to prepare

**près (de)**  near (to)
**présenter**  to present, introduce
**presque**  almost
**pressé(e)**  hurried, rushed
**prêt(e)**  ready
**prêter**  to lend
**printemps (m.)**  spring
**prise de courant (f.)**  socket
**privé(e)**  private
**prix (m.)**  price, prize
**prochain(e)**  next
**proche**  near, neighboring
**profession (f.)**  profession
**promenade (f.)**  walk; **faire une promenade**  to take a walk
**promesse (f.)**  promise
**promettre**  to promise
**prononcer**  to pronounce
**propre**  clean
**propriétaire (m.)**  owner
**propriété (f.)**  property
**protéger**  to protect
**protester**  to protest
**provisoire**  temporary
**provisoirement**  temporarily
**prudence (f.)**  carefulness
**prune (f.)**  plum
**pruneau (m.)**  prune
**public(ique)**  public
**pyjama (m.)**  pyjamas

# Q

**quai (m.)**  platform
**qualité (f.)**  quality
**quand**  when
**quantité (f.)**  quantity
**quarante**  forty
**quart (m.)**  quarter
**quartier (m.)**  district

**quatorze**  fourteen
**quatre**  four
**quatre-vingt-dix**  ninety
**quatre-vingts**  eighty
**que**  that
**que?**  what?
**quel(le)**  which
**quelque chose**  something
**quelquefois**  sometimes
**quelque part**  somewhere
**quelques**  some
**quelequ'un**  someone
**question (f.)**  question
**queue (f.)**  line (of people); tail; **faire la queue**  to form a line
**qui**  who
**quincaillerie (f.)**  hardware store
**quinze**  fifteen
**quitter + place *or* person**  to leave
**quoi**  what
**quotidien(ne)**  daily

# R

**rabais (m.)**  reduction
**raconter**  to tell
**radio (f.)**  radio, X-ray
**radis (m.)**  radish
**rafraîchissements (m. pl.)**  refreshments
**ragoût (m.)**  stew
**raifort (m.)**  horseradish
**raisin (m.)**  grape
**raison (f.)**  reason; **avoir raison**  to be right
**raisonnable**  reasonable
**rang (m.)**  row
**rapide**  fast, express train
**rapidement**  quickly

**rappeler: se rappeler** to remember

**rare** rare

**raser: se raser** to shave oneself

**rasoir (m.)** razor; **le rasoir électrique** electric razor

**rayon (m.)** shelf; department (of a store)

**rayure (f.)** stripe; **à rayures** striped

**récemment** recently

**recevoir** to receive

**réclame (f.)** advertisement

**recommander** to recommend

**récompense (f.)** reward

**récompenser** to reward

**reçu (m.)** receipt

**récupérer** to recuperate

**refuser** to refuse

**regarder** to look at

**règle (f.)** rule, ruler

**régler** to settle, adjust, regulate; **régler une affaire** to settle an affair

**regretter** to regret, be sorry

**régulier(ière)** regular

**régulièrement** regularly

**relier** to connect

**remarquer** to notice

**rembourser** to reimburse, refund

**remède (m.)** remedy

**remercier** to thank

**remettre** to put back; **se remettre** to recover (health)

**remplacer** to replace

**remplir** to fill (out)

**rencontrer** to meet

**rendez-vous (m.)** meeting

**rendre** to return, give back

**renseignement (m.)** a piece of information; **les renseignements** information

**renvoyer** to send back

**réparer** to repair

**repas (m.)** meal

**repasser** to iron; **ne pas repasser** wash and wear

**répéter** to repeat

**répondre** to answer

**réponse (f.)** the answer

**repos (m.)** rest, relaxation

**reposer: se reposer** to rest

**représentation (f.)** performance

**requin (m.)** shark

**réservation (f.)** reservation

**réserver** to reserve

**résoudre** to resolve

**responsable** responsible

**ressembler à** to resemble, look like

**restaurant (m.)** restaurant

**rester** to stay, remain

**résultat (m.)** result

**retard (m.)** delay; **en retard** late

**retenir** to retain

**retourner** to return, go back

**réveil (m.)** alarm clock

**réveiller: se réveiller** to wake up

**revenir** to come back, return

**rez-de-chaussée (m.)** ground floor

**rhume (m.)** cold; **rhume de cerveau** head cold; **rhume des foins** hay fever; **rhume de poitrine** chest cold

**rien** nothing; **ne . . . rien** nothing; **de rien** you're welcome

**rire** to laugh

**rive (f.)** bank, shore

**rivière (f.)** river, stream

**riz (m.)** rice

**robe (f.)** dress; **robe de chambre** bathrobe; **robe de soir** evening gown

**robinet (m.)** faucet

**roman (m.)** novel; **roman policier** detective story

**rond(e)** round

**rose** pink, rose

**rôti(e)** roasted

**rouge** red

**route (f.)** route, road

**rue (f.)** street

**ruelle (f.)** lane, alley

# S

**sable (m.)** sand

**sac (m.)** bag, pocketbook

**saignant(e)** rare (food)

**saison (f.)** season

**salade (f.)** salad

**sale** dirty

**salé(e)** salted

**salle (f.)** room; **salle à manger** dining room; **salle d'attente** waiting room; **salle de bains** bathroom; **salle de concert** concert hall

**salon (m.) de beauté** beauty parlor

**saluer** to greet

**samedi** Saturday

**sang (m.)** blood

**sans** without

**santé (f.)** health

**sardine (f.)** sardine

**satin (m.)** satin

**satisfait(e)** satisfied

**saucisse (f.)** sausage

**saumon (m.)** salmon

**savoir** to know (facts)

**savon (m.)** soap

**sec, sèche** dry

**sèche-cheveux (m.)** hair dryer

**sécher** to dry

**secours (m.)** help; **au secours!** help!

**sécurité (f.)** security; **la ceinture de sécurité** seat belt

**seize** sixteen

**séjour (m.)** stay, sojourn

**sel (m.)** salt

**selon** according to

**semaine (f.)** week

**sembler** to seem

**sentir: se sentir** to feel

**sept** seven

**sérieux(ieuse)** serious

**serrure (f.)** lock

**serveuse (f.)** waitress

**service (m.)** service

**serviette (f.)** towel, napkin, briefcase

**serviette hygiénique (f.)** sanitary napkin

**servir** to serve

**seul(e)** alone, only (adj.)

**seulement (adv.)** only

**si** if; yes (to a negative question)

**siège (m.)** seat

**signer** to sign

**signification (f.)** meaning

**signifier** to mean

**s'il vous plaît** please

**six** six

**ski (m.)** ski; **les skis nautiques** water skis

**slip (m.)** panties

**soda (m.)** soda

**soeur (f.)** sister

**soie (f.)** silk

**soif (f.)** thirst; **avoir soif** to be thirsty

**soin (m.)** care; **avec soin** carefully

**soir (m.)** evening

**soixante** sixty

**soixante-dix** seventy

**soldes (m. pl.)** sales, bargains

**sole (f.)** sole, flounder

**soleil (m.)** sun; **il fait du soleil** it is sunny; **les coups (m. pl.) de soleil** sunburn

**sommeil (m.)** sleep, sleepiness; **avoir sommeil** to be sleepy

**sommelier (m.)** wine waiter

**somnifère (m.)** sleeping pill

**sonner** to ring

**sorbet (m.)** sherbert

**sortie (f.)** exit

**sortir** to leave

**souhaiter** to wish (someone something)

**soûl(e)** drunk

**soulier (m.)** shoe

**souper (m.)** supper

**souper** to have supper

**sous** under

**sous-titre (m.)** subtitle

**sous-vêtement (m.)** undergarment; **les sous-vêtements (m. pl.)** underwear

**soutien-gorge (m.)** bra

**souvent** often

**spectacle (m.)** show

**stade (m.)** stadium

**station-service (f.)** service station; gas station

**stylo à bille (m.)** ball-point pen

**succursale (f.)** branch of a bank, etc.

**sucre (m.)** sugar

**sud (m.)** south

**suivant(e)** following, next

**suivre** to follow

**supermarché (m.)** supermarket

**supporter** to tolerate

**sur** on

**sûr(e)** sure

**surnom (m.)** last name, nickname

**surtout** especially

**surveiller** to watch, supervise

**synagogue (f.)** synagogue

**syndicat (m.) d'initiative** tourist office

**synthétique** synthetic, polyester

# T

**tabac (m.)** tobacco

**table (f.)** table

**tableau (m.)** picture, painting

**tache (f.)** stain

**taille (f.)** size, figure (body), waist

**taille-crayon (m.)** pencil sharpener

**tailleur (m.)** tailor, woman's suit

**talon (m.)** heel (of foot)

**tampon (m.) périodique** tampon

**tapis (m.)** rug

**tard** late

**tarif (m.)** rate

**tartan (m.)** plaid

**tarte (f.)** pie

**tasse (f.)** cup

**taxi (m.)** taxi

**teinturerie (f.)** dry cleaner's

**télégramme (m.)** telegram

**téléphone (m.)** telephone; **cabine (f.) téléphonique** telephone booth

**téléphoner** to call on the phone

**téléphoniste (f.)** operator

**téléski (m.)** ski lift

**télévision (f.)** television

**tempête (f.)** storm

**temple (m.)** church (Protestant)

**temps (m.)** weather, time; **de temps en temps** from time to time

**tenir** to hold

**tente (f.)** tent

**terminer** to finish

**terrain (m.)** ground; **terrain de camping** camping grounds; **terrain de golf** golf course **terrain de sport** playing field;

**terre (f.)** land, earth; **par terre** on the ground

**tête (f.)** head

**thé (m.)** tea; **au citron** with lemon; **au lait** with milk; **glacé** iced; **sucré** with sugar

**thon (m.)** tuna fish

**timbre (m.)** stamp

**tire-bouchon (m.)** corkscrew

**tirer** to pull

**tissu (m.)** material

**tissu-éponge (m.)** terry cloth

**titre (m.)** title

**toit (m.)** roof

**tomate (f.)** tomato

**tomber** to fall; **tomber malade** to become ill

**tort: avoir tort** to be wrong

**tôt** early

**toucher** to touch; **toucher un chèque** to cash a check

**toujours** always

**tour (f.)** tower

**tour (m.)** trip, turn

**touriste (m./f.)** tourist

**tourner** to turn

**tout (m. s.); tous (m. pl.); toute (f. s.); toutes (f. pl.)** all, every; **tous les jours** every day; **tout le monde** everybody; **tout le temps** all the time

**tousser** to cough

**toux (f.)** the cough; **la pastille contre la toux** cough drop; **le sirop contre la toux** cough syrup

**traduire** to translate

**train (m.)** train; **être en train de** to be in the act of

**traitement (m.)** treatment

**trajet (m.)** distance, journey, trip

**tranche (f.)** slice

**travail (m.)** work

**travailler** to work

**travers: à travers** across, through

**traverser** to cross, go across

**treize** thirteen

**trente** thirty

**très** very; **très bien** very well

**triste** sad

**trois** three

**tromper** to deceive, trick; **se tromper** to be mistaken, make a mistake

**trop (de)** too much, many (of)

**trottoir (m.)** sidewalk

**trou (m.)** hole

**trouver** to find

**truite (f.)** trout

**tu** you

# U

**un (m.)** a, an, one

**une (f.)** a, an, one

**uni(e)** solid (color)

**unique** only (adj.)

**urgent(e)** urgent; **cas urgent (m.)** emergency; **d'urgence** urgently

**usage (m.)** custom, practice

**usagé(e)** secondhand

**usé** worn out, threadbare, hackneyed

**usine (f.)** factory

**utile** useful

**utiliser** to use

# V

**vacances (f. pl.)** vacation

**valable** valid

**valeur (f.)** value

**valise (f.)** suitcase

**varié(e)** varied

**veau (m.)** veal

**velours (m.)** velvet; **velours côtelé** corduroy

**vendeur(euse)** salesman, saleswoman

**vendre** to sell

**vendredi** Friday

**venir** to come; **venir de** to have just; **faire venir** to send for

**vent (m.)** wind; **il fait du vent** it is windy

**vente (f.)** sale; **en vente** for sale

**ventilateur (m.)** fan, blower

**verglas (m.)** ice, frost

**vérifier** to check

**vérité (f.)** truth

**verre (m.)** glass; **le verre de contact** contact lens

**vers** towards

**vert(e)** green

**vestiaire (m.)** coat checkroom

**veston (m.)** jacket

**vêtements (m. pl.)** clothing

**viande (f.)** meat

**vide** empty

**vie (f.)** life

**vieille (f.)** old

**vieux (m.)** old

**village (m.)** village

**ville (f.)** city

**vin (m.)** wine; **vin blanc** white wine; **vin mousseux** sparkling wine; **vin rosé** rosé wine; **vin rouge** red wine; **le négociant en vins** wine merchant

**vinaigre (m.)** vinegar

**vingt** twenty

**violet** purple

**virage (m.)** turn, bend, corner

**visage (m.)** face

**vitamine (f.)** vitamin

**vite** quickly

**vitesse (f.)** speed

**vitrine (f.)** shop window

**vivre** to live

**voici** here is, are

**voie (f.)** route, path, track

**voilà** there is, are

**voir** to see

**voisin(e)** neighbor

**voiture (f.)** car

**vol (m.)** flight

**volant (m.)** steering wheel

**voler** to fly, steal

**voleur (m.)** thief, robber

**volontiers** gladly, with pleasure, willingly

**vouloir** to wish, want; **vouloir dire** to mean, signify

**vous** you

**voyage (m.)** trip; **voyage d'affaires** business trip

**voyager** to travel

**voyageur (m.)** traveller

**vrai(e)** true

**vraiment** really

**vue (f.)** view

# W

**wagon (m.)**  railroad car
**wagon-lit (m.)**  sleeping car
**wagon-restaurant (m.)**  dining car
**W.C.**  toilet

# Y

**y**  there
**yaourt (m.)**  yogurt
**yeux (m. pl.)**  eyes

# Z

**zéro**  zero
**zone (f.)**  zone
**zoo (m.)**  zoo

# INDEX

# READY REFERENCE KEY

Here are some phrases and words from the book that you are
likely to use often. For a more extensive list of phrases, refer to
the appropriate chapter within the book.

## SIMPLE WORDS AND PHRASES

Do you speak
English?

**Parlez-vous anglais?** *pahr-lay voo
ahn-gleh*

Do you understand?

**Comprenez-vous? (Vous compren-
ez?)** *kohn-pruh-nay voo (voo kohn-
pruh-nay)*

I don't speak French.

**Je ne parle pas français.** *zhuh nuh
pahrl pah frahn-sseh*

I don't understand.

**Je ne comprends pas.** *zhuh nuh
kohn-prahn pah*

Please speak slowly.

**Parlez lentement s'il vous plaît.**
*pahr-lay lahnt-mahn seel voo pleh*

Please repeat.

**Répétez, s'il vous plaît.** *Ray-pay-tay,
seel voo pleh*

## BEING POLITE

Please

**S'il vous plaît** *seel voo pleh*

Thank you very
much.

**Merci beaucoup** *mehr-ssee boh-koo*

Excuse me.

**Excusez-moi.** *ehkss-kew-zay
mwah*

**Pardon** *pahr-dohn*

Good morning
(afternoon).

**Bonjour.** *bohn-zhoor*

Good evening
(night).

**Bonsoir.** *bohn-swahr*
**Bonne nuit.** *bohn nwee*